Of this first English edition Radishchev's JOURNEY FROM ST. PETERSBURG TO MOSCOW the *American Historical Review* said: "This short volume, felicitously tra 'ated [is] a valuable historical so landmark in Russian intellect Primarily an attack on se appeal to the Sovereig were wickedly gentry to free the JOURNEY at-JOURNEY has a Russian U Published had no choice but to institute reforms at once. Radishchev did not want a revolution, although he felt one would have been justified. He wanted reforms, and he wanted them in time.

This edition of the *JOURNEY* offers a complete and accurate English translation of the original work. The introduction includes an account of Radishchev's life, the feelings and beliefs which led him to write this and other important works, and a complete analysis of the *JOURNEY* — its content and background, historical source material and points of departure, literary analogues or sources, Radishchev's language, style, and literary technique, and the influence and aftermath of it all. Extensive notes clarify points which might not be immediately clear to English readers and often make reference to the Empress Catherine II's own notes on the *JOURNEY*, which appear in translation at the back of the book.

Roderick Page Thaler is Associate Professor of History, Bishop's University, Lennoxville, Quebec, Canada. This book is a revision of the translation begun by the late Leo Wiener and left uncompleted at his death.

A JOURNEY FROM
ST. PETERSBURG TO MOSCOW

ALEKSANDR NIKOLAEVICH RADISHCHEV

From an engraving by Vendramini in the State Historical Museum, Moscow

ALEKSANDR NIKOLAEVICH RADISHCHEV

A JOURNEY FROM ST. PETERSBURG TO MOSCOW

"A grim monster, savage, gigantic, hundred-mouthed, and bellowing —"

Telemakhida, Vol. II
Book XVIII, verse 514

TRANSLATION BY
LEO WIENER

EDITED WITH
AN INTRODUCTION AND NOTES BY
RODERICK PAGE THALER

HARVARD UNIVERSITY PRESS
Cambridge, Massachusetts
1966

© Copyright 1958
By the President and Fellows of Harvard College

Second Printing

Distributed in Great Britain by
Oxford University Press
London

Library of Congress Catalog Card Number 58–6580

Printed in the United States of America

TO
MY FATHER AND MOTHER

PREFACE

Radishchev's *Journey from St. Petersburg to Moscow* made educated Russians think about the problem of serfdom. It did not, like *Uncle Tom's Cabin*, lead to emancipation within a decade, but it looked in that direction. Serfdom in Russia was not abolished until more than seventy years after the appearance of the *Journey*. Still, the book presented a serious criticism of serfdom and of the entire Russian social order, a criticism which helped to make many intelligent and influential Russians aware of much that was wrong in their country and led them to think of reforms. Radishchev was one of the earliest of the liberal Russian intelligentsia, and his book is often made the starting point in the study of Russian intellectual history. There is ample reason for this, because ever since his own time Russians have looked upon Radishchev as the man who "first proclaimed liberty to us." When Pushkin proudly claimed that he had spoken out for liberty, he proudly added that he had followed in the footsteps of Radishchev. Radishchev, however, had condemned equally the sovereign's despotism, the gentry's tyranny, and the peasants' violence. He did not want a revolution. He wanted to make a revolution unnecessary. He wanted reforms, and wanted them in time.

The present translation was first prepared by Professor Leo Wiener of Harvard University, who unhappily did not live to see it published. Professor Wiener was one of the pioneers of Slavonic studies in the United States, and scholars in the field are deeply indebted to him. His *Anthology of Russian Literature* has helped give English readers over the last fifty years an idea of its wonderful scope and richness. A selection from the *Journey* was included in the *Anthology*. The translation of the *Journey* was thoroughly revised by the editor, who used a photolithographic reprint (Moscow and Leningrad: "Academia," 1935) of Radishchev's own edition (*Puteshestvie iz Peterburga v Moskvu*, St. Petersburg, 1790). The editor is solely responsible for the Introduction and Notes. Full information about later editions, translations, and the present text is given in the Bibliography. The *Journey* has never before been published in English. As in the original, Radishchev's own footnotes are indicated by asterisks and appear at the bottom of the pages annotated. The editor's notes are indicated by numbers and appear in a separate section at the end of the book. The corresponding pages of the text of Radishchev's own edition of the *Journey* are always preceded by an asterisk and are given in square brackets in the body of the text of each page of the translation.

I am very grateful to the Committee for the Promotion of Advanced Slavic Cultural Studies, and especially to its chairman, Mr. R. Gordon Wasson, for a generous grant-in-aid toward the publication of this volume.

I am deeply grateful, also, to my father, Professor Alwin Thaler of the University of Tennessee, for steadfast help, encouragement, and good counsel; and to Professor Robert Lee Wolff of Harvard University for careful and constructive criticism. I am chiefly indebted, however, to Professor Michael Karpovich of Harvard University. From start to finish, his learning, his wisdom, and his unfailing kindness have pointed the way and illuminated the course of this study.

R. P. T.

NOTE ON DATES AND TRANSLITERATION

Dates. The Old Style (Julian) Calendar prevailed in Russia until 1918. In the eighteenth century, this calendar was eleven days behind the New Style, or Gregorian, Calendar; in the nineteenth century, it was twelve days behind; and in the twentieth, thirteen. Dates after 1752, when the New Style was adopted in England, are given in both styles.

Transliteration table:

Russian		English		Russian		English	
А	а	A	a	С	с	S	s
Б	б	B	b	Т	т, ш	T	t
В	в	V	v	У	у	U	u
Г	г	G	g	Ф	ф	F	f
Д	д	D	d	Х	х	Kh	kh
Е	е	E	e	Ц	ц	Ts	ts
Ж	ж	Zh	zh	Ч	ч	Ch	ch
З	з	Z	z	Ш	ш	Sh	sh
И	и	I	i	Щ	щ	Shch	shch
I	i	I	i		ъ	Omitted	
	й		y		ы		y
К	к	K	k		ь		,
Л	л	L	l	Ѣ	ѣ	E	e
М	м	M	m	Э	э	E	e
Н	н	N	n	Ю	ю	Yu	yu
О	о	O	o	Я	я	Ya	ya
П	п	P	p	Ѳ	ѳ	F	f
Р	р	R	r	V	v	I	i

The adjectival endings -ий and -ый are both transliterated simply as -y, as in russky, novy. The ending -ой is transliterated as -oy, as in Tolstoy. Place names which have an accepted form, such as St. Petersburg, Moscow, and Archangel, are given in the familiar English form. The names of sovereigns are also given in the familiar form, as the Empresses Elizabeth and Catherine, the Emperors Paul and Alexander. Other names are strictly transliterated, as Elizaveta, Ekaterina, Pavel, and Aleksandr. The Russian Translation Project of the American Council of Learned Societies has been the model.

CONTENTS

Introduction   1

A JOURNEY FROM ST. PETERSBURG TO MOSCOW   39

    DEDICATION   40

THE DEPARTURE [*1]	41	EDROVO [*210]	131
SOFIYA [*4]	42	KHOTILOV [*236]	142
TOSNA [*9]	44	VYSHNY VOLOCHOK [*268]	156
LYUBANI [*14]	46	VYDROPUSK [*278]	160
CHUDOVO [*21]	49	TORZHOK [*289]	164
SPASSKAYA POLEST' [*41]	57	MEDNOE [*341]	187
PODBEREZ'E [*86]	77	TVER' [*350]	191
NOVGOROD [*99]	82	GORODNYA [*370]	201
BRONNITSY [*113]	89	ZAVIDOVO [*395]	212
ZAYTSOVO [*119]	91	KLIN [*401]	215
KRESTTSY [*154]	107	PESHKI [*410]	219
YAZHELBITSY [*197]	125	CHERNAYA GRYAZ' [*417]	221
VALDAI [*204]	128	EULOGY ON LOMONOSOV [*419]	222

The Empress Catherine II's Notes on the *Journey*   239
Bibliography   251
Notes   257
Index   281

INTRODUCTION

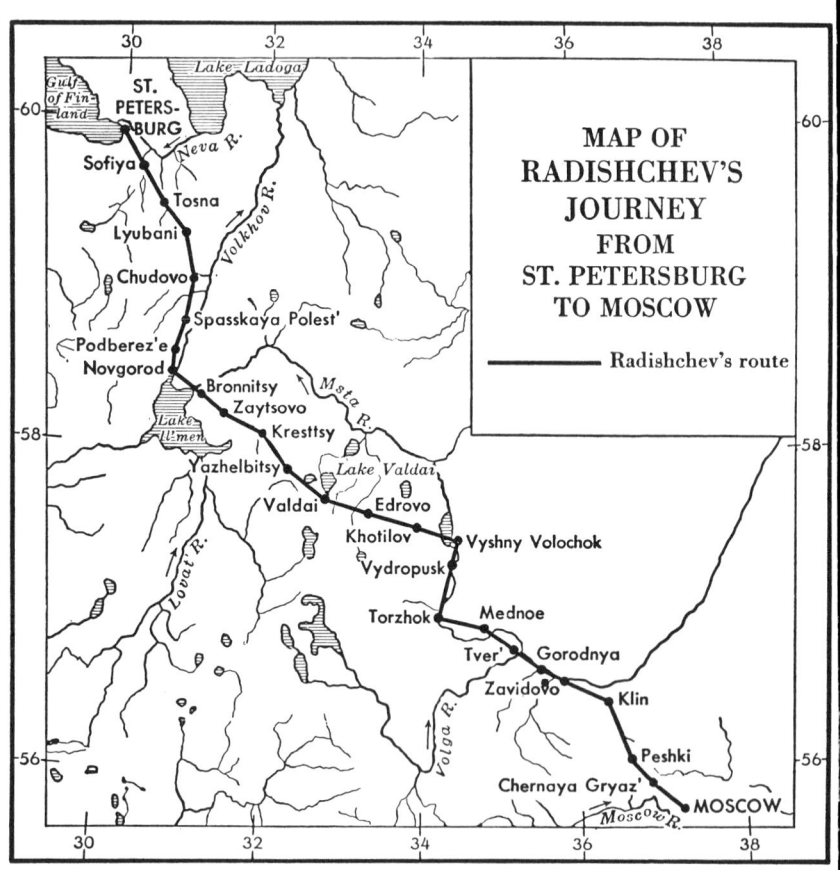

From Yakov Lazarevich Barskov and M. V. Zhizhka, *Materialy k izucheniyu "Puteshestviya iz Peterburga v Moskvu" A. N. Radishcheva*, Moscow and Leningrad, 1935, p. 208.

INTRODUCTION

The background of Radishchev's *Journey from St. Petersburg to Moscow* is bleak. Its historical and political aspects were significantly affected by the economic policy of Peter the Great, which was admirably summed up by the late Professor Sumner in one sentence: "In his eyes, just as the landowner was to be tied to service, the townsman to his trade or handicraft, so the peasant was to be tied to the land."[1] The culmination of Peter's efforts to compel the gentry to serve the state was his law of 1722, establishing the famous Table of Ranks.[2] This was a list, in parallel columns, of equivalent ranks in the Military, Civil, and Court Services, ranging from grade 1, field marshal or chancellor, and grade 2, full general or privy councillor, down to grade 13, second lieutenant or senatorial registrar, and grade 14, ensign (or cornet) or collegiate registrar. Persons who reached any of the upper eight grades became gentry, with that group's privileges of owning serfs and exemption from the capitation tax. (Radishchev, already of the gentry by birth, reached the sixth grade, collegiate councillor, equivalent to colonel.) A man's power, importance, and prestige were thus made to depend, not on his birth, but on his rank in the Service. For English-speaking readers, it may be well to stress strongly that the word "Service," which is very often used in the *Journey*, does not connote only the Military Service. "The Service" means *any* service to the state, military, civil, or at court, under the Table of Ranks.

In the same year, 1722, Peter the Great contributed to the long, gradual process of binding the peasants to the soil. So that men would be constantly available for military service and to pay the capitation tax, he ordered that no manorial serf should move from the estate on which he worked without the written permission of his master. The basic tax on the peasants was changed: it had been calculated on the acreage cultivated or the number of farm buildings; it became a tax per person, or "head": a capitation tax, sometimes called a "poll tax." The landlord was made responsible for the collection of this tax from his serfs.[3]

Theoretically, the basic reason for turning over peasants as serfs to the gentry had been to enable the gentry to serve the state. But immediately after the death of Peter the Great there began the gradual process commonly known as the "emancipation of the gentry," the freeing of the gentry from any obligation to serve the state, while they kept intact and even increased their power over their serfs. The Empress Anna, in 1736, legalized exemptions of gentry from the obligation to service and shortened the term of service for those who did serve. In the same year, the landed gentry were given the power personally to impose whatever punishment they pleased on any of their serfs who ran away. The uncertainty of succession to the throne, the frequency of palace revolutions, and the fact that sovereigns were overthrown and proclaimed, not by vote of the peasants, but by a handful of people in the Imperial guards regiments, who were gentry, all may help to explain why most of the sovereigns after Peter the Great yielded to the gentry. Many of Peter's successors had poor titles to the throne and were in no position to stand up to the gentry. And the laws, though made by the sovereign, had to be enforced by officials who, like the Imperial guards, were gentry. The fact that the requirement of service could not be enforced and was being evaded on a large scale was finally recognized in a law of the Emperor Peter III in 1762, completely freeing the gentry from the obligation to service. And the Empress Catherine II, in 1765, permitted the gentry to send peasants to forced labor in Siberia.[4]

By the reign of Catherine II, then, the landed gentry held

the whip hand, literally over their peasants, figuratively over the sovereign. The gentry could, and some of them occasionally did, require their peasants to give all their time to work on the manorial land, leaving them no time to work on their own. Or in lieu of compulsory labor, they could demand whatever they pleased, in money or in kind, from the peasants. If peasants were disobedient or tried to run away, their masters could punish them in almost any way they pleased, short of actually killing them. The gentry could send them, as a punishment, to Siberia or to the army. In some cases, masters were known to have abused their power so far as to take advantage of women serfs. Appeals by the peasants to the courts were very difficult to make and unlikely to achieve anything: the judges were gentry. In all but the most extreme cases, the landlords themselves had jurisdiction over their peasants.

During Catherine's reign, some attempts were made at legislative reform, but these largely died *in camera*. For example, in 1767 Catherine summoned the Legislative Commission to which she issued her famous *Instruction* (*Nakaz*), largely based on the works of Montesquieu and Beccaria. But before the Commission had been able to make any substantial improvement in the laws, its session was prorogued upon the outbreak of war with Turkey in 1768, and it was never reconvened. Radishchev's *Journey* is full of projects for new laws, and he was deeply interested in legal reform to the very end of his life. But although he had made a special study of law, he never had the satisfaction of seeing the Russian law improved as he felt that it should be, and as he felt that he himself could help to improve it.

From 1771 to 1773 (while Radishchev was a clerk of the Senate), the Senate tried the cases of a number of serf-owners who had harshly mistreated or, in some cases, even killed their serfs. But those serf-owners who were found guilty were let off with what appeared to be unjustly light sentences.

It is not surprising, then, that when Emel'yan Pugachev, in 1773, pretended that he was the Emperor Peter III and began burning down manor houses and killing gentry, he found many followers among the peasants. The Pugachev Rebellion was centered in the eastern and southern parts of European Russia, including the very region where Radishchev's parents lived. As Radishchev later said of the peasants who followed Pugachev, "Enticed by a crude pretender, they hastened to follow him, and wished only to free themselves from the yoke of their masters; and in their ignorance they could think of no other means to do this than to kill their masters. . . . This is what awaits us [the gentry], this is what we must expect." [5]

The Pugachev Rebellion was eventually suppressed, but nothing was done about the grievances of the peasants. Instead, Catherine II attempted, through a series of measures culminating in the Charter to the Gentry in 1785,[6] to strengthen the position of the gentry, and perhaps to give them some sense of class responsibility as well as class consciousness. The gentry were to elect provincial and district marshals of their class, who, with other officers, were to be elected at regular triennial assemblies of the gentry. These assemblies of the gentry were to have easy access to the sovereign or the provincial governor, who, in turn, might consult them. The gentry's privileges of exemption from personal taxation and from compulsory service were confirmed, as was their privilege of owning serf villages. They were exempted from corporal punishment. They could not be deprived of life, rank, or landed property except by trial in court, and even then the verdict would have to be approved by the sovereign. It was against this background of everything for the gentry and nothing for the peasants that the *Journey* was written.

To do justice to the quality and range of the book, one must know something of the man who wrote it, and of his other work.

Aleksandr Nikolaevich Radishchev was born in Moscow

on August 20/31, 1749, three days after Goethe, six years after Jefferson, ten years before the younger Pitt. Until he was eight years old, he lived on his father's estate at Verkhnee Oblyazovo in what was then Saratov province (now in Penza *oblast'*), some three hundred miles north of present-day Stalingrad, two hundred miles south of Kazan', and one hundred miles west of the Volga River. His father was a well-educated landed gentleman who seems to have been liked and trusted both by his own peasants and by the gentry of his district. His peasants protected him during the Pugachev Rebellion, when many peasants were only too happy to murder their proprietors. In 1787 he was elected marshal of the gentry of his district, Kuznetsk, in Saratov province.

From 1757 to 1762, between the ages of eight and thirteen, Radishchev lived in Moscow with his mother's relatives, the Argamakov family. The head of the Argamakov family was the curator of the newly founded Moscow University, and their home was always full of teachers and students. From 1762 to 1766 Radishchev was in the Corps des Pages in St. Petersburg, where he may have acquired some of his intense dislike for the Court Service. He was in St. Petersburg in 1765 when Mikhaylo Vasil'evich Lomonosov, the Russian Benjamin Franklin, died there. Lomonosov, a very different sort of man from most of those at court, embodied many of the qualities Radishchev most admired, and to him Radishchev devoted the last chapter of his *Journey*.

In 1766 Radishchev was one of twelve Russians sent by the government to study at the University of Leipzig. Among his fellow students at Leipzig were Aleksey Mikhaylovich Kutuzov, to whom the *Journey* was dedicated; Pyotr Ivanovich Chelishchev, who figures prominently in the *Journey*; Matvey Kirilovich Rubanovsky, whose niece Radishchev later married; Fyodor Vasil'evich Ushakov, whose biography Radishchev later wrote, telling particularly about their years at the University; and Goethe. Like Goethe, Radishchev particularly enjoyed Professor Christian Fürchtegott Gellert's lectures on poetry and rhetoric, and Professor Ernst Platner's lectures in philosophy and physiology. The Russian students had been sent "to study the Latin, German, French, and, if possible, Slavonic languages, . . . moral philosophy, history, but particularly natural and international law, as well as the law of the Roman Empire. Each one is free to study the other sciences as he wishes."[7] Accordingly Radishchev studied many of the French philosophers, not only Montesquieu, Voltaire, and Rousseau, but the now less well-known Bayle, Fénelon, Helvétius, Mably, and Raynal.

In 1771 Radishchev returned to Russia and entered the Civil Service as a clerk of the Senate. He was transferred to the Military Service, to the staff of General Bruce, in 1773. In this same year, when he was twenty-four, he published his first book: a translation, with introduction and notes, of Mably's *Observations sur l'histoire de la Grèce*. What I have seen of this translation is a very fair rendering of the original, not slavishly literal, but certainly close to Mably's meaning. Perhaps the most striking passage in the work is one in which Radishchev renders Mably's word "despotisme" by the Russian word "samoderzhavstvo," which means "autocracy." The Russian government at this time, and down to 1917, officially called itself an autocracy. In one of his numerous notes, Radishchev comments at length on this word. "Autocracy," he says, "is the state of affairs most repugnant to human nature. . . . The injustice of the sovereign gives the people, who are his judges, the same or an even greater right over him than the law gives him to judge criminals. The sovereign is the first citizen of the people's commonwealth."[8]

In 1775, the war with Turkey won and the Pugachev Rebellion suppressed, Radishchev received his honorable discharge with the rank of second major. He married Anna Vasil'evna Rubanovskaya, with whom he was very happy until her death in 1783. In 1777 their first child, Vasily, was born, and Radishchev went back into the Civil Service, in the Department of Commerce. He had a successful career in the Service, was promoted in 1780, 1782, 1784, and finally, in 1790, became Chief of the St. Petersburg Custom House. He won honor as well as rank, being made a Knight of the Order of St. Vladimir in 1785.

When he resigned from the Service in 1775, Radishchev made a journey from St. Petersburg to Verkhnee Oblyazovo to ask his parents' blessing for his marriage. On the way, he traveled through some of the country ravaged by the Pugachev Rebellion in the past two years. When he reached home, he was told how his father's peasants had helped his father hide out safely in the woods and had disguised his younger brothers and sisters as peasant children while Pugachev's men were near their estate. But he also heard of things that had happened to many another landlord, less enlightened and less generous to the peasants than his father. In the *Journey* Radishchev, referring more than once to the Pugachev Rebellion, warns his fellow serf-owners, in vivid and striking language, that a far worse and more terrible rebellion awaits them. Only by prompt and substantial reforms — above all, by freeing the serfs — can they hope to avert revolution. But he says himself that he does not mean to appeal primarily to the fear or self-interest of the serf-owners. Rather he appeals to their essential decency and sense of justice in asking them voluntarily to forswear a whole system that is manifestly wrong. In great detail he shows why serfdom was wrong, on three main grounds. It was a violation of natural right; it was economically wrong, cutting down food production and the growth of the population; and it was morally wrong, corrupting both masters and serfs. Radishchev was not a revolutionary, nor a prophet of revolution in the usual sense. He did predict revolution, if a whole series of liberal reforms were not made, and made in time. But he wanted the reforms, not the revolution. He felt that if his own class resisted and delayed the needed reforms, the revolution would come, inevitably, as a just punishment. While he felt that the peasants would be justified in revolting, he condemned revolutionary violence just as vigorously as he did royal violence and tyranny. Having real faith in human nature, he hoped that men could be persuaded to be reasonable, to do what he felt must be done. In the dedication of the *Journey* to his friend Kutuzov, Radishchev set forth his reasons for writing it: "I felt that it was possible for anyone to strive for the well-being of his fellows."

It is worth noting that Radishchev deeply loved his country, knew its history well, and was proud of what was good and honorable in it. He loved Russia enough to recognize her faults, point them out, and try to correct them. He wanted education to be as good in Russia as in Germany. He wanted the Russian legal system to be good enough to satisfy a Grotius, Montesquieu, or Blackstone. Above all, he wanted the press and the people to be as free in Russia as in England.

During the years 1781–1783, he wrote *Liberty: An Ode*, after reading Raynal's *The Revolution in America*, and included part of the Ode in the *Journey*. The whole poem, however, was not published until after the Revolution of 1905. The Empress Catherine II's note on this part of the *Journey* helps to explain why: "Pages 350 to 369 contain . . . an ode most clearly, manifestly revolutionary, in which Tsars are threatened with the block. Cromwell's example is cited and praised. These pages are of criminal intent, completely revolutionary. . . ."[9] Radishchev had pictured a wicked Tsar, who had abused the power given him to serve his people, being dragged to trial before his people, and condemned by them to death; he had praised Cromwell for trying and executing King Charles I by legal procedure. But he also condemned Cromwell for "destroying the citadel of liberty" by setting up a new tyranny of his own. Another part of the Ode, summarized in prose in the *Journey*, contains the interesting prophecy that the farther Russia expands, the weaker will be her control over outlying parts, and that the whole state will disintegrate: "all the sooner, the greater it grows." Though she did not refer to it in her notes, this, too, can hardly have been pleasing to the Empress, for she had already added extensive and distant territories to the Empire, and was just then in the process of adding more.

The parts of the Ode having to do with America are completely omitted from the *Journey*. In one stanza he apostrophizes Washington: "Thou wert and art invincible: *Thy leader, Washington, is Liberty.*" Later he apostrophizes the American people, urging them to preserve in their hearts God's gift of liberty. Still addressing the American people, he adds: "Your example has set a goal for us — we all wish for the same. I have no part in your glory, but since the soul is subject to no one, allow at least my ashes to rest in your soil!" But Radishchev, a true son of his fatherland, went on in the next stanza: "But no! Where fate decided that I should be born, there let me end my days. Let my cold ashes be overshadowed by the greatness of which I sing to-day, so that a young man, thirsting for glory, may come to my deserted grave and feelingly may say: 'He who was born here under the yoke of tyranny and bore gilded fetters was the first to proclaim liberty to us.'" [10]

Radishchev worked at the *Journey* intermittently over the course of ten years, beginning part of it as early as 1780. One of his own footnotes, which refers to the death of the Austrian Emperor Joseph II, must have been written after February 20, 1790. Part of the chapter "Podberez'e" was written no later than 1782, while another chapter, "Torzhok," contains a reference to "the late Frederick II, King of Prussia," who died in 1786. There are only two brief references to the French Revolution, which in any case was only in its early stages by the time the *Journey* was published, in May 1790. Russia had been at war with Turkey since 1787 and with Sweden since 1788, a fact which should be kept in mind when reading Radishchev's account of a sale of serfs as recruits for the army, and his particular rejoicing at Russian victories over the Turks in earlier wars.

Much the greater part of his book, however, was written by 1788. It would have been better for Radishchev had he published it then, before the French Revolution had gotten under way at all. It had not yet gone very far by 1790, but it had gone far enough to frighten Catherine II, to make her expect to see its poisonous, subversive contagion everywhere. "The purpose of this book," she wrote in her Notes on the *Journey*, "is clear on every page: its author, infected and full of the French madness, is trying in every possible way to break down respect for authority and for the authorities, to stir up in the people indignation against their superiors and against the government." In one of his two brief references to the French Revolution, Radishchev had simply listed Mirabeau, along with Demosthenes, Cicero, Pitt, Burke, and Fox, as a great orator to whom Lomonosov was comparable. The Empress was furious at Radishchev's "praise of Mirabeau, who deserves not once but many times over to be hanged. . . ."[11]

At the end of the book was the usual imprimatur, the statement that it was printed "With the permission of the Department of Public Morals." The Empress, noting this, said: "This is probably a lie, or else carelessness."[12] It was actually carelessness. Radishchev had submitted the manuscript to the censor, who had cut out substantial parts of it. But Radishchev had nevertheless printed it all, on his own press. He then submitted the whole thing to the police, who gave it their official stamp of approval without reading it again. It never occurred to them that anyone would dare to print anything they had cut out.

Radishchev had printed the *Journey* anonymously, but it was a very simple matter for the Empress to discover who had written it. Frank, straightforward, outspoken, Radishchev had none of the instincts of a revolutionary. In 1789 he had dedicated his *Life of Fyodor Vasil'evich Ushakov* to Aleksey Mikhaylovich Kutuzov, whom he addressed as "my best beloved friend." In 1790 he dedicated the *Journey* "To A. M. K., My Best Beloved Friend," using exactly the same words. He went on to say: "Everything my mind and heart may wish to produce shall be dedicated to you, my comrade." Radishchev and Kutuzov were both well known in St. Petersburg, and Catherine herself had sent them off as comrades to the University of Leipzig. They had been good friends ever since. If this were not enough, the author of the *Journey* calls himself an inhabitant of St. Petersburg and later speaks of walking down the customs pier and looking at the ships, with more than a mere layman's knowledge of the ships and their cargoes. It was earlier in this very year 1790 that the Empress had made Radishchev Chief of the St. Petersburg Custom House. If it be objected that an editor with nothing else to do might notice such details in a book, but that an Empress with two wars to fight and a fair-sized country to govern would hardly have time, the editor must ruefully reply that the Empress found time to write ten closely printed pages of notes on the *Journey*, and that she noticed some things in it which he had missed.

The Empress's private secretary, Aleksandr Vasil'evich Khrapovitsky, noted in his diary that "She was graciously pleased to say that he [Radishchev] was a rebel, worse than Pugachev."[13] On June 30/July 11, 1790, Radishchev was arrested and imprisoned in the Fortress of St. Peter and St. Paul. On July 24/August 4, he was condemned to death. Ten days later, Russia and Sweden made peace in the Treaty of Verela. In honor of the peace, the Empress, on September 4/15, mercifully commuted Radishchev's sentence to banishment for ten years to Ilimsk in eastern Siberia, some three hundred miles north of Irkutsk and forty-five hundred miles east of St. Petersburg. She also deprived him of his status as a member of the gentry, of his rank in the service, and of his order of knighthood. But she did not confiscate his property, and she permitted him to travel without wearing fetters, after the first day.

Less than a year before the *Journey* appeared, Radishchev had published "A Conversation about Who Is a True Son of the Fatherland." This had appeared in the December 1789 number of the St. Petersburg magazine, The Citizen in Conversation (*Beseduyushchy grazhdanin*, part III, pp. 308ff.). "Not everyone born in the fatherland," he said, "deserves the glorious name of a son of the fatherland (a patriot). Those who live on under the yoke of slavery do not deserve to be honored with this name. . . . The name of a son of the fatherland belongs to man, and not to beasts or cattle. . . . The essential quality of man is freedom, and man was given a mind, reason, and free will . . . that he might always strive after what is more beautiful, greater, and more nearly perfect." So Radishchev strove in his next work, the *Journey*, and for his pains he was sent on another journey, to Ilimsk.

Less than a month after the commutation of Radishchev's sentence, Count Semyon Romanovich Vorontsov, the Russian ambassador to England, wrote a letter to his brother, Count Aleksandr Romanovich Vorontsov, President of the Commerce Collegium, Radishchev's superior officer in the Service and lifelong friend. The ambassador wrote from Richmond, England, on October 1/12, 1790: "The condemnation of poor Radishchev hurts me deeply. What a sentence and what a commutation for a mere blunder! What will they do for a crime or for a real revolt? Ten years of Siberia is worse than death for a man who has children from whom he must part, or whom he will deprive of an education and a chance to enter the service if he takes them with him. It makes one shudder."[14] But now, in time of trouble, Radishchev was very fortunate in his family and friends. His brother, a government official in Archangel, took care of his two elder sons. His deceased wife's sister, Elizaveta Vasil'evna Rubanovskaya, took care of his youngest son and his only daughter, and with them followed him into exile. In 1791 she married him, and they had three children in Siberia: two girls and a boy. Count Aleksandr Vorontsov proved to be a faithful friend, sending money, books, and news, and using his influence to make things easier for the exile. It was Vorontsov who prevailed upon the Empress to allow Radishchev to travel to Siberia unfettered, and who persuaded the Siberian authorities to let Radishchev go off on long walks and hunting trips.

Radishchev reached Ilimsk on January 3/14, 1792. Twelve days later, he started writing his next work, "On Man, on his Mortality and Immortality." Professor Lapshin, analyzing this work in detail, described it as "one of the first original Russian philosophical works." All that had happened to Radishchev had failed to destroy his faith in the essential goodness and potential greatness of man. A bird, he says, can sing gloriously, but what bird can produce such sounds as Gluck, Mozart, and Haydn do? An eagle can soar into the empyrean, and can see wonderfully clearly, but Sir William Herschel with his telescope can go still farther into the heavens, and Anton van Leeuwenhoek with his microscope can see still more clearly.[15]

In Siberia Radishchev was not able to accomplish the things he wanted to do, but he was free to move about, within reasonable limits, and he did a great deal of reading and some writing of his own. He volunteered his services as an amateur doctor, taking care of the sick at Ilimsk. The greater part of what we know of his life in Siberia comes from his letters to Count Aleksandr Vorontsov, which are preserved in the fifth volume (pp. 284-389) of the *Archive of Prince Vorontsov*. They show Radishchev as sincerely grateful but by no means servile to a nobleman who was in very truth a noble man. They show Radishchev's lively interest in the country and people around him, and also his desire to keep up with what was going on in Europe. In one letter he tells Vorontsov how much he has enjoyed a work by Condorcet, and then admits, in answer to the Count's question, that he would also enjoy reading Condorcet's commentaries on "the book of the Englishman Smith." Scotsmen will graciously forgive a poor exile for referring thus to Adam Smith's *The Wealth of Nations*.[16]

Count Vorontsov was also responsible for another work of Radishchev's, his "Letter on Chinese Trade." As President of the Commerce Collegium, the Count had excellent grounds for asking Radishchev for information on this subject. But knowing Radishchev as well as he did, and being his good friend, he may very likely have thought this would help to keep him busy in Siberia, and make him feel he was doing something useful. Whatever the Count's motives, he got a great deal of detailed information about what quantities of what goods came over which routes, what they were worth, and what items of trade might profitably be encouraged by the government.[17]

Fortunately for Radishchev, the Empress Catherine II died, November 6/17, 1796. Her son and successor, the Emperor Paul, had been treated abominably by his mother and hated everything that she had done. Accordingly, on November 23/ December 4, 1796, Paul issued an Imperial rescript permitting Radishchev to leave Siberia and to live on his estate in European Russia, where his "conduct and correspondence" would be "under observation" by the governor of the province. Radishchev therefore went to live on his estate of Nemtsovo, near Maloyaroslavets in Kaluga province, some seventy-five miles southwest of Moscow, where he arrived in June 1797. His wife had died on the way back from Siberia, but in January 1798 Radishchev and all his children — four sons and three daughters — set off for Verkhnee Oblyazovo to see his parents. He stayed with them for a whole year, returned to Nemtsovo in 1799, and remained there until 1801.

While he was at Nemtsovo, Radishchev wrote a poetic fairy tale on Bova Korolevich, Bova the King's Son. "Bova" is the

English "Bevis of Hampton," of the Anglo-Norman metrical romance. Sir Bevis himself traveled widely in his time, from Southampton to Armenia, but his story did almost as well, and lived longer. From England and France to Italy, where it was called "Bovo d'Antona," the story made its way through Bohemia and Belorussia, and so to Russia. During the course of the seventeenth and eighteenth centuries, it gradually grew to be a popular Russian fairy tale, changing considerably from the original. So well known was Bova in Russia by the late eighteenth century that Radishchev could refer to him offhandedly in the *Journey* (p. *43) and assume that his readers would know whom he was talking about. Then, in 1799, he started to write his own version of the tale.[18] As excellent a judge of the merit of Russian poetry as Pushkin found that "*Bova* . . . has real merit. The character of Bova is sketched out in an original manner, and his conversation with Karga is entertaining." [19]

The Emperor Paul was assassinated on March 11/23, 1801. Four days later, the Emperor Alexander I freed Radishchev from being "under observation" and restored to him his status as one of the gentry, his rank in the Service, and his order of knighthood. On August 6/18, 1801, on the recommendation of Count Aleksandr Vorontsov, Radishchev was appointed a member of the Commission on Revision of the Laws. Four years earlier, the Emperor Paul, at his coronation, had issued one new law of whose purpose Radishchev had heartily approved. On April 5/16, 1797, Paul had forbidden that peasants be required to work more than three days a week on their master's land. Radishchev, in the *Journey*, had particularly attacked landlords who required their peasants to give all their time to work on their master's land and allowed them no time to work their own. Now Radishchev hoped that under the reputedly more liberal Emperor Alexander I it would be possible to take further steps to protect the peasants.

In the very year of Alexander's accession, Radishchev wrote

a poem expressing his pride in the achievements — particularly those of Russia — in the century just ended. Pushkin said that "generally Radishchev wrote better in verse than in prose" and that "his best work in verse is *The Eighteenth Century*, a lyrical poem, written in the ancient elegiac metre." In the opinion of the present writer, it is a better poem than Coleridge's *Ode to the Departing Year* (1796). It is certainly more generous, though it might be argued that Coleridge's treatment of the Empress Catherine II was more nearly the kind she deserved. However that may be, Radishchev was a great enough man and a good enough Christian to praise, without any suspicion of servility, the worthwhile achievements of the dead Empress, in spite of all the misery she had caused him. And he looked forward with high hopes to the new century under the guardian genius of the new Emperor Alexander I.[20]

Two statements made by Radishchev as a member of the Commission have been preserved. The Commission debated at length the question of recommending a change in the law regulating the compensation to be paid to a serf-owner whose serf had been unintentionally killed. The Commission, including Radishchev, finally recommended a substantial increase in the amount of compensation. But Radishchev also sent to the Senate his own supplementary "minority report," in which he said that if a serf were killed, money should be paid, not to his owner, but to his parents, wife, or children. Although he approved of the increase in compensation, he wrote that "the value of human blood cannot be measured in terms of money." Again, Radishchev disagreed with the rest of the Commission as to the proper methods of trying persons accused of blasphemy, acts of rebellion, murder, robbery, and other capital offenses. The Commission recommended that the law should remain as it was, and specifically, that such accused persons should neither be permitted to challenge their judges nor be given a list of the charges against them. Radishchev, in a dissenting opinion worthy of Holmes or Brandeis, held that in every such trial the accused should be allowed to choose someone to defend him, and that if he could find no one, the court itself must provide someone to defend him; that the accused should have the right to challenge his judges; and that no one should be condemned to death by less than a two-thirds majority of the judges.[21]

The Commission seems to have accomplished very little. The chairman, Count Pyotr Vasil'evich Zavadovsky, eventually got around to writing an apologetic letter to the Emperor, trying to explain why they had spent so much time and done nothing. Radishchev's son, writing in 1858, said that his father, by contrast, had wanted to do a great deal, to make really substantial reforms in the law. He says that Radishchev drew up a "Project of a Civil Code," which he summarizes in nine points:

1. Make all classes of people equal before the law, and do away with corporal punishment.
2. Abolish the table of ranks.
3. In criminal cases, do away with threatening interrogations, and introduce public court proceedings and trial by jury; otherwise there can be no justice.
4. Establish complete religious toleration, and set aside everything which restricts freedom of conscience.
5. Establish freedom of the press, with limitations and clear regulations on the degree of responsibility.
6. Emancipate the manorial serfs, and put an end to the sale of men as recruits.
7. Introduce a tax per unit of land instead of per cultivator.
8. Establish freedom of trade.
9. Repeal the severe laws against usurers and against insolvent debtors, and have something on the order of Habeas corpus.

A Russian scholar writing in 1912 published a tenth point of this "Project," which he said was in the manuscript of Radishchev's son's article, but which did not appear in the published version. It reads: "Radishchev said that in her provision for elections of their officers by the gentry [the Charter to the Gentry of 1785], Catherine II had laid the foundation of the future constitution of Russia. He proposed that, abandoning unlimited monarchical power in Russia, they should introduce democratic institutions. Let the Tsar still be great, but let Russia be free (like England)." [22]

The "Project" itself is not extant, but the ideas of the ten points are perfectly in accord with Radishchev's ideas as expressed in the *Journey*. At his death it was discovered that he had a number of books on the English government, the English criminal code, the functioning of justices of the peace, and others. If Radishchev sounds like more of an Anglophile in the "Project" than in the *Journey*, we may recall that in the dozen years between, he had kept up a steady correspondence with his faithful friend, Count Aleksandr Vorontsov, who was one of a family of ardent Anglophiles, and who had sent him many of his books. Radishchev's son says that when his father was appointed to the Commission in 1801, he actually wanted to go to England to study at first hand the jury system and the practice of conducting trials in public.[23]

In short, Radishchev had very high hopes for reform, but he was deeply discouraged and depressed by the attitude of the other members of the Commission, especially the chairman, Count Zavadovsky. One of the best Russian authorities on Radishchev, Professor Borozdin, accepted as "very probably correct" Pushkin's account of Radishchev's death. Pushkin said that the Emperor Alexander I ordered Radishchev to set forth his ideas on certain questions of government. Poor Radishchev, carried away by the subject, . . . remembered the old days and, in a project presented to the government, revealed his old opinions. Count Z[avadovsky] was astonished at the youthfulness of his gray hairs and said to him in friendly reproof: "Eh, Aleksandr Nikolaevich, do you still want to talk the same old nonsense? Or didn't you have enough of Siberia?" In these words Radishchev saw a threat. Distressed and terrified, he went home, remembered the friend of his youth, the student at Leipzig [probably Fyodor Vasil'evich Ushakov] who had first suggested to him the thought of suicide . . . and took poison. He had foreseen his end long before and had prophesied it himself!

The *Journey* is full of Radishchev's view of suicide. In one place he advised his sons: "If there is no refuge left on earth for your virtue, if, driven to extremes, you find no sanctuary from oppression, then remember that you are a man, call to mind your greatness, and seize the crown of bliss which they are trying to take from you. Die. As a legacy I leave you the words of the dying Cato." When he had committed suicide, Cato had said: "Now I am my own master." And so, on September 12/24, 1802, Radishchev became his own master.[24]

In content, Radishchev's *Journey from St. Petersburg to Moscow* is ostensibly an account of people and things he saw while traveling through Russia, from her newer to her older capital. Throughout the book there is abundant analysis and exposition. For example, there are descriptions of a peasant plowing a field, barges carrying grain through a canal to supply St. Petersburg, an auction sale of serfs, the recruiting of peasants for the army, the furnishings of a peasant hut, the forced marriage of two peasants who do not love one another. The Vyshny Volochok Canal, an important part of the developing network of inland waterways, is described with the natural enthusiasm of a Commerce Department official. In another place, in a sort of flashback, Radishchev describes the harbor, naval base, and fortress of Kronstadt, the key point in the defense of Russia's foreign trade. He gives an account of the historically opulent but commercially decayed city of Novgorod, and looks down from her ancient and famous bridge (so renowned in the Chronicles) over the Volkhov River. There are excursions into local history or folklore at several places along the way. He climbs the hill at Bronnitsy and tells the story of the old Slavonic temple there. He visits the Lake of Valdai, points out the Iberian Monastery on its island in the lake, and tells the story of its monk who fell in love with a girl from Valdai. Later we listen to a singer of folk songs at Klin and share Radishchev's impressions of him. And Radishchev's impressions could be strikingly vivid. In short, the book is full of interesting descriptions of people, places, customs, and institutions in Russia in the 1780's.

It is obvious, however, that the main purpose of these descriptive passages is not to give historical information or to entertain the reader, but to serve as launching platforms for attacks on the Russian government and institutions. Radishchev's prime concern was with the peasants, that 95 per cent of the Russian people who not only had no voice in their government but were not even their own masters. The institution of serfdom and the government that backed it up with military force were the chief objects of his attack. His description of the peasant's plowing affords him an opportunity to attack landlords who preëmpted nearly all of their peasants' time. The sight of barges carrying grain to St. Petersburg at first makes him proud of his country's progress in canal building, but his pride becomes anger when he realizes that the grain moving over the canal was grown by men who were the property of other men, and how much human misery this process entailed. An auction sale of serfs graphically shows forth the brutal selfishness of their masters. The master, in this case, is not merely willing to sell human beings to the highest bidder; he is selling his devoted retainers, almost members of his family, people who have risked their lives for him. Moreover, though these people are themselves a family, he does not hesitate to break up this family and sell each one to a different master. The recruiting of peasants for the army also illustrates several different forms of cruel injustice to the peasants. One serf has to go off to the wars even though he is the sole support of his family. A landlord sells three of his serfs as recruits because he wants money to buy a new carriage. Another serf is sent off to the army as a punishment, because his behavior was not servile enough to satisfy his imperious owners.

The point can and should be made that not all landlords were vicious and cruel, just as not all Southerners were like Simon Legree. Certainly Radishchev's father, and probably many others, were thoroughly decent people. But the *Journey*, like *Uncle Tom's Cabin*, is an abolitionist tract, and Radishchev, like Mrs. Stowe, is thoroughgoing and relentless in his attack against a pernicious wrong. He was not writing a judiciously balanced and objective history; he was a reformer, attacking, in its head and members, what he considered an entirely evil system.

The sovereign is explicitly attacked at least three times in the *Journey*, and several times more by implication. In the chapter "Spasskaya Polest'," Radishchev dreams of himself as a sovereign, sitting on his throne, surrounded by sycophantic courtiers. He imagines himself great, glorious, beloved by all his people, the source of their happiness. The servile flatterers around him encourage him in all his worst impulses, and are leading him and the country straight to ruin. The fairy Truth appears, shows him that he has been blinded by flattery, removes the cataracts from his eyes, lets him see how frightfully bad things really are in his country, and warns him that the cataracts will grow back again if he succumbs to flattery again and ignores honest and courageous criticism. The entire chapter "Vydropusk" is an attack on the Court Service and the dangerous effect of flattery on the sovereign, making him unaware of his people's needs and suffering, encouraging him to think only of his own satisfaction, vanity, and pleasure. The sovereign's tendency to reward the toadies around his person rather than men who truly serve him comes in for particular attack. The chapter "Tver'" contains the excerpts from the ode *Liberty*, which deal, as we have seen, with a tyrannical Tsar. The fact that Russia is an autocracy, the recognition of the sovereign as the source of the laws, the belief that the sovereign alone has power enough to right wrongs and to render justice to the poor and the oppressed, are expressed in various ways throughout the *Journey* (pp. *58–*59, *184).

The officials beneath the sovereign also are fully criticized. Radishchev attacks judges who have been so brutally unjust as to deprive people of property, honor, and life itself to fill the treasury and satisfy the demands of the government. He praises one judge who had had the courage to temper justice with mercy by declaring innocent some peasants who had murdered their landlord after what any fair-minded person would have to admit was more than ample provocation (pp. *58, *119–*147). But he shows how this rare good official's life was made so miserable that he was driven out of the Service and replaced by one who would please his superiors by his unrelenting cruelty and harshness to the peasants. Officials time and time again are pictured as lacking in any concern for the welfare of the people subject to their authority, and concerned only for their own wealth, comfort, and position in the Service.

Since most officials were drawn from the gentry, one would hardly expect the gentry to be shown in a more favorable light than the officials. They are not. Radishchev represents them as neither gentle nor even men. They treat their peasants not as their fellow men, but simply as tools to produce more wealth for their masters. The landlords are shown as local autocratic rulers over their peasants, possessing unlimited power and constantly abusing it. Again it should probably be noted that not all landlords were in fact as Radishchev pictured them.

It is a refreshing change indeed to turn from Radishchev's landlords to his peasants, although their originals were doubtless not by any means so good as he makes them. The peasants generally are hard-working, honest, simple, straightforward, incorruptible, not given to deceitfulness and trickery, and wonderfully patient. They are truly nature's noblemen. They share what little they have. They endure terrible suffering before they finally rise up in righteous wrath and smite their oppressors. The influence of Rousseau is obvious, but there are many small details that do distinguish Radishchev's peasants from peasants in abstract theory, and give them life. The peasant's condition as a serf, the fact that this best of men has the worst lot of all, the ruinous, degrading, brutalizing effects of serfdom on master and serf alike, are the main theme and the chief object of attack throughout the *Journey*.

In this connection it is noteworthy that Radishchev repeatedly and bitterly attacked America (pp. *251, *270, *348). We have already noted that he omitted from the *Journey* all parts of the ode *Liberty* in which he had spoken favorably of America. He went much farther. The most opprobrious and vicious thing he could think of with which to compare and equate Russian serfdom was American Negro slavery. On the other hand, he was not completely anti-American. He praised John Dickinson, Benjamin Franklin, the Quakers, and the freedom of the press in America (pp. *301, *450, *347, *334–*335).

Radishchev attacked not only the sovereign, officials, and gentry, but also the clergy — chiefly as obscurantists, standing in the way of the enlightenment and full liberation of the people. He attacked the servants of the God of love and Father of all men for persecuting those of His children whose religious beliefs were not precisely orthodox. He also excoriated the clergy for serving the interests of the rich and powerful, and for not having the courage to stand up and denounce oppressors. But he made it very clear that he considered the landed gentry far worse than the clergy, whose offense was the secondary one of collaboration in and winking at evil done by and for the chief benefit of the gentry. He warmly praised individual clergymen, ranging from the Metropolitan of Moscow to a village priest at Sestroretsk. Whatever his feeling was toward priests, Radishchev made it thoroughly clear that he did not hold against their Master the shortcomings of His servants and their failure to live up to their high calling. The *Journey* is to some degree anticlerical; it is not at all antireligious (pp. *349, *447-*448, *39).

One part of Radishchev's anticlerical feeling appears in his attack on the Russian monastic schools, which he twice criticizes for teaching according to the rules of medieval scholasticism. (On the other hand, he tries to be fair, pointing out that Lomonosov derived great benefit from reading the Church books and advised others to read them.) He wants all teaching in Russia to be in the vernacular, so that more people can learn more, sooner. He wants new universities founded, in addition to the University of Moscow, and he particularly wants them to give instruction in the sciences. He is opposed to the use of corporal punishment in the schools (pp. *89, *428, *427, *90, *91, *294).

But the greatest bar to the education and enlightenment of the people, he feels, is the censorship. "Torzhok," the longest chapter in the *Journey*, contains an historical account of the origins and development of the censorship, and the struggle for freedom of the press in many countries. In a great many details, both of fact and of argument, it is strongly reminiscent of Milton's *Areopagitica*. We know, both from Radishchev himself and from his son, that he had read some of Milton's works and had the highest opinion of him: indeed he speaks of Milton, Shakespeare, and Voltaire (in that order) as the three supremely great writers. While many of Radishchev's factual data on censorship come from Johann Beckmann's *Beiträge zur Geschichte der Erfindungen*, it is quite possible that his inspiration comes from Milton.[25]

Among the written works of history which provided Radishchev with ideas, information, and inspiration for writing his *Journey*, probably the most important was the Abbé Raynal's *History of the Two Indies.* Horace Walpole gave a classic description of this work,

> a most amusing book in six volumes. . . . It tells one everything in the world; — how to make conquests, invasions, blunders, settlements, bankruptcies, fortunes, &c.; tells you the natural and historical history of all nations; talks commerce, navigation, tea, coffee, china, mines, salt, spices; of the Portuguese, English, French, Dutch, Danes, Spaniards, Arabs, caravans, Persians, Indians; of Louis XIV and the King of Prussia; of La Bourdonnais, Dupleix, and Admiral Saunders; of rice, and women that dance naked; of camels, gingham, and muslin, of millions of millions of livres, pounds, rupees, and cowries; of iron cables and Circassian women, of law and the Mississippi; and against all governments and religions. This and everything else is in the first two volumes. I cannot conceive what is left for the four others. And all is so mixed, that you learn forty new trades, and fifty new histories, in a single chapter. There is spirit, wit, and clearness — and, if there were but less avoirdupois weight in it, it would be the richest book in the world in materials. . .

In a far more serious and scholarly account, published in 1891, Edmond Scherer says: "I am persuaded that the *Histoire philosophique des deux Indes* had more influence on the French Revolution than the *Contrat social* itself." The driving force, the moving power in Raynal's work is a burning hatred of slavery, tyranny, and oppression in all forms. This comes out strongly in the one passage from Raynal which Radishchev directly quotes in the *Journey*. Raynal's work is certainly not great, either as history or as literature. But the idea that is the essence of the work, the desire to free mankind, and the conviction with which Raynal expressed this idea throughout the work made a deep impression on Radishchev, and led him to classify Raynal, along with Tacitus and Robertson, as one of the three greatest historians.[26]

Professor Black, in his work on great historians of the eighteenth century, ranks Robertson along with Voltaire, Hume, and Gibbon. One instance (not heretofore noted by editors of Radishchev) will serve to show how Radishchev borrowed both factual information and ideas from Robertson. In his discussion of the Incas in Peru, Robertson said: "Manco Capac and his consort, taking advantage of the propensity in the Peruvians to superstition, and particularly of their veneration for the Sun, pretended to be children of that glorious luminary, and to deliver their instructions in his name and authority. The multitude listened and believed." And Radishchev: "The weak Peruvians readily believed Manco Capac when he told them that he was the son of the sun and that his laws came from heaven." [27]

We have already referred to Radishchev's translation of Mably's work on Greek history, and to the fact that both men hated despotism, in any language. Mably hated the power of rich landlords over poor peasants, hated the fact that some men should own and derive the fruits from great lands which they did not work themselves, while other men should have to work those lands and derive from their labor only what their landlord graciously permitted them to keep. Mably felt that this system was not only unjust but unproductive. "The cultivation of the land is neglected, and the fields produce a meagre harvest under the work of hands not animated by a sense of ownership; for one does not work for others with the same ardor as for oneself." "Thus we find the agriculturists in our country," says Radishchev. "The field is not their own, the fruit thereof does not belong to them. Hence they cultivate the land lazily and do not care whether it goes to waste because of their poor work." [28]

We have already noted the source of the greater part of Radishchev's information on the censorship. He was thoroughly familiar with Bayle's *Historical Dictionary*, and seems to have done some reading of the Novgorod Chronicles. His work demonstrates his interest in, and in some cases considerable knowledge of, a wide range of significant people: statesmen like Cromwell, Pitt, Burke, Fox, Lafayette, Mirabeau, and Dickinson; scientists like Bacon, Franklin, Marggraf, Rüdiger, Richmann, and Lomonosov; and artists like Hogarth, Vernet, and Lavater. The Empress Catherine II was absolutely right when she said of Radishchev: "He has learning enough, and has read many books." [29]

The *Journey*, as a literary work, is hard to classify. In form, it is modeled on Sterne's *Sentimental Journey*. The form of the journey enabled Radishchev to comment on and criticize a great variety of things, without being troubled about any logical sequence. Radishchev does not seem to treat subjects in any particular order, nor does he bring up a subject, treat it fully, and then move on to another. Forced marriages of the peasants appear in "Edrovo," again in "Mednoe," again in "Gorodnya," and once again in "Chernaya Gryaz'." In "Zaytsovo," at what would seem to be sufficient length, he attacks the custom of making calls on great personages; yet in "Kresttsy," after considering a variety of other subjects, he returns unwearied to the same attack and pursues it for two pages more. From Zaytsovo to Tver' he takes up, in order, the Service, the abuse of peasants by landlords, calling on great personages, the Service, education, calling on great personages, venereal disease, a monk, an admirable peasant girl, the emancipation of the serfs, trial by jury, canal building, the emancipation of the serfs, the abolition of the Court Service, censorship, an auction sale of serfs, and prosody.

One passage in Radishchev's *Journey* is reminiscent of Sterne's. In his chapter "The Snuff-Box. Calais," Sterne tells how he offered his snuff-box as a gift to the old Franciscan monk, Father Lorenzo. The monk would not take it as a gift, but exchanged snuff-boxes with him. Thereafter, whenever Sterne used the snuff-box, he thought of the monk. The last time he went through Calais, he heard, to his grief, that Father Lorenzo was dead. He went to the monk's grave, looked at the snuff-box again, and "burst into a flood of tears." [30] Radishchev, in his chapter "Klin," has a similar experience which moves him in much the same way.

As we have already noted, the *Journey* is something of a literary travelogue. Although its main purpose is very different, it does frequently remind one of such works as Drayton's *Poly-Olbion* and Defoe's *Tour through the Whole Island of Great Britain*. Even before the seventeenth century and increasingly throughout the eighteenth and after, from Defoe's all-British *Tour* to the larger ranges of *Gulliver's Travels*, Montesquieu's *Persian Letters*, and Goethe's *Italian Journey*, accounts of travels, voyages, and journeys of all kinds, real and fictitious, sentimental and satirical, pastoral, comical, tragical, historical, had become immensely popular. English-speaking students of the literature of travel have paid little attention to Russian works in this field. Radishchev's *Journey*, for example, is not mentioned in Edward Godfrey Cox's three-volume *Reference Guide to the Literature of Travel* (Seattle, 1935–1949). Yet the tradition and influence of other distinguished literary travelers, especially Montesquieu, left their mark not only upon Radishchev's zealously idealistic political journeyings, but also upon the more factual and descriptive north Russian *Journey* by his friend Chelishchev and the *Letters of a Russian Traveler* by the famous Karamzin.[31]

The *Journey* certainly was influenced by Goethe's *Sorrows of Young Werther*. Like it, the *Journey* contains elements of fictionalized and sentimentalized near-autobiography, especially in the chapters "Kresttsy," "Yazhelbitsy," and "Edrovo." But Radishchev, like Goethe, was not writing a formal, factual autobiography, and often wrote things about himself which were not true at all, but simply designed to move his readers to tears. Thus, in "Yazhelbitsy," when he tearfully said that he had condemned himself to premature old age and decrepitude, and had poisoned his sons with a loathsome disease, condemning them to poor health and cutting short their lives, he was simply indulging in a sentimental pose. To put it more charitably, we might say that he was trying to attack a prevalent and common evil by attributing it to himself, making it sound more horrible by describing it in the first person. For the fact is that Radishchev enjoyed robust good health and was not too decrepit to enjoy taking long walks in Siberia in winter. The two sons he referred to were in fact both vigorously healthy, and one of them lived to be over eighty. The suicide motif, which crops up several times through the *Journey*, is again reminiscent of *Werther*. But Radishchev's only actual reference to Werther in the *Journey* is perhaps most revealing of all. Addressing his friend Kutuzov, Radishchev tells him how he listened to a blind old singer of folk songs at Klin. "I wept in company with all the others at the post station, and my tears were as sweet to me as those which had once been called forth by Werther. . . O my friend, my friend! Why did you not see this picture? You would have shed tears with me, and the bliss of mutual feeling would have been even sweeter."

By the same token, Radishchev would seem to have remembered something of the tears and self-reproachful agonizings of Rousseau's *Confessions*. The *Journey*'s nature-worship also reflects Rousseau's, and the chapter "Kresttsy" in particular reminds one of *Emile*. Like Rousseau, Radishchev would have mothers suckle their own babies and fathers tutor their own children. Both would have the children acquire some trade or handicraft, and learn to take care of themselves in difficult conditions. But unlike Rousseau, Radishchev wanted children to learn foreign languages, history, logic, ethics, and even metaphysics.

Again, the *Journey* is comparable to More's *Utopia* and to Swift's *Modest Proposal* and *Gulliver's Travels*. It contains political and social satire, and an ideal vision of the future. There is particularly savage satire, sometimes almost worthy of Swift, in the chapters "Spasskaya Polest'," "Zavidovo," and

"Peshki." The *Journey* is one of the works considered in a recent study of utopian fantasy in Russian literature. The chapters "Khotilov" and "Vydropusk" each contain "A Project for the Future." These "projects" look forward to the abolition of serfdom, the individual ownership of the land by the peasants who cultivate it, trial by jury, with peasants to serve on juries when peasants are tried, the prohibition of arbitrary punishment without due process of law, and the abolition of the Table of Ranks and the Court Service. Three specific proposals (for moderation in punishment, for popular education, and for bondage to be reserved only as the extreme punishment for the worst criminals and for enemies captured in battle), and the reasons advanced in support of these proposals, do remind one strongly of *Utopia*. But they were probably inspired rather by the actual conditions of Russian life, or, in the case of the proposal for moderation in punishment, possibly also by Beccaria.[32]

In the *Journey*, Radishchev refers to, and occasionally quotes (though without always using quotation marks or mentioning his source) from the works of a great many famous authors, including Homer, Pindar, Demosthenes, Cicero, Virgil, Horace, Livy, Tacitus, Tasso, Cervantes, Shakespeare, Grotius, Milton, Racine, Addison, Montesquieu, Voltaire, Blackstone, Herder, and Goethe. Of these his favorites seem to have been Virgil, Horace, Shakespeare, Milton, and Voltaire.[33]

Unfortunately, Radishchev's style is not the best thing about the *Journey*. Pushkin, who admired Radishchev and agreed with his ideas, did not think he had expressed them well.[34] The *Journey* tends to be repetitious. Landlord after landlord, with monotonous consistency, is cruel, wicked, grasping, brutal, and rapacious. In "Zaytsovo" Radishchev spells out the theory of the social contract in wearisome detail. In "Khotilov" he does it all over again, in very nearly the same words.

Radishchev uses a great deal of Church Slavonic, which is sometimes effective, but more often sounds archaic, and occasionally heavy. His language appears distinctly more old-fashioned than that of his approximate contemporaries Fonvizin and Karamzin, and much more so than the English of Johnson and Boswell.[35] Yet paradoxically, English readers of Radishchev, by virtue of his passionate intensity will be reminded of a later English writer. In mood, occasion, and style, in oracular vehemence and prophetic rhapsody, Radishchev curiously anticipates Thomas Carlyle. Witness, for example, the turgid eloquence of *Past and Present*'s protest against the social-economic misery of the "masses" in the England of 1843.

Radishchev's language sometimes looks strange to a modern Russian reader. The verb "to be," hardly used at all in modern Russian except in the third person singular, appears in almost all its forms throughout the *Journey*. Radishchev's sojourn in Germany may have given him his taste for heavy, intricately constructed sentences, with long-drawn-out adjectival modifiers. He frequently uses a construction like the Latin ablative absolute. It may also have been from the Latin that Radishchev learned to be fond of long, elaborate similes in the manner of Virgil.[36]

Radishchev seems also to be fond of the long sentence. In "Vydropusk" one sentence ambles along for two whole pages. Another, in "Zavidovo," occupies an entire page. But while this would not have been to the liking of nineteenth-century American critics (compare Mark Twain's unkind remarks about transcontinental German sentences), those of the twentieth century can scarcely find serious fault with Radishchev on this ground. For a writer no less universally acclaimed than William Faulkner has turned out far longer sentences than any that Radishchev ever dreamed of.[37]

At the time Radishchev wrote, it should be remembered, the Russian literary language as used by the great writers of the nineteenth century had not yet been developed. Lomonosov had done some very important pioneering work, which Radishchev appreciated and warmly praised. The next great molder of the language, Karamzin, did most of his writing only after the *Journey* was published. Karamzin greatly enriched the language, forming Russian equivalents for many Western words. But Radishchev used the language as it was in the 1780's, Church Slavonic, foreign words, Russian folk expressions, and all, without attempting a synthesis or trying, as Karamzin did, to form a modern, secular, uniform literary language. By the time Pushkin wrote his criticism of Radishchev's style in 1836, the language, thanks to the work of Karamzin and Pushkin himself, had become an incomparably richer and greater literary vehicle.

Radishchev is fond of poetic rhapsodizing. He lyrically apostrophizes God, liberty, Peter the Great, Lomonosov. Like Derzhavin, he was fond of writing odes. Like Derzhavin's, these had none of the courtier's servility in them, and they sometimes mixed Church Slavonic and peasant expressions, solemn reflections and satire. But Radishchev lacked Derzhavin's sense of humor and the terse mastery which enabled him to express a great idea in a very few words. Radishchev as a poet was thoughtful, sincere, and honorable, but not great.

His fictional characters, however, are more convincingly portrayed than Karamzin's. The peasant girl Anna in the chapter "Edrovo" is a more real person than Karamzin's heroine in *Poor Liza*. The merchant family in "Novgorod" and the *filles de joie* in "Zaytsovo" come to life so vividly that they seem almost to anticipate some of Ostrovsky's characters.

The worst fault of the *Journey* is its lack of humor. There is sharp irony, as in the account of the Viceroy who had such an all-consuming passion for oysters that he turned the whole administration upside down to get them, and in the lord admiral's flowery description of the globe-girdling voyage of discovery that he had made — while he had actually been coasting just outside the harbor of St. Petersburg the whole time. But there is no warm, genial humor in the *Journey*. Radishchev was well aware of the possibilities of ridicule as a weapon. One only wishes that he might have tempered ridicule with kindly understanding, with more willingness to make allowances for other people's shortcomings. On the whole, the people in the *Journey* tend to be altogether good or altogether bad. They (and the *Journey*) would be more effective if they had elements of both. In short, the *Journey* contains Tartuffes and Candides. It contains no Falstaff, no Mr. Micawber.

To present-day taste, the *Journey* is certainly marred by its sentimentality. This sometimes sounds almost falsetto. In "Chudovo," Pavel, a peasant fisherman, tells his companions the story of how he brought them help when they were shipwrecked. He tells it all not merely with immaculately perfect grammar but with such lofty sentiment as would have done credit to the most highly educated nobleman. He concludes: " 'If you had drowned, I would have hurled myself into the water after you.' So saying, Pavel burst into tears." In "Gorodnya," a peasant woman is shown saying farewell to her son as he is taken away to the army. What she says to him can only be described as maudlin. At the time the *Journey* appeared, of course, sentimentality was as much the fashion as brutality is the fashion nowadays.

It should also be remembered, of course, that even sentimentality — oversensitive sympathy, exaggerated "sensibility" — such as Richardson popularized for men of feeling all over Europe, was a not altogether unwholesome offset to the harsh actualities faced by the poor and humble in the eighteenth century. Radishchev's sensibility helped to inspire him to write a book primarily concerned with the peasants. They were to become tremendously important in the great

Russian literature of the nineteenth century. But in Radishchev's time the peasants had been so little noticed that Karamzin found it necessary, even two years after the *Journey* appeared, to tell the readers of *Poor Liza* that "even peasant women know how to love." [38]

With all its faults as a literary work, the over-all impression that the *Journey* gives is one of burning sincerity and high purpose. And indeed Radishchev had everything to lose and nothing to gain for himself by writing the *Journey*. It is a deeply moving book, inspired by his heartfelt sympathy for the sufferings of his fellow men and his desire to do what he could to bring about a more merciful, more rational, more hopeful, and more nearly just state of affairs.

Radishchev was and is remembered by Russians as he himself wished to be remembered, as the man who "first proclaimed liberty to us." In 1802 his friend Pnin wrote a poem "On the Death of Radishchev," who, he said, spoke the truth, bravely cried out for justice, strove not for his own but for the general welfare, and pointed the way to liberty.[39]

Pushkin was strongly influenced by Radishchev. In 1814, while he was at the Imperial Lyceum in Tsarskoe Selo, Pushkin, like Radishchev, wrote a poem called "Bova." Pushkin appeals to his muse, says he too has decided to be a poet, but adds, "Shall I be compared to Radishchev?" In 1817 he wrote "Liberty: An Ode," with the same title as Radishchev's work and very much the same ideas. Regicide is justified, but only as a last resort against an intolerable tyranny. Like Radishchev, Pushkin was equally opposed to royal and revolutionary violence and despotism. The firm alliance of law and freedom, he felt, would guarantee the safety of the ruler and the welfare of his subjects. In 1819 Pushkin wrote a poem, "The Village," which reminds one strongly of the *Journey*'s chapters "Vyshny Volochok" and "Mednoe." Pushkin paints an idyllic picture at first, but then his picture is all poisoned by the realization that there is serfdom in the village. At the end he expresses his humanitarian hope for the freeing of the serfs, not by revolution, but from above, by the Tsar himself.[40]

Pushkin had a copy of Radishchev's own edition of the *Journey*. He made a great many marginal notes in it and knew it through and through. In 1826, in a poetical epistle to his friend Sobolevsky, he told him where to go and what to see on a journey from Moscow to St. Petersburg. The most amusing part of it is where he tells him to be sure not to miss certain delicacies in Valdai — the very delicacies that Radishchev had not missed when he was there. Another amusing recollection of Radishchev's *Journey* appears in Pushkin's historical novel, *The Captain's Daughter*. There, as I have pointed out elsewhere, Pushkin paid his respects to the censor by an oblique but unmistakable allusion to Radishchev's anecdote of the French tutor in Russia. In the years 1833 to 1835, Pushkin worked intermittently at "A Journey from Moscow to St. Petersburg." This was intended to be the return journey that Radishchev had suggested at the end of his. It covers much of the same material, such as serfdom, censorship, forced marriages of the peasants, and the recruiting of peasants for the army, often in the same spirit as Radishchev. But Pushkin did not hesitate to disagree with Radishchev. Though he also considered serfdom utterly wrong, he felt that Radishchev had somewhat exaggerated the wickedness of the landlords and the miseries of the serfs. He also felt that Radishchev had not done sufficient honor to Lomonosov. Referring to Radishchev's last chapter, his "Eulogy on Lomonosov," Pushkin says: "Lomonosov was a great man. . . He founded our first university. To put it better, he was our first university." Pushkin completed only one chapter of his "Journey," but left notes for, or incomplete versions of, twelve chapters in all. Pushkin being the man he was, it of course contains a great deal of fresh material and many new ideas, and is not simply a restatement of Radishchev, though it was inspired by him.[41]

In 1836 Pushkin wrote a biographical sketch, "Aleksandr

Radishchev," which included a critique of Radishchev's works. It was intended for publication in Pushkin's magazine, The Contemporary (*Sovremennik*), but was rejected by the censorship. Annenkov was permitted to publish it in 1857, in the seventh volume of his edition of Pushkin's complete works. It was this article of Pushkin's which inspired Radishchev's son Pavel to write his biographical sketch of his father for The Russian Messenger (*Russky vestnik*) in 1858.

In 1836 Pushkin also wrote his famous poem bearing the Horatian subtitle "Exegi Monumentum." (One notes Radishchev's closing allusion in the *Journey* to Horace's "Odi Profanum Vulgus.") In his fourth stanza, Pushkin said that he would be remembered for having sung the praises of liberty and for having appealed for mercy to those who had fallen. In a variant form of this stanza, he said he would be remembered "because, following in the footsteps of Radishchev, I sang the praises of liberty." [42]

Herzen was deeply moved by Radishchev. *My Past and Thoughts*, for example, contains many passages reminiscent of Radishchev's concern for the hardships inflicted upon peasants by the brutality or thoughtless selfishness of their masters. In London in 1858 Herzen published the first edition of the *Journey* to appear since Radishchev's own in 1790. In his preface to this edition, Herzen says that Radishchev "sympathizes with the sufferings of the masses, he talks with coachmen, serfs, and recruits, and in his every word we find a hatred of arbitrary power and a sturdy protest against serfdom." After giving a sketch of Radishchev's life and death (based on Pushkin's sketch), Herzen concludes: "How can the memory of this martyr be anything but dear to our hearts?" [43]

Dobrolyubov carried admiration for Radishchev to extremes. In 1857 he reviewed the seventh volume of Annenkov's edition of Pushkin, containing the article on Radishchev. For seven pages, with considerable heat, Dobrolyubov berates Pushkin for having dared to criticize Radishchev's literary style. The basic idea is that Radishchev was right: he was trying to change the old order, which was wrong; therefore any criticism of Radishchev, on any ground whatsoever, was disloyal, a betrayal of the cause. From what we have already said, of course, it is sufficiently clear that Pushkin was thoroughly loyal to the ideals of Radishchev. He was, in fact, so loyal that he wished Radishchev had expressed them more effectively. As Pushkin himself said it: "How is it possible in an article on Russian literature to forget Radishchev? Whom, then, should we remember?" [44]

A JOURNEY FROM
ST. PETERSBURG TO MOSCOW

BY

ALEKSANDR NIKOLAEVICH RADISHCHEV

To A. M. K.
My Best Beloved Friend

Everything my mind and heart may wish to produce shall be dedicated to you, my comrade! Although my opinions on many subjects differ from yours, your heart beats sympathetically with mine — and you are my friend.

I looked about me — my heart was troubled by the sufferings of humanity. I turned my eyes inward — I saw that man's woes arise in man himself, and frequently only because he does not look straight at the objects around him. Is it possible, I said to myself, that nature has been so miserly with her children as to hide the truth forever from him who errs innocently? Is it possible that this stern stepmother has brought us into the world that we may know only calamities, but never happiness? My reason trembled at this thought, and my heart thrust it far away. I found a comforter for man in himself: "Remove the veil from the inward eye — and I shall be happy!" This voice of nature resounded loudly within me. I arose from the despair into which sensitivity and compassion had plunged me; I felt within me strength enough to withstand this delusion, and — unspeakable joy! I felt that it was possible for anyone to strive for the well-being of his fellows. Such is the thought which moved me to sketch out what you are going to read. But, I said to myself, if I find a man who will approve of my intention, who for the sake of the good cause will not condemn my imperfect rendering of my thoughts, who will share my compassion for the sufferings of his fellow beings, who will support me in the quest before me: will not my undertaking have borne abundant fruit? Why, why should I seek some one who is far away? My friend, you live close to my heart — and may your name illumine this beginning!

[*1] THE DEPARTURE

Having supped with friends, I took my place in the post chaise. As was his custom, the driver urged the horses on to the utmost, and in a few minutes I was outside the city. It is hard to part, even briefly, from someone who has become necessary to us in every moment of our being. It is hard to part, but blessed is he who can part without smiling, for love or friendship will console him. You weep as you say farewell, but think of your return, and may your tears vanish at the thought of it as the dew vanishes before the face of the sun. Blessed is he who sobs, hoping for a consoler; blessed is he who sometimes lives in the future; blessed is he who lives in dreams. His whole being is enriched, his joys multiply, and calm soothes the gloom [*2] of sorrow, creating images of gladness in the mirror of the imagination.

I lay back in the carriage. The ringing of the post bell, after tiring my ears, at last summoned kindly Morpheus. The sadness of parting remained with me in my deathlike slumber and made me feel utterly alone. I beheld myself in a broad valley, which from the sun's heat had lost all its charming and variegated verdure; there was no spring in which to cool myself, no shade trees to temper the heat. Alone, deserted, a hermit amidst nature! I shuddered.

"Miserable one," I cried, "where are you? Where is everything that used to attract you? Where is that which used to make your life pleasant? Is it possible that the joys which you once felt were only dreams and fancies?"

Fortunately a rut in the road, which jarred my carriage, awakened me. [*3] The carriage stopped. I raised my head. I saw in an open space a three-story building.

"What is it?" I asked my driver.

"The post station."

"Where are we?"

"In Sofiya."

Meanwhile he was unhitching the horses.

[*4] SOFIYA

Silence everywhere. Lost in contemplation, I had not noticed that my carriage had been standing for some time without its horses. The driver who had brought me thither roused me from my reverie.

"A few kopeks, Master, for a drink?"

Although such exactions are not legal, everybody pays willingly to avoid vexatious travel regulations. Twenty kopeks served me well. He who has traveled by post knows that the permit to use post horses is a protective letter, without which any purse, excepting possibly a general's, is subject to great strain. Taking the permit from my pocket, I carried it the way they sometimes carry a cross for protection.

I sought the stationmaster and found him snoring. I touched him lightly on the shoulder.

"Is the Devil after you? What's the idea of leaving the city at night? There aren't [*5] any horses. It's still very early; so please go to the inn and have some tea, or go to sleep." Saying this, Mr. Stationmaster turned to the wall and started snoring again. What was to be done? Once more I shook him by the shoulder.

"What do you mean, waking me up again? I've already told you there aren't any horses," and Mr. Stationmaster covered his head with a blanket and turned away from me.

"If all the horses are out," I thought, "it is not fair to disturb the stationmaster's slumber. But if the horses are in the stable —"

I made up my mind to find out whether Mr. Stationmaster had told me the truth. Stepping into the yard, I hunted up the stable, where I discovered some twenty horses. True enough, you could count their bones, but they could have dragged me to the next station. From the stable I returned to the stationmaster and shook him harder than before. It seemed to me I had a right to, since I had caught him lying. He jumped up quickly and, still half asleep, [*6] asked me who had arrived — but on coming to his senses and seeing me, he said:

"My good fellow, you seem to have been used to treating drivers like this in the old days. They used to beat them with sticks, but the times have changed."

And Mr. Stationmaster angrily went back to bed. I felt like treating him the way they used to treat drivers whom they caught cheating; but my generosity to the city driver had inspired the Sofiya drivers to hitch up the horses in a hurry, and at the very moment that I was going to commit a crime on the stationmaster's back, a bell tinkled in the yard. I remained a good citizen. Thus the twenty copper kopeks saved a peaceable man from judicial investigation, my children from an example of uncontrolled anger; and I learned that reason is a slave to impatience.

The horses carry me quickly; my driver has started a song, as usual [*7] a melancholy one. He who knows the melodies of Russian folk songs must admit that there is something in them which suggests spiritual sorrow. Nearly all the tunes of such songs are soft and melancholy. Learn how to establish governmental rule in accord with this musical inclination of the people. In these songs you may discover the very soul of our people. Look at a Russian; you will find him pensive. If he wishes to purge his melancholy, or, as he would say, to have a good time, he goes to the tavern. In his pleasures he is impulsive, daring, quarrelsome. If anything happens not to suit him, he immediately starts an argument or a fight. A barge-hauler who goes to the tavern with downcast head and returns blood-spattered from blows in the face may help to explain much that has seemed puzzling in Russian history.

[*8] My driver was singing. It was past two in the morning. His song lulled me to sleep as the bell had done before. O nature, who wrappest man in a shroud of sorrow at his birth, and draggest him over the rugged crags of fear, boredom, and grief all through his life, thou hast given him sleep as a consolation. When one falls asleep, all is over. Intolerable to the unfortunate one is his awakening. O how pleasant death is to him! But is it the end of sorrow? Most gracious Father, wilt Thou turn Thine eyes away from him who manfully puts an end to his miserable existence? This sacrifice is offered unto Thee, the source of all good things. Thou alone givest strength when nature quakes and trembles. It is the Father's voice calling His child unto Himself. Thou gavest me life, and I return it unto Thee, for on earth it has become useless.

[*9] TOSNA

When I set out from Petersburg, I flattered myself that I was going on the best of roads. Such it was considered to be by everyone who had traveled on it in the wake of the Emperor. Such indeed it had once been, but only for a short time. The dirt, which covered the road and made it smooth in dry weather, turned it into a muddy bog under the softening rains of summer, and made it impassable. — Wearied by the bad road, I left the carriage and entered the post hut in order to take a rest. In the hut I found a traveler who, as he sat at the usual long peasant table in the front corner, was looking through some papers and was asking the stationmaster to let him have some horses as quickly as possible. When I asked who he was, I learned that he [*10] was a lawyer of the old school, going to Petersburg with a great heap of ragged papers, which he was then sorting. I immediately entered into a conversation with him, and here is the substance of what he said:

"My dear sir! As a registrar in the Razryadny Archive,[1] I, your most humble servant, had an opportunity to use my place to good advantage. With great effort I have collected the genealogies of many Russian families, based on indisputable evidence. I can prove their princely or noble ancestry for several centuries. Frequently I can establish princely dignity by proving descent from Vladimir Monomakh or Rurik himself.[2] My dear sir!" he continued, pointing to his papers, "all the Great Russian nobility ought by rights to buy my work at a better price than they [*11] would give for any other wares. But with your permission, Your Honor, Your Excellency, or Your Highness (for I do not know your rank), they do not know what is good for them. You know how the Orthodox Tsar Fyodor Alekseevich,[3] of blessed memory, offended the Russian nobility by abolishing *mestnichestvo*.[4] This severe legislation placed many princely and royal families on a par with the Novgorod nobility.[5] The Orthodox Sovereign Emperor Peter the Great threw the old nobility into total eclipse by his Table of Ranks.[6] Through the military and civil service he opened the way for everyone to obtain a noble title, and, so to speak, trampled the old nobility into the mud. Now our most gracious Reigning Mother has confirmed the former decrees by an Imperial Charter to the Gentry,[7] which has distressed our ancient [*12] noble families, because they have been placed below all the others in the Book of the Nobility. But it is rumored that a new, complementary decree will soon be issued, whereby those families that can trace their line for two or three hundred years will be granted the title of marquis or some other illustrious title and will thus have some distinction from the other families. For that reason, dear sir, my work should be very acceptable to all the old noble society; but everyone has his enemies.

"In Moscow I fell in with a company of young gentlemen and offered them my work, hoping by their favor to make up at least for the paper and ink which I had used; but instead of a warm response I met only with derision, and I sorrowfully left that elder capital, and am now on my way to Petersburg, where, as you know, there is a great deal more enlightenment." [*13] So saying, he made me a low obeisance and then, straightening up, stood before me in a most respectful attitude. I knew what he was thinking, took something out of my purse — and giving it to him, advised him, on his arrival in Petersburg, to sell his notes to the peddlers by the pound, for wrapping paper; for the prospective marquisates would turn many a head, and he would be the cause of a recrudescence of an evil eradicated from Russia: boasting of one's ancient lineage.

[*14] LYUBANI

I suppose it is all the same to you whether I traveled in winter or in summer. Maybe both in winter and in summer. It is not unusual for travelers to set out in sleighs and to return in carriages. In summer. The corduroy road tortured my body; I climbed out of the carriage and went on foot. While I had been lying back in the carriage, my thoughts had turned to the immeasurable vastness of the world. By spiritually leaving the earth I thought I might more easily bear the jolting of the carriage. But spiritual exercises do not always distract us from our physical selves; and so, to save my body, I got out and walked. A few steps from the road I saw a peasant ploughing a field. The weather was hot. I looked at my watch. It was twenty minutes before one. I had set out on Saturday. It was now Sunday. [*15] The ploughing peasant, of course, belonged to a landed proprietor, who would not let him pay a commutation tax.[1] The peasant was ploughing very carefully. The field, of course, was not part of his master's land. He turned the plough with astonishing ease.

"God help you," I said, walking up to the ploughman, who, without stopping, was finishing the furrow he had started. "God help you," I repeated.

"Thank you, sir," the ploughman said to me, shaking the earth off the ploughshare and transferring it to a new furrow.

"You must be a Dissenter,[2] since you plough on a Sunday."

"No, sir, I make the true sign of the cross," he said, showing me the three fingers together.³ "And God is merciful and does not bid us starve to death, so long as we have strength and a family."

"Have you no time to work during the week, then, and can you not have any rest on Sundays, in the hottest part of the day, at that?"

"In a week, sir, there are six days, and we go six times a week [*16] to work on the master's fields; ⁴ in the evening, if the weather is good, we haul to the master's house the hay that is left in the woods; and on holidays the women and girls go walking in the woods, looking for mushrooms and berries. God grant," he continued, making the sign of the cross, "that it rains this evening. If you have peasants of your own, sir, they are praying to God for the same thing."

"My friend, I have no peasants, and so nobody curses me. Do you have a large family?"

"Three sons and three daughters. The eldest is nine years old."

"But how do you manage to get food enough, if you have only the holidays free?"

"Not only the holidays: the nights are ours, too. If a fellow isn't lazy, he won't starve to death. You see, one horse is resting; and when this one gets tired, I'll take the other; so the work gets done."

"Do you work the same way for your master?"

"No, sir, it would be a sin to work the same way. On his fields there are [*17] a hundred hands for one mouth, while I have two for seven mouths: you can figure it out for yourself. No matter how hard you work for the master, no one will thank you for it. The master will not pay our head tax; but, though he doesn't pay it, he doesn't demand one sheep, one hen, or any linen or butter the less. The peasants are much better off where the landlord lets them pay a commutation tax without the interference of the steward. It is true that sometimes even good masters take more than three rubles a man; but even that's better than having to work on the master's fields. Nowadays it's getting to be the custom to let villages to tenants, as they call it. But we call it putting our heads in a noose. A landless tenant skins us peasants alive; even the best ones don't leave us any time for ourselves. In the winter he won't let us do any carting of goods and won't let us go into town to work; all our work has to be for him, because he pays our head tax. It is an invention of the Devil to turn your peasants over to work for a stranger. You can make a complaint against [*18] a bad steward, but to whom can you complain against a bad tenant?"

"My friend, you are mistaken; the laws forbid them to torture people."

"Torture? That's true; but all the same, sir, you would not want to be in my hide." Meanwhile the ploughman hitched up the other horse to the plough and bade me good-bye as he began a new furrow.

The words of this peasant awakened in me a multitude of thoughts. I thought especially of the inequality of treatment within the peasant class. I compared the crown peasants with the manorial peasants.[5] They both live in villages; but the former pay a fixed sum, while the latter must be prepared to pay whatever their master demands. The former are judged by their equals; the latter are dead to the law, except, perhaps, in criminal cases. A member of society becomes known to the government protecting him, only when he breaks the social bonds, when he becomes a criminal! This thought made my blood boil.

[*19] Tremble, cruelhearted landlord! on the brow of each of your peasants I see your condemnation written.

While absorbed in these thoughts I happened to notice my servant, who was sitting up on the box in front of me, swaying from side to side. Suddenly I felt a chill coursing through my veins, sending the blood to my head and mantling my cheeks with a blush. I felt so ashamed of myself that I could scarcely keep from bursting into tears. "In your anger," I said to myself, "you denounce the proud master who wears out his peasants in the field; but are you not doing the same or even worse yourself? What crime has your poor Petrushka committed that you should deny him sleep, the consolation for our miseries, and nature's greatest gift to the unfortunate? He gets pay, food, and clothing, and you never [*20] beat him with a whip or cudgel. (O moderate man!) And you think that a piece of bread and a scrap of cloth give you the right to treat your fellow human being as though he were a top, and you merely boast that you do not often whip it up while it is whirling. Do you know what is written in the fundamental law, in the heart of every man? He whom I strike has the right to strike me. Remember the day when Petrushka was drunk and did not come in time to dress you. Remember how you boxed his ear. If only he had then, although intoxicated, come to his senses and answered you as your question deserved! And who gave you power over him? The law. The law? And you dare to defile that sacred name? Miserable one!" — Tears gushed from my eyes, and while I was in this state the post nags brought me to the next station.

[*21] CHUDOVO

I had barely entered the post hut when I heard the sound of a post bell in the street, and a few minutes later my friend Ch——[1] came in. When I had left him in Petersburg, he had had no intention of leaving there so soon. It was an extraordinary occurrence which had caused a man of firm habits, like my friend, to leave Petersburg, and here is what he told me.

"You were ready to depart when I betook myself to Peterhof. I spent the holidays as happily as possible in the smoke and swirl of pleasures. But wanting to turn my journey to advantage, I decided to go down to Kronstadt and Sisterbek, where they told me great changes had been made lately. I spent two very pleasant days [*22] in Kronstadt, feasting my eyes on all the foreign ships, the stone enclosures of the Kronstadt fortress, and the rapidly rising buildings. I was curious to see the plan of the new Kronstadt, and happily I saw in my mind's eye the beauty of the future development; in a word, the second day of my visit ended happily and pleasantly. The night was calm and bright, and the fragrant air permeated my senses with a peculiar gentleness which it is easier to experience than to describe. I intended to make the best use of nature's favor and at least once more in my life to enjoy the superb spectacle of the rising sun, which I had never yet been able to see over the smooth horizon of the water. I hired a twelve-oared marine sloop and set out for S———.

[*23] "For about four versts [2] everything went well. The monotonous sound of the oars made me sleepy, and my drowsy eyes hardly noticed the momentary gleam of the drops of water falling from the raised oars. A poetic fancy was already transporting me to the lovely meadows of Paphos and Amathus.[3] Suddenly the shrill whistle of the wind rising in the distance dispelled my dreams, and before my drowsy eyes appeared a mass of dense black clouds which seemed to be gathering and threatening to break over our heads. The mirror-like surface of the water began to ripple, and the calm gave place to an incipient plashing of the waves. I rejoiced at this spectacle, too; and watching the majestic features of nature, I confess without boasting that what was beginning to frighten the others was giving me pleasure. Now and then I cried out, like Vernet, 'Oh, how beautiful!'[4] But as the wind grew [*24] steadily stronger, we had to think about getting to shore. Dense, opaque clouds completely obscured the sky. The impetuous motion of the waves deflected the direction of the rudder, and the gusts of wind, now raising us on the watery crests, now plunging us into the steep furrows of the swelling sea, inhibited the forward movement of the rowers. We followed willy-nilly the direction of the wind and drifted at ran-

dom. Then we began to be afraid of the shore; indeed the very thing which would in favorable sailing have given us hope now threw us into despair. It seemed to us that nature was miserly at this hour, and we were indignant that she did not reveal her awful majesty in flashes of lightning and did not make our ears ring with peals of thunder. But hope, which follows man in his extremity, now gave us strength, and we encouraged one another as much as we could.

[*25] "Borne by the waves, our vessel suddenly came to a stop and was stuck fast. All our combined efforts failed to dislodge it from the place where it was stranded. While trying to get our boat off the shoal, as we thought it was, we did not notice that in the meantime the wind had almost completely died down. The sky was gradually cleared of the clouds which had veiled its azure. But the returning light, instead of bringing joy, only revealed our perilous situation. We saw clearly that our sloop was not on a shoal, but jammed in between two large rocks, and that no force could release it intact. My friend, imagine our situation! Anything I might say would be feeble compared to what I felt. Even if I were able to give an adequate account of all my sensations, it would [*26] still be too weak to arouse in you feelings like those which then arose and stirred within my soul. Our vessel stood in the middle of a rocky bank which shut in the bay and extended as far as S——. We were about a verst and a half from the shore. The water began to enter the boat from all sides and threatened ultimately to sink us. At the last hour, when our flame sinks low and eternity opens before us, all the distinctions invented by men's minds begin to disappear. Man becomes simply man: thus as we saw our end drawing near, we all forgot our rank and stations and thought only how we might save ourselves, helping to bail the water as best we could. But what was the use? As fast as the water was bailed out by our combined efforts, it poured in again. To the extreme [*27] distress of our hearts there was no ship to be seen passing by us, either

near or far. But even if one had given us hope by heaving into sight, it would only have deepened our despair by forsaking us in order that they might not share our fate.

"At last the captain of our boat, who was more accustomed to the dangers of the sea than anyone else, and who, in the various marine engagements in the late Turkish War in the Archipelago,[5] had probably been forced to learn to look with indifference upon death, decided either to save us by saving himself, or to perish in this noble endeavor: for if we stayed in that place, we were doomed to perish. He left the boat and, making his way from rock to rock, walked toward the shore, accompanied by our heartfelt prayers. At first he went rapidly on his way, leaping from stone to stone, fording the [*28] water where it was shallow, and swimming where it was deep. We did not take our eyes off him. At last we saw that his strength was beginning to fail, for he went from rock to rock more deliberately and frequently stopped and sat down on a rock to rest. It seemed to us that he was lingering in doubt and indecision whether to continue on his way. This impelled one of his comrades to follow the captain in order to help him if he found him exhausted before he could reach the shore, and, in that case, to try to reach the shore himself. Our eyes followed now one, now the other, and we devoutly prayed for their safety. Finally the second of these emulators of Moses in crossing the watery depths on foot (though without a miracle) stopped still on a rock, and we entirely lost sight of the first one.

[*29] "The secret, innermost emotions of each one of us, heretofore imprisoned, so to speak, by terror, started to come to the surface as our hopes waned. Meanwhile, the water was rising in our boat, and our straining efforts to bail it out were clearly exhausting our strength. An excitable and impatient man tore his hair, bit his fingers, and cursed the hour of his departure. A man with a timid soul, who, perhaps, had long felt the weight of crushing oppression, wept bitterly, and

drenched with his tears the bench on which he sprawled with his face downward. Another, remembering his home, his children, and his wife, sat as if petrified, thinking not of his own destruction but of theirs, for they were supported by his labors. You yourself, my friend, may guess what was the condition of my mind, for you know me well. All I will say to you is that I fervently prayed to God. At last we all began to give way to despair, for our vessel was more [*30] than half filled, and we were standing up to our knees in water. Frequently we thought of leaving the boat and proceeding over the stony ridge to the shore, but our fellow traveler's long hours of waiting upon that rock and the disappearance of the captain made the danger seem greater to us than it perhaps was in reality. In the midst of these woeful reflections, we observed near the opposite shore, although I could not definitely determine at what distance, two black spots which seemed to be moving on the water. The moving black spots appeared to grow larger as we watched them; at last as they came nearer we clearly saw two small boats making straight for the very place where we were waiting in a despair which surpassed our hope a hundredfold. As when a door is suddenly opened in a dark temple that is utterly impervious to light, [*31] and a ray of sunlight in a twinkling penetrates and dispels the darkness and spreads over the whole building to its farthest corners — so, at the sight of the boats, a ray of hope penetrated our souls. Despair gave way to exaltation, sadness to joy, and there was danger that our joyous bodily movements and splashings might cause our destruction before we could be removed from jeopardy. But the returning hope of life brought back the memory of our distinctive stations in life, which had been dormant while we were in danger. For the present it redounded to our common advantage. I restrained the excessive rejoicing, which might have been a cause of injury. After a while we beheld two large fishing smacks, and, when they reached us, we saw in one of them our savior who, having reached the shore over the stony ridge, had found these boats to save us [*32] from our imminent danger. We abandoned our vessel without delay and made for the shore in the fishing smacks, not forgetting, however, to take off from the rock our comrade, who had been there for about seven hours. Not half an hour had elapsed when the sloop, relieved of the weight of its passengers, floated out from between the rocks and fell completely to pieces. As we approached the shore in joy and exaltation at being saved, Pavel, our companion who had brought us rescue, told us the following tale:

" 'When I left you in imminent danger, I hurried over the rocks to the shore. My desire to save you gave me supernatural strength, but about seven hundred feet from the shore my strength began to give out, and I began to despair of saving you or myself. But after resting on a rock for about half an hour, I leaped up with renewed vigor, and, without resting any more, crawled, so to speak, [*33] up to the shore. There I stretched out on the grass and, after ten minutes' rest, got up and ran as fast as I could along the shore to S——. Although fairly exhausted, I thought of you and continued running until I reached the place. It seemed that Heaven wanted to put your firmness and my patience to the test, for neither along the shore nor in S—— itself did I find any boat with which to save you. Almost in despair, I thought there was no better place to look for help than at the local commander's. I ran to the house where he lived. It was already after six o'clock. In the anteroom I found a sergeant of the local command. I briefly explained to him your plight and the reason for my coming, and I asked him to wake Mr. ———, who was still sleeping. The sergeant said to me: "My friend, I do not dare to."

" ' "What? You do not dare to? When twenty men are drowning, you do not [*34] dare to wake the man who can save them? But you, worthless fellow, are lying; I will go wake him myself—." The sergeant took me by the shoulder, not very politely, and pushed me out the door. I almost burst with anger. But thinking more of your danger than of the insult to me and the hardheartedness of the commander to his subordinate, I ran to the guardhouse, which was about two versts distant from the accursed house whence I had been ejected. I knew that the soldiers living there had boats in which they rowed about the bay collecting cobblestones to sell for paving, and I was not mistaken in my hope. I found these two small boats, and now, to my unutterable joy, you are all saved. If you had drowned, I would have hurled myself into the water after you.' So saying, Pavel burst into tears.

"Meanwhile we reached the shore. Upon leaving the boat, I fell upon my knees and raised my hands to [*35] Heaven. 'Almighty Father,' I cried, 'it is Thy will that we live; Thou hast tried us; Thy will be done.' This, my friend, is a feeble description of what I felt. The terror of the last hour had pierced my soul, and I saw the moment when I should cease to exist. But what shall I be? I do not know. A terrible uncertainty. Now I feel; the hour strikes; I am dead; motion, life, feeling, thought, all vanish in an instant. Imagine yourself, my friend, at the brink of the grave: will you not feel a withering chill flowing through your veins and cutting life off before its time? O my friend! But I have strayed from my story.

"After I had finished my prayer, fury seized my heart. 'Is it possible,' I said to myself, 'that such inhumanity should occur in our time, in Europe, next door to the capital, under the eyes of the Great Sovereign?' It reminded me [*36] of the English shut up in the dungeon of the Bengal Subab.*

* The English in Calcutta had taken under their protection a Bengal official who had fled to them to escape punishment for bribery. The Subab, justly irritated, put himself at the head of his army, attacked the place, and took it. He threw the garrison into a close dungeon, where they were suffocated in the space of twelve hours. Three and twenty of them only remained alive. These wretched people offered large sums to the keeper of their prison, to prevail upon him to get their deplorable situation represented to the prince. Their cries and lamentations were sufficient informations to the

[*37] "I sighed from the depths of my soul. Meanwhile we reached S———. I thought that when the commander awoke, he would punish his sergeant and would at least give the shipwrecked men a chance to rest. In this hope I went straight to his house. But I was so irritated by the conduct of his subordinate that I was unable to moderate my speech. When I saw him, I said, 'Sir, have you been informed that a few hours ago twenty men were in danger of losing their lives [*38] at sea, and appealed to you for help?' Smoking away at his pipe, he answered me as coolly as possible, 'I have been told of it since, for then I was asleep.' At that I trembled with the anger of outraged humanity. 'If you are a hard sleeper, you should have yourself waked with a hammer on your head when people are drowning and crying for your help.' My friend, guess what his answer was! I thought I would have a stroke from what I heard. He said to me: 'That is not my duty.' I lost my patience. 'Is it your duty to kill people, you vile man? And you wear tokens of distinction, you are in command of others! — ' I was unable to finish my speech, almost spat in his face, and walked away. I tore my hair with rage. I made a thousand plans to wreak vengeance on this beastly commander, not on my account but on behalf of all humanity. But when I came to my senses, I realized, from many similar instances, [*39] that my revenge would be fruit-

---

people, who were touched with compassion; but nobody wanted to approach the potentate. The expiring English were told that he was asleep; and there was not, perhaps, a single person in Bengal who thought that the tyrant's slumbers should be interrupted for one moment, even to preserve the lives of one hundred and fifty unfortunate men.

What then is a tyrant? Or rather, what are a people accustomed to the yoke of tyranny? Is it respect, or fear, that makes them bend under it? If it [*37] be fear, the tyrant then is more formidable than the gods, to whom man addresses his prayers, or his complaints, at all times of the night, or at every hour of the day. If it be respect, mankind may then be brought even to revere the authors of their misery, a prodigy which superstition alone could accomplish. Which is it that astonishes us most, the ferocity of the Nabob who sleeps, or the baseness of the man who does not dare to wake him? — Raynal, *History of the Indies*. Volume II.⁶

less and that I would only be taken for a madman or an evil-doer; so I calmed myself.

"Meanwhile my men went to the priest, who received us with great joy, warmed us, fed us, and gave us a place to rest. We passed a whole day with him, enjoying his hospitality and good cheer. Next day we found a large sloop, in which we reached Oranienbaum without any mishap. In Petersburg I told this tale to one man after another. They all sympathized with my plight and berated the commander's hardheartedness, but no one would speak up to him. If we had drowned, he would have been our murderer. 'But his duty does not prescribe that he should save you,' someone said. Now I am bidding the city good-bye forever. Never again will I enter that den of tigers. Their sole joy is in devouring one [*40] another; they delight in torturing the weak to their last gasp and in groveling before the powers that be. And you wanted me to settle in the city! No, my friend," said the story-teller, jumping up from his chair, "I will go where people do not go, where they do not know what man is, where his name is unknown. Farewell!" With these words he got into his carriage and was off.

[*41] SPASSKAYA POLEST'

I drove so fast after my friend that I overtook him at the next post station. I tried to persuade him to return to Petersburg, tried to prove to him that small and occasional imperfections in society do not destroy its bonds, just as a pebble falling upon the expanse of the sea cannot disturb its surface. But he cut me off sharply, saying, "If I, a small pebble, had gone to the bottom, of course it would not have caused any storm in the Gulf of Finland, and I would have gone to live with the seals." And with an indignant look he bade me good-bye, lay back in his carriage, and hastily departed.

The horses were already hitched up, and I was on the point of stepping into my carriage when it suddenly began to rain.

"No great misfortune," I thought; [*42] "I will cover myself with matting and keep dry." But this thought had barely entered my mind, when I felt as though I had been immersed in an ice-hole. Without asking my advice, the sky unloosed the clouds and the rain poured down in buckets. You can't argue with the weather, and, considering the proverb, "the slower you travel, the farther you'll get," I left the carriage and ran to the nearest hut. The proprietor had already gone to bed, and it was dark in the hut. But even in the darkness I obtained permission to dry myself. I took off my wet clothes, put what was still dry under my head, and soon went to sleep on a bench. But as my bed was not made of down, I could not pamper myself very long. As I awoke I heard some whispering. I could distinguish the voices of two people conversing with each other.

"Go ahead, husband, and tell me," said a woman's voice.

"Listen, wife. Once upon a time — and really it goes like a fairy tale."

"But how can you believe a fairy tale?" said the wife, half-aloud, yawning from [*43] sleepiness. "You can't make me believe there was a Polkan, Bevis, or Nightingale the Robber." [1]

"Who's making you? You may, if you want to. This much is certain, that in the old days bodily strength was respected, and strong men used it for evil. There you have Polkan. As for Nightingale the Robber, my dear, read those who tell about Russian antiquity. They will tell you that he was called Nightingale because of his eloquence. Now don't interrupt my story. And so, once upon a time there lived a Viceroy.[2] In his youth he had loafed around in foreign countries, had learned to eat oysters, and had become very fond of them. So long as he had but little money of his own, he restrained his passion and ate only ten at a time, and that only when he was in Petersburg. As soon as he began to climb up the ladder of ranks, the number of oysters at his table began to increase. And when he became Viceroy and had a lot of his [*44] own money and government funds at his disposal, he craved oysters like a pregnant woman. Asleep or awake, he thought only of eating oysters. While they were in season nobody had any rest. All his subordinates became martyrs. No matter what happened, he had to have oysters. He would send an order to the office to furnish him a courier at once, to dispatch with important reports to Petersburg. Everybody knew that the courier was sent to fetch oysters, but he had his traveling expenses granted anyhow. The government's purse has many holes. The courier is provided with a traveling permit and money; he is all ready, and appears before His Excellency in a tunic and riding breeches.

" 'Be off, my good fellow,' says he of the string of medals, 'take this packet to the Great Morskaya.'

" 'To whom shall it go, sir?'

" 'Read the address.'

" 'To His ——— His ———'

[*45] " 'You are not reading it right.'

" 'To the Honorable ———'

" 'Wrong again. It goes to Mr. Korzinkin, honorable shopkeeper, in St. Petersburg, Great Morskaya.'

" 'I know, Your Excellency.'

" 'Then be off, my good fellow, and as soon as you get it, return at once, without delay. I'll show my gratitude to you.'

"And he gallops and gallops, as fast as the troika [3] can carry him, to Petersburg and right into Korzinkin's yard.

" 'Welcome! What a joker His Excellency is, to send you a thousand versts for some trash or other. But he is a good master. I am happy to serve him. Here are the oysters, fresh from the market. Tell him I can't sell them for less than 150 a keg; they come pretty high to me. We will settle the account with His Grace later.'

"They loaded the keg in the carriage, turned the shaft about, and off went the courier again; he barely [*46] had time to go to the inn and drink two cups of brandy.

"Tinkle, tinkle — As soon as they caught the sound of the post bell at the city gates, the officer on duty ran to the Viceroy (nothing like doing everything properly) and reported to him that the carriage had been seen in the distance and the post bell could be heard. He had not finished his report when — whish — the courier was at the door.

" 'I have brought it, Your Excellency.'

" 'Most opportunely,' and, turning to those present, 'indeed a worthy, dependable man, and not a drunkard. How many years now, he has been making two trips a year to Petersburg, and I cannot even remember how many to Moscow. Secretary, take down this recommendation: "For his numerous missions as a courier and their punctual execution, I recommend him for advancement in rank." '

"In the treasurer's record of disbursements it is written: 'At the recommendation of His [*47] Excellency, courier N. N., sent to St. Petersburg with most important dispatches, was granted traveling expenses from the special funds for journeying both ways with three horses.' The treasurer's record has gone to the audit, but there is no odor of oysters in it.

" 'At the recommendation of His Excellency, General, etc., etc., IT IS ORDERED, that Sergeant N. N. be promoted to the rank of Lieutenant.'

"You see, wife, how they manage to get their promotions. What good does it do me to serve honestly and not get ahead by a finger's breadth? According to the regulations, I should have been rewarded for good service. But the Tsar is merciful, while the dogkeeper is not.[4] Neither is our treasurer: this is the second time that they have sent me to the criminal court on his recommendation. If I were in cahoots with him, life would be a regular carnival."

"Klement'ich, stop talking nonsense! If you want to know

why he doesn't like you, it's because you [*48] take tips from everybody and don't share with him."

"Softly, Kuzminichna, talk softly. Somebody might hear you." Both voices fell silent, and I fell asleep again.

In the morning I learned that the couple who had passed the night with me in the hut were a courthouse functionary and his wife, and that at daybreak they had left for Novgorod.

While they were hitching the horses to my carriage, another equipage, drawn by a troika, drove up. From it leaped a man in a large cloak, and his broad-brimmed hat pulled down over his head made it impossible for me to see his face. Without a traveling permit he asked for horses; and while a number of drivers were standing around him haggling about the price, he did not wait for the end of their bickering, but impatiently exclaimed to one of them: "Hitch the horses at once. I'll give you four kopeks for every verst." The driver ran away to fetch the horses. The others, seeing that [*49] there was no use making any new offer, all left him.

I was not more than ten yards away from him. He came up to me and, without taking off his hat, said: "Dear Sir, won't you give something to an unfortunate man?"

This surprised me beyond measure, and I could not help saying to him that I was surprised at his appeal for help, since he had not haggled about the stage fees and had offered double the usual rate.

"I see," he said to me, "that you have never had any hard luck in your life."

I was pleased with this firm reply, and without hesitation took something from my purse —. "Pardon me," I said, "I cannot help you out with more at present, but when we reach our destination I may be able to do a little better by you." I hoped in this way to make him more open-hearted, and I was not [*50] disappointed.

"I see," he said to me, "that you still have generous feeling, that contact with the world and the pursuit of your own advantage have not barred the way to your heart. Permit me to take a seat in your carriage, and let your servant ride in mine." Meanwhile our horses were hitched up, I carried out his wish — and we're off.

"Oh, sir, I can hardly realize yet that I am unhappy. Not more than a week ago I was gay and cheerful, I felt no want, I was loved, or at least so it seemed; for my house was filled every day with people who had already attained proofs of distinction, and my table was always like some glorious feast. But if pride had such a measure of satisfaction, my soul likewise enjoyed true bliss. After many false starts, attempts, [*51] and failures, I had finally won as my wife the lady whom I desired. Our mutual passion, satisfying us in body and soul, presented everything to us in a bright light. We beheld no clouded day. We had reached the acme of our bliss. My wife was with child and the hour of her delivery was near. Fate had decided that all this happiness should be destroyed in an instant.

"I gave a dinner, and a multitude of so-called friends had come to glut their idle appetites at my expense. One of those present, who secretly disliked me, began to talk to his neighbor, in a whisper, but loudly enough so that my wife and many others could hear him. 'Don't you know that our host's case in the criminal court has already been decided?'

[*52] "It must seem strange to you," said my fellow traveler, addressing his words to me, "that a man not in the government service and in the situation I have described [5] could be subjected to criminal prosecution. For a long time I thought so myself, even when my case had gone through the lower courts and reached the court of highest instance. This is how it happened: I was registered in the merchants' guild; putting my capital into circulation, I became a partner in a lease concession. My inexperience led me to trust a dishonest man who, having been personally caught in a crime, was excluded from the concession, and who, as his books showed, had large debts.

He went into hiding; I was on hand; and they decided to recover the debts from me. I looked into the matter as best I could and found that in fact either none of the debt at all or only a very small part of it was mine, and so I petitioned for a proportionate settlement, [*53] since I was surety for him. But instead of granting my petition, the authorities ordered me to make good the losses. This was the first injustice. But to it they added a second. At the time when I had become a surety for the lease, I had had no landed property; but now, under the usual rules, my landed property was attached in the civil court. A strange thing, to forbid one to sell what one does not own! After that I bought a house and made other acquisitions. At the very same time chance permitted me, upon my receiving rank,[6] to pass from the merchants' guild to the gentry. Watching my chances, I took the opportunity to sell my house on favorable terms and passed the deed in the very same court where the attachment was entered. This was held against me as a crime; for there were people whose pleasure was [*54] darkened by the happiness of my life. The government attorney reported against me, claiming that in selling the house I had tried to evade paying the debts due to the treasury, and that I had deceived the civil court by giving my present status rather than my status at the time I had purchased the house. In vain did I plead that there could be no attachment of that which had not been part of the estate;[7] in vain did I plead that at least the rest of the estate should be sold first and the debts paid out of the proceeds of this sale, and that only after that should other measures be taken; and that I had not deceived them about my status, since I was already a nobleman when I bought the house. All this was disallowed, the sale of my house was voided, for my dishonest behavior I was sentenced to be deprived of my ranks, and" — the storyteller proceeded — " 'our host is now summoned to court to be held under arrest until final disposition of the case.' [8]

[*55] "While telling this last part of the tale, our dinner

guest had raised his voice. My wife had scarcely heard it when she embraced me and cried out: 'No, darling, I will go with you.' She could not utter another word. Her body grew limp and she fell senseless into my arms. I lifted her from the chair and carried her into the bedroom. I do not know how the dinner ended.

"When she came to after a while, she felt the pains which heralded the imminent birth of the fruit of our love. But however severe they were, the thought that I should be under arrest troubled her so much that she kept repeating: 'I will go with you.' This unfortunate affair hastened the birth of the child by a whole month, and all the efforts of the midwife and doctor who were called in to help were in vain, and could not keep my wife from giving birth to the child within twenty-four hours. Her anguish of soul was not assuaged [*56] by the birth of the child; indeed it grew even more violent and threw her into a fever. What is the use of dragging out the miserable story? My wife died the third day after the child was born. Seeing her suffering, you may believe me, I did not leave her for a moment. In my grief I had completely forgotten my trial and the decision against me. On the day before the death of my beloved, the premature fruit of our union had also died. I was completely absorbed in the sickness of his mother, and the child's death did not at that time appear so great a loss to me. Imagine, imagine," cried the narrator, pulling his hair with both his hands, "imagine my situation when I saw my beloved leaving me forever. Forever!" he cried out in a wild voice. "But why am I running away? Let them put me in prison; I am no longer vulnerable; let them take my life. O cruel barbarians, tigers, [*57] serpents, gnaw my heart, inject your slow poison! Forgive my outbreak; I think I shall soon lose my mind entirely. Whenever I think of the moment my beloved left me, I forget everything, and the light in my eyes is extinguished. But I shall finish my story. While I lay prostrate in deep despair over the lifeless body of my beloved, one of my true friends came running up to me and said, 'They've come to arrest you; they're waiting for you outside. Run from here; a carriage is ready for you at the back gate; go to Moscow or wherever you want and stay there until it is possible to get your sentence reduced.' I paid no attention to his remarks, but, with the help of his servants, he carried me out by force and put me in the carriage. Then, remembering that I would need money, he gave me a purse, which, however, contained only fifty [*58] rubles. He went to my study to get me more money, but finding an officer already in my bedroom, managed only to send me word that I should get away. I do not remember how I got to the first station. My friend's servant told me all that had happened and bade me farewell, and now I am going, as the proverb says, whither my eyes look." [9]

My fellow traveler's story moved me inexpressibly. "Is it possible," I said to myself, "that such cruelties could be perpetrated in such a merciful reign as ours? Is it possible that there can be judges so brutally unjust that, to fill the treasury (indeed one may thus dignify every illegal seizure of property to satisfy the demands of the government), they would deprive people of their property, honor, life?" I considered how this incident might be brought to the ears [*59] of the supreme power. For I justly believed that in an autocratic government only the supreme power could be impartial. "Why can I not undertake his defense myself? I will write a petition to the highest governmental authorities. I will give a detailed account of the whole matter and demonstrate the injustice of the judges and the innocence of the defendant. But they will not accept the petition from me. They will ask what right I had to draw it up; they will demand a power of attorney from me. What right have I? Why, that of suffering humanity! A man deprived of his property, his honor, half his life, in voluntary exile to escape a disgraceful incarceration. And for this you need a power of attorney? From whom? Is it not enough that one of my fellow citizens is suffering? But there is no need of that. He is a man: therein is my right, therein is my power of attorney. O God-man! Wherefore didst Thou write Thy [*60] law for barbarians? They make the sign of the cross in Thy name and bear bloody sacrifices to evil. Wherefore wert Thou merciful to them? Instead of threatening future punishment, Thou shouldst have increased their present punishment and, tormenting their conscience in proportion to their wickedness, Thou shouldst have given them no rest by day or night until by their suffering they had atoned for all the evil they had wrought." These reflections so wearied my body that I fell sound asleep and did not wake up for a long time.

While I was sleeping, the humors stirred up by my thoughts streamed to my head and, stimulating the tender substance of my brain, aroused a variety of images. In my dream appeared innumerable pictures, but they disappeared like light vapors in the air. At last, as often happens, a certain fiber of my brain, firmly touched by the fluids arising from the internal vessels of my body, throbbed more than the others, and this is what I dreamed.

[*61] I imagined that I was a tsar, shah, khan, king, bey, nabob, sultan, or some such exalted being, sitting on a throne in power and majesty.

My throne was of pure gold and, cleverly set with vari-colored precious stones, it shone resplendent. Nothing could compare with the luster of my raiment. My head was crowned with a laurel wreath. Around me lay the regalia of my power. Here lay a sword on a column wrought of silver, on which were represented battles at sea and on land, the capture of cities, and other triumphs of this sort; everywhere my name could be seen on high, borne by the Genius of glory, who was hovering over all these exploits. Here one could see my scepter resting upon sheaves heavy with abundant ears of grain, wrought of pure gold and perfectly imitating nature. [*62] A pair of scales hung from a rigid beam. In one of the scales lay a book with the inscription "The Law of Mercy"; in the other likewise there was a book with the inscription "The Law of Conscience." The orb was carved from a single stone and was supported by a circlet of cherubim sculptured in white marble. My crown was raised above everything else and rested on the shoulders of a mighty giant, and its rim was supported by Truth. A serpent of enormous size, forged of gleaming steel, wound all about the foot of my throne and, holding the tip of its tail in its jaws, represented eternity.

Not these lifeless emblems alone proclaimed my power and majesty. About my throne stood the estates of the realm, timidly submissive and anxious to catch my glance. At some distance from my throne crowded a countless multitude of people, whose [*63] various attires, facial features, bearing, appearance, and stature indicated their diversity of race. Their trembling silence assured me that they were all subject to my will. On the sides, upon a somewhat higher level, stood a great number of charming, splendidly garbed women. Their glances expressed their delight upon seeing me, and their very wishes strove to anticipate mine ere they arose.

The deepest silence reigned in this assembly; it seemed that all were anxiously expecting an important event upon which depended the peace and happiness of the whole commonwealth. Self-centered and bored to the bottom of my soul by the cloying monotony of existence, I paid my debt to nature and, opening my mouth from ear to ear, I yawned with all my might. They all [*64] responded to my mood. Suddenly confusion spread its somber veil over the face of joy, the smile flitted away from the lips of tenderness and the sparkle of merriment from the cheeks of pleasure. Twisted and furtive glances betrayed the sudden approach of terror and imminent misfortune. Sighs were heard, the stinging forerunners of grief; and groans, restrained by fear. Despair and mortal terror, more agonizing than death itself, rushed in with giant strides to take possession of all hearts. I was moved to the depths of my soul by this sad spectacle; my facial muscles involuntarily contracted toward my ears and, stretching my lips, produced in my features a twitch that resembled a smile, after which I sneezed loudly. Just so the midday sun breaks through the thick, dark, foggy atmosphere. [*65] Its vital heat disperses the condensed moisture, which, divided into its component particles, is in part lightened and swiftly borne into the immeasurable space of ether, while the rest, retaining in itself only the weight of its earthly particles, swiftly falls down. The darkness, which had prevailed everywhere before the radiant globe broke through, suddenly disappears and, hastily throwing off its impenetrable shroud, flies away on rushing wings, leaving no trace of its presence. Even thus my smile dispelled the looks of sadness which had settled on the faces of the assembled company; joy quickly filled the hearts of all, and not an oblique sign of displeasure was left. All began to cry: "Long live our mighty Sovereign! May he live forever!" Like the gentle midday breeze which stirs the foliage and produces [*66] an amorous whisper in the oak grove was the joyful murmur that passed through the gathering.

One said in a low voice: "He has subdued our enemies abroad and at home, he has expanded the frontiers of the fatherland, he has subjected thousands of men, of many races, to his power." Another exclaimed: "He has enriched the realm, he has expanded internal and foreign commerce, he is a patron of the arts and sciences, he encourages agriculture and industry." Women tenderly said: "He has saved thousands of useful citizens from destruction by preventing their death even at the breast." One announced with dignity: "He has increased the income of the government, he has reduced the people's taxes, he has provided the people with a secure livelihood." Youths, ecstatically raising their hands to heaven, cried: "He is merciful and just, his law is equal for all, and he considers himself its first servant. [*67] He is a wise legislator, a righteous judge, a zealous executive, he is greater than all other kings, he gives liberty to all men."

Speeches like these, striking my eardrum, resounded loudly in my soul. To my mind the praises seemed true, since they were accompanied by outward expressions of sincerity. Receiving them as such, my soul rose above the usual circle of vision, expanded in its essence, and, embracing all, touched the threshold of divine wisdom. But nothing could be compared with my self-satisfaction as I uttered my commands. I ordered my commander-in-chief to proceed with an innumerable host to the conquest of a country separated from me by a whole celestial zone. "Sovereign," he replied, "the glory of thy name alone will conquer the people who inhabit that land. Terror will [*68] go before thine arms, and I will return bearing the tribute of mighty kings." To my lord admiral I spake: "Let my ships spread sail over all the seas, so that strange peoples may see them; let my flag become known in the north, east, south, and west." "It shall be done, Your Majesty." And he flew to execute my command like a wind sent to swell the sails of a ship. "Proclaim to the farthest limits of my realm," I said to the keeper of the laws, "that this is the day of my birth; let it be forever famous in the chronicles as the day of universal amnesty. Let the prisons be thrown open, set the prisoners free to return to their homes as people who have strayed from the true path." "Thy mercy, O Sovereign, is the mark of an infinitely generous being. I hasten to publish the glad tidings to the fathers grieving for their children, to the wives grieving for their husbands." To my chief architect I said, "Let magnificent buildings be erected [*69] as homes for the Muses, let them be adorned with various imitations of nature; and may they be as inviolate as the celestial beings for whom they were built." "O wise ruler," he replied, "even as the elements have obeyed thy commands and, joining forces, have in swamps and solitudes founded vast cities which surpass in magnificence the most famous cities of antiquity, so this labor will be light to the zealous executors of thy commandments. Thou hast spoken, and the raw building materials are already hearkening to thy voice." "Let the hand of generosity be opened now," I said, "and let the surplus of superabundance flow out to the needy, let the treasure which we do not need return to its source." "O most gracious ruler, given us by the Almighty, father of thy children, enricher of the poor, thy will be done!" At each of my commands all the people there shouted for joy, and [*70] applause not only accompanied my speech but even anticipated my thoughts. Of all this company, one woman alone, who stood leaning hard against a column, sighed grievously, while scorn and anger flashed across her countenance. Her features were stern and her garments simple. Her head was covered with a hat, while all the others stood with their heads bare. "Who is she?" I asked one who was standing near me. "She is a pilgrim, a stranger to us; she says she is an oculist, named Clear-of-Eye. But she is a very dangerous witch who carries venom and poison, and gloats over grief and affliction; she is always frowning, and she scorns and reviles everyone; in her abuse she spares not even thy sacred head." "Wherefore, then, is this evildoer tolerated in my realm? But we shall deal with her tomorrow. This is a day of grace and rejoicing. Come, my comrades in bearing the heavy burden of government, receive the rewards your labors and [*71] accomplishments deserve." Then I arose from my throne and conferred various honors upon those present; nor were the absent ones forgotten, but those who had received my commands with joyful countenance were granted ampler signs of grace.

Then I continued my speech: "Let us go, props of my power, buttresses of my rule, let us go and be merry after our labor. For he who has labored deserves to partake of the fruit of his labors. The Monarch should partake of joy, since he dispenses joy so bountifully to all. Show us the way to the feast you have prepared," I said to the master of the revels. "We shall follow you." "Wait," the pilgrim called to me from her place, "wait, and come to me. I am a physician sent to thee and thy like to open thine eyes. Oh, what blindness! " she exclaimed. An invisible power urged me to approach [*72] her, although all those who surrounded me held me back and some even used force.

"On both thine eyes there are cataracts," said the pilgrim, "and yet thou hast passed unhesitant judgment upon everything." Then she touched both my eyes and took off from them a thick film, like horny skin. "Thou seest," she said to me, "that thou hast been blind, stone-blind. I am Truth. The Almighty, moved to pity by the groans of thy subject people, has sent me down from the heavenly regions to drive away the darkness which impenetrably obscured thy vision. I have done so. Now everything will appear before thine eyes in its true form. Thou shalt see into the heart of things. No longer will the serpent that hides in the deep recesses of the soul escape thee. Thou shalt know thy faithful subjects who, far from thee, love not thee, but their country; [*73] who are always ready for thy defeat, if it will avenge the enslavement of man.[10] But they will not stir up untimely sedition to no purpose. Call them to thee, to be thy friends. Drive away this haughty mob that stand before thee and hide the infamy of their souls under gilded garments. They are thy real enemies, who dim thine eyes and bar my entry to thy palace. Once only do I appear to kings during their whole reign, that they may know me in my true form; but I never abandon the dwellings of mortals. My stay is not in royal palaces.[11] The guard that surrounds and watches them with a hundred eyes by day and by night bars my entry thither. If and when I succeed in breaking through this dense crowd, all those who surround thee raise the scourge of persecution and seek to cast me out of thy dwelling; therefore beware lest I leave thee again. For then [*74] words of flattery, emitting poisonous vapors, will again bring back thy cataracts, and a film impenetrable to light will cover thine eyes. Then will thy blindness be very great and thy vision barely suffice for one step. Everything will seem joyful to thee. Thine ears will not be troubled by groans; every hour thy hearing will be soothed by sweet songs. The sacrificial incense of flattery will hover about thy vulnerable soul. Thy touch will always feel smooth softness. Never will beneficent roughness irritate thy sense of feeling. Tremble now in the face of this imminent peril. A storm cloud will rise above thy head, and avenging thunderbolts will be ready to strike thee down. But I promise thee, I will remain within the borders of thy realm. Whenever thou desirest to see me, whenever thy soul, besieged by the wiles of flattery, thirsts for the sight of me, call [*75] me from afar; wherever my harsh voice is heard, there wilt thou find me. Never be afraid of my voice. If from the midst of the people there arise a man who criticizes thy acts, know that he is thy true friend. With no hope of reward, with no servile trembling, with a sturdy voice he will proclaim me to thee. Beware and do not dare to put him to death as a rebel.[12] Call him to thee, be hospitable to him as to a pilgrim. For everyone who criticizes the Sovereign in the fullness of his autocratic power is a pilgrim in the land where all tremble before him. Treat him well, I say, honor him, so that he may return and tell thee ever more truth. But such stout hearts are rare; hardly one in a whole century appears in the world's arena. But in order that the impassioned delight in the exercise of power may not put thy vigilance to sleep, I give thee this ring, which will warn thee against thine [*76] injustice, if thou wilt fight against it.[13] For know that thou hast it in thy power to be the greatest murderer in the commonweal, the greatest robber, the greatest traitor, the greatest violator of the public peace, a most savage enemy who turns his malice against the lives of the weak. Thine is the blame if a mother lament for her son, or a wife for her husband, killed on the field of battle, for the danger of being subjected to a conqueror's yoke hardly justifies the murder called war.[14] Thine the blame if the field be deserted, if the peasant's little ones starve at their mother's breast, withering from lack of food. But look now at thyself and those around thee, observe how thy commands are executed, and if thy soul quake not with terror at the sight, I will leave thee and forget thy palace forever."

[*77] As she spoke, the pilgrim's countenance seemed radiantly happy. The sight of her filled my soul with joy. No longer did it feel the surge of vanity and the swell of pride. I felt at peace; the tumult of vainglory and the storm of ambition no longer disturbed my soul. My glittering garments seemed to be stained with blood and drenched with tears. On my fingers I saw fragments of human brains; my feet were standing in slime. The people around me looked still more odious. They seemed all blackened and seared within by the dark flame of greed. At me and at one another they threw fierce looks full of rapacity, envy, sly cunning, and hate. My commander-in-chief, whom I had sent forth to conquer, was wallowing in luxury and pleasure. The army was without discipline; my soldiers were [*78] valued less than cattle. No pains were taken to care for their health or their provisioning; their lives counted for nothing; they were deprived of their fixed and proper pay, which was misspent on unnecessary military frippery. A majority of the new recruits died as a result of neglect by their superiors or because of their unnecessary and untimely severity. The money intended for the maintenance of the troops was in the hands of the master of the revels. Medals for military distinction were awarded, not for bravery, but for base servility. I saw before me a renowned military commander, whom I had honored with outstanding marks of my favor. Now I saw clearly that his whole distinction lay in pandering to the lust of his superior.[15] He had had no occasion to show bravery, for he had

not even seen the enemy from a distance. From such warriors [*79] I had expected new laurels. I turned away from a thousand calamities that unfolded before my eyes.

My ships, which I had ordered to sail the farthest seas, I saw coasting near the mouth of the harbor. The admiral who had flown on the wings of the wind to carry out my orders was stretching his limbs on a soft bed, intoxicated with voluptuous desire, in the embraces of a hired inciter of his lust. On a chart, executed at his command, of a completely imaginary voyage, there were already visible in all parts of the world new islands abounding in fruits appropriate to their various climates. Vast lands and innumerable peoples were created by the pens of these new voyagers. By the gleam of nocturnal lights they had already written a glowing description, in a flowery and splendid style, [*80] of this voyage and the discoveries made on it. Golden covers had already been prepared to adorn this very important work. O Cook! Why did you pass your life in travail and privations? Why did you end it so miserably? If you had boarded these ships, you would have begun your voyage in delightful ease, and in delightful ease you would have ended it, and you would have made just as many discoveries while sitting in one place, and (in my kingdom) you would have been just as famous, for you would have been honored by your Sovereign.[16]

The achievement of which, in my blindness, my soul was most proud, namely, the abolition of the death penalty and the granting of amnesty to prisoners, had hardly any visible effect on the vast complex of governmental activities. My commands had either been completely violated by being misapplied, or had not had the desired effect because of distorted interpretation and dilatory execution. Mercy had come to be bought and sold, and [*81] the auctioneer's hammer knocked down compassion and generosity to the highest bidder. Instead of being thought merciful by my subjects because of the amnesty I had ordered, I passed among them for a cheat, hypocrite, and wicked play-actor. "Keep thy mercy," thousands of voices shouted, "do not proclaim it to us in high-sounding words, if thou dost not intend to carry it out. Do not add insult to injury, do not make our burden heavier by making us feel it more keenly. We were peacefully asleep; thou hast disturbed our sleep when we did not want to wake up, since we had nothing to wake up for." In the construction of cities I saw only the waste of the government's money, frequently drenched with the blood and tears of my subjects. In the erection of magnificent buildings the waste was often accompanied by a misunderstanding of true art. I saw that their internal and external arrangements lacked even the slightest particle of taste. They seemed to belong to the age of the Goths and Vandals. In the home prepared for the Muses [*82] I did not see the inspiring streams of Castalia and Hippocrene; [17] limping art crept, earthbound, scarcely daring to raise its glances above the levels sanctioned by tradition. Bending over the drawings of the building, the architects were not thinking about how to make it beautiful but about how to make money out of it. I was nauseated with my ostentatious vanity and turned my eyes away. But my soul was hurt most of all by the results of my liberality. In my blindness I had thought that public funds not needed for governmental purposes could not be spent in any better way than on succour for the indigent, clothing for the naked, food for the hungry, rescue for those suffering under adverse circumstances, or to reward excellence and merit that do not find their joy in wealth. But how sad it was to see that my generosity poured more wealth upon the rich, the flatterer, the false friend, the murderer, sometimes indeed the secret murderer, [*83] the traitor and violator of the public trust, the clever sycophant who knew my desires and pandered to my weaknesses, the woman who gloried in her shamelessness. Barely, almost imperceptibly, the thin wellsprings of my generosity trickled down to modest worth and bashful merit.

Tears poured from my eyes and hid from me the miserable objects of my foolish generosity. Now I saw clearly that the honors I had given out always fell into the hands of the unworthy. In the quest for honors, which mortals dream of, inexperienced worth, struck with the first gleam of these supposed blessings, began the race evenly with flattery and meanness of soul. But starting awkwardly, it was always exhausted after the first few steps and was fated to content itself with its own approval, in the conviction that [*84] worldly honors are dust and ashes. Seeing that the world was out of joint as a result of my weakness and the trickery of my ministers; that my affection was wasted upon a woman who sought in my love satisfaction only for her vanity and who sought to please me only with her outward appearance, while her heart felt only loathing for me, I shouted in the madness of my anger. "Unworthy criminals, evildoers! Tell me, wherefore have you abused your Sovereign's trust? Stand now before your judge. Tremble, ye who have grown hardened in evil. How can you justify your deeds? What can you say in excuse? Here he is; I will call him from his hut of humility.[18] Come," I called to an old man whom I saw at the border of my vast realm, half-hidden in a moss-covered hut, "come and lighten my burden; come and restore peace to my anxious [*85] heart and troubled mind." As I said this, I saw afresh the responsibility of my high office, recognized the vastness of my duty, and understood whence proceeded my right and my power. I trembled inwardly and was terrified by the responsibility of my stewardship. My blood surged wildly, and I awoke. Even before I was fully conscious, I clutched my finger, but it bore no ring of thorns.[19] If only it would always stay on the little finger of a King!

Ruler of the world, if, when you read my dream, you smile scornfully or knit your brow, know that the pilgrim whom I saw has flown far away from you and disdains your palace.

[*86] PODBEREZ'E

I could hardly wake up from the heroic sleep in which I had dreamt so much. My head was heavier than lead, worse than a drunkard's head would be after a drunken bout a week long. I was in no condition to continue my journey and be jolted in a hard wooden cart (for my carriage had no springs). I picked up my book of home remedies and looked for a cure for headache caused by delirium while asleep or awake. Although I always carry a stock of medicine with me, yet, in accordance with the proverb, "enough stupidity in every wise man,"[1] I had taken no precautions against delirium; hence my head, when I reached the next post station, was worse than a wooden block.

I recalled that my nurse of blessed memory, [*87] Praskov'ya Klement'evna, called Pyatnitsa in honor of the Saint,[2] had been very fond of coffee, and that she used to say it was good for a headache. "When I have drunk five cups," she would say, "I can see straight again, but without it I'd be dead in three days."

I was taking my nurse's medicine, but, not being used to drinking down five cups in a row, I offered what was left of the coffee they had made for me to a young man who was sitting on the same bench with me but in the other corner by the window. "Thank you very much," he said, as he took the cup of coffee. His friendly appearance, frank expression, and polite manner seemed out of keeping with his long coat and hair slicked down with kvas.[3] Reader, forgive my inference: I was born and grew up in the capital, and if a man's hair is not curled and powdered, I think he is not worth noticing. If you too are a country bumpkin and do not powder your hair, do [*88] not condemn me if I do not notice you and pass by on the other side.

After exchanging a few words with my new acquaintance, we soon found ourselves on friendly terms. I learned that he was from the Novgorod Seminary and was walking to Petersburg to visit his uncle, who was a secretary in the provincial administration. But his chief purpose was to find a chance to study. "We still need a great deal of aid to learning in our country," he said. "The knowledge of Latin alone cannot satisfy a mind hungry for learning. Virgil, Horace, Livy, even Tacitus I know almost by heart, but when I compare the information of my fellow seminarists with what I have had the good luck to learn, I see that our school belongs to a bygone age. We know all the classical authors, but we know more of the critical interpretation of their texts [*89] than of what still makes them so appealing today, and promises them eternal life. We are taught philosophy, we go through logic, metaphysics, ethics, theology, but, as Kuteykin says in 'The Minor,'[4] we shall reach the end of our philosophical training and then turn back again. Is it any wonder? Aristotle and scholasticism still hold sway in the seminaries. By good luck I became acquainted with the family of a government official in Novgorod, had a chance to read some of his books, and learned some French and German. What a difference there is between the enlightenment of the times when Latin alone was used in the schools, and the present! What a help it is to learning, when the sciences are not mysteries open only to those who have mastered Latin, but are taught in the native tongue! But why," he continued, [*90] after interrupting his own speech, "why do they not, in our country, institute higher schools of learning in which the sciences are taught in the vernacular, in Russian? The instruction would be more accessible to all; enlightenment would reach everyone sooner, and after one generation there would be two hundred educated men instead of one Latin scholar; at least in every court there would be one member who understood what jurisprudence or legal science is. My God!" he continued excitedly, "if one were to cite examples from our judges' decrees and opinions on cases! What would Grotius, Montesquieu, or Blackstone say?"

"Have you read Blackstone?"

"I have read the first two parts, in the Russian translation.[5] It would not be a bad idea to compel our judges to have this book instead of the calendar of saints, and to make them consult it more frequently than the calendar. [*91] How can one help being sorry," he repeated, "that we have no schools in which the sciences are taught in the native tongue!"

The entrance of the postilion made it impossible to continue our conversation. I had just time enough to tell the seminarist that his wish would soon be fulfilled, that a decree had already been issued for the foundation of new universities where the sciences would be taught as he wished.[6] "It's high time, sir, it's high time — ."

While I was paying my fare to the postilion, the seminarist went out. As he left, he dropped a small bundle of papers. I picked them up and did not give them back to him. Don't give me away, gentle reader. On this condition I'll tell you what I pilfered. When you have read it, I am sure you will not betray my theft,. for it is written in the Russian law that not only he who has stolen is a thief, but also he who has received the stolen goods. I must confess that my hands are [*92] not clean: whenever I see something that looks sensible, I immediately appropriate it; see to it that you do not leave your ideas lying around unguarded. Read what my seminarist has to say:

"He who compared the moral world to a wheel expressed a great truth. Perhaps he did nothing else but this: he observed the circular shape of the earth and of the other great bodies borne in space and simply gave expression to what he saw. Advancing in the knowledge of nature, men may perhaps discover the secret connection between spiritual or moral and physical or natural substances, and learn that the cause of all changes, transformations, and perversions in the moral or spiritual world may perhaps be dependent on the circular form of our terrestrial abode and of the other bodies belonging to the solar system, which, like the earth, are globular and revolve [*93] on their axes. This sounds like a Martinist, a pupil of Swedenborg.[7] No, my friend, I eat and drink not merely to sustain life, but because in doing so I find a considerable sensual enjoyment. And I will confess to you, as I would to my spiritual father, that I would much rather spend the night with a pretty girl and fall asleep in her embrace, intoxicated with passion, than bury myself in Hebrew or Arabic letters, in ciphers, or Egyptian hieroglyphics, or try to separate my soul from my body and wander about over the vast stretches of fantastic speculation, like the ancient and modern spiritual knights. When I die there will be time enough for the incomprehensible, and my soul will have its fill of wandering about.

"Look back; the time is still close behind our shoulders when superstition reigned, and all its followers: ignorance, slavery, the Inquisition, and many others. Has it been long [*94] since Voltaire cried out till he was hoarse, against superstition? Has it been long since Frederick was its implacable enemy not only in his words and deeds, but, with still more terrible effectiveness, by his sovereign example?[8] But in this world everything reverts to its former state, for everything has its origin in destruction. An animal, a plant, is born, and grows, in order to beget its kind; then dies and yields its place to them. Nomadic peoples gather in cities, found kingdoms, mature, become famous, grow weak, become exhausted, and fall. Their dwellings are lost to sight, their very names are forgotten. Christian society at first was meek and peaceful, and hid in desert places and caves; then grew strong, strayed from its path, and fell into superstition. In its deviation it went the usual way of all nations; it exalted its chieftain, [*95] extended his power, and the Pope became the mightiest of kings.

Luther began the reformation, created a schism, withdrew from under the papal power, and had many followers. The structure of prejudice in favor of the papal power began to crumble, and superstition, too, began to disappear. Truth found its devotees, made a breach in the thick wall of prejudices,[9] but did not long persist in this path. Freedom of thought turned into unbridled license. Nothing was sacred; violent hands were laid on everything. When it reaches its utmost limits, free thought will turn back in the other direction. This change in the manner of thinking is imminent in our time. We have not yet reached the farthest extreme of unchecked free thought, but already many are beginning to turn to superstition. Open the latest mystical works, and you will think we are back in the days of scholasticism and disputations, when the human mind busied itself with arguments without considering whether there was any sense in [*96] these arguments; when, as a problem worthy of philosophy, to be solved by seekers after truth, they posed the question how many angels could stand on the point of a pin.

"If aberration is to be the fate of our descendants, if they abandon nature and chase after phantoms, then it would be a very useful labor for a writer to show us from former events the progress of the human mind, when it broke through the mist of prejudices and began to pursue truth in its loftiest flights, and when, so to speak, wearied by its vigils, it began once again to abuse its strength, and, gripped by fear, to descend into the mist of prejudice and superstition. The work of such a writer will not be in vain, for, in disclosing the progress of our thoughts toward truth and falsehood, he will save at least some from following the path of destruction and will obstruct the advance of ignorance. Happy [*97] the author if by his work he is able to enlighten even one man, happy if he has implanted virtue even in one heart.

"We may consider ourselves fortunate, for we shall not live to see the extreme disgrace of intelligent beings. Our immediate descendants may be even more fortunate than we. But the miasma which has been gathering in the mire of decay is already seeping up and is predestined to overcast the whole horizon. We shall be fortunate if we do not live to see the new Mohammed; the hour of aberration will be delayed for a time. Know that when in speculative thought, in judgments of things moral and spiritual, there begins a ferment, and a strong and enterprising man appears — a man strong for truth or for falsehood — then there will follow a change of powers, and a change of creeds.

"If, on the ladder on which human reason must descend into the darkness of error, we point out [*98] what is ridiculous and do some good by laughing at it, we shall be thought worthy of praise.

"Wandering from speculation to speculation, my beloved brethren, beware lest you stray into the path of the following investigations.

"Akiba said: 'I once followed Rabbi Josua into the secret place and learned three things from him. I learned, (1) that we must turn ourselves, not Eastward and Westward, but Northward and Southward. I learned, (2) that we must evacuate, not standing, but sitting. I learned, (3) that we should wipe our rear not with our right hand, but with our left.' Upon this Ben Hasas objected, 'Are you so hardened in impudence as to watch your master when he is evacuating?' He replied, 'These are secrets of our Law, to learn which I was obliged so to do.' " *

[*99] NOVGOROD

Be proud, ye vain founders of cities, be proud, ye founders of kingdoms! Dream that the glory of your name will endure forevermore. Pile stone upon stone, to the very clouds. Carve in stone images of your exploits, and inscriptions that proclaim your deeds. Lay firm foundations of government in unchange-

* See *Bayle's Dictionary*, the article "Akiba." [10]

able laws. Time with its sharp rows of teeth laughs at your presumption. Where are the wise laws of Solon and Lycurgus, which established the liberties of Athens and of Sparta? In books. And in their former abode slaves are pastured under the scepter of autocracy. Where is rich Troy? Where is Carthage? You can hardly see the place where once they proudly stood. Does the imperishable sacrifice send its smoke to the One Being in the famous temples of ancient Egypt? Their magnificent ruins serve [*100] as a place of refuge for bleating cattle at the time of the midday heat. They are not watered by joyous tears of thanksgiving to the Almighty Father, but by the stinking evacuations of animals. O pride, O human arrogance, behold this and learn how contemptible you are!

With such thoughts I reached Novgorod and looked at the multitude of monasteries which lay around it.

They say that all these monasteries, even those which now are fifteen versts distant from the city, were at one time within its precincts, and that a hundred thousand warriors could come forth from within its walls. It is known from the Chronicles that Novgorod had a popular government. They had princes, but these had little power. All the power of government was centered in the *posadniki* and *tysyatskie*.[1] The people in its assembly, the Veche, was the real sovereign. The territory of Novgorod extended [*101] even beyond the Volga in the north. This free state belonged to the Hanseatic League.[2] The ancient saying, "Who can stand against God and Great Novgorod?" may serve as proof of its power. Trade was the cause of its rise. Internal discord and a rapacious neighbor brought about its fall.

While crossing the bridge, I left my carriage to enjoy the sight of the flowing Volkhov. I could not help remembering the deed of Tsar Ivan Vasil'evich after the capture of Novgorod. Stung by the resistance of the republic, this proud, bestial, but clever ruler wanted to destroy it completely. I can see him standing on the bridge with his battle axe, as some report, sacrificing the elders and chief men of Novgorod to his fury. But what right did he have to rage against them? What right [*102] did he have to take Novgorod for himself? ³ Was it because the first Russian grand princes had lived in this city? Or because he styled himself Tsar of all Russia? Or because the Novgorodians were of Slavic origin? But what avails right, when might prevails? Can right live, when a decision is sealed with the blood of the nations? Can right exist, when no force exists to make it effective? Much has been written about the law of nations, and it is often referred to, but the teachers of the law have not considered whether there can be a judge between nations. When hostility arises between them, when hatred or self-interest drives one against another, their judge is the sword. He who has fallen or been disarmed is guilty, and without gainsaying obeys this decision, and there is no appeal from it. That is why Novgorod belonged to Tsar Ivan Vasil'evich. [*103] That is why he destroyed it and appropriated its smoking ruins. Necessity, the desire for safety and security build kingdoms; discord, cunning, and force destroy them. What then is the law of nations?⁴ The nations, say the learned in the law, stand in the same relationship to each other as one man to another in the state of nature. Question: What are man's rights in the state of nature? Answer: Look at him. He is naked, hungry, thirsty. He appropriates everything he can seize for the satisfaction of his needs.⁵ If anything tries to stand in his way, he removes the obstacle, destroys it, and takes what he wants. Question: If, on the way to satisfy his needs, he meets his like, if, for example, two hungry men try to satisfy their appetite with the same morsel, [*104] which of them has the greater right to it? Answer: The one who takes it. Question: Who takes the morsel? Answer: The stronger one. Is it possible that this is the law of nature, is it possible that this is the foundation of the law of nations? The examples of all times bear witness to the fact that law without power has always been considered, in practice, as an empty word. Question: What is civil law? Answer: He who travels by post does not trouble himself about nonsense but thinks only about getting his horses as quickly as possible.

From the Chronicle of Novgorod. The Novgorodians waged war with the Grand Prince Yaroslav Yaroslavich and concluded a written treaty of peace.

The Novgorodians composed a charter for the defense of their liberties and confirmed it with fifty-eight seals.

The Novgorodians prohibited the circulation within their territory of coined money introduced by the Tatars.

[*105] Novgorod began to coin its own money in the year 1420.

Novgorod belonged to the Hanseatic League.

In Novgorod there was a bell, at the tolling of which the people assembled at the Veche for the consideration of public business.

Tsar Ivan took the charter and the bell away from the Novgorodians.

Then: In the year 1500, in the year 1600, in the year 1700, in the year —, in the year —, Novgorod still stood in the same old place.[6]

But one can't think always of times past, one can't always think hopefully of the morrow. If — I reflected — I look at the sky all the time, without noticing what's under foot, I'll soon stumble and fall into the mire. No matter how concerned I am, Novgorod cannot be restored to its ancient glory. The future will show what God will grant. Now it is time for supper. I will go to see Karp Dement'ich.

"Well, well! Welcome! Whence has God brought you?" my friend Karp Dement'ich, formerly a merchant of the third guild, but now an honorable citizen,[7] said to me. As the proverb has it, [*106] the lucky fellow arrives when the table is set. "I beg you to dine with us."

"But what is the occasion for this feast?"

"My benefactor, I married off my son yesterday."

"Benefactor indeed," I thought; "not without good cause does he call me that." I helped him, together with many another, to be enrolled as an honorable citizen. In 1737, I think, my grandfather apparently gave somebody a promissory note for one thousand rubles; to whom he gave it, I do not know. In 1780 Karp Dement'ich bought the note somewhere and had it protested. He came to me with a clever lawyer, and they were exceedingly kind to me, for they took only the interest for fifty years, and let me keep the principal. Karp Dement'ich is a grateful man. "Daughter-in-law, some vodka for the unexpected guest!"

"I do not drink vodka."

"At least a sip."

"To the health of the newlyweds!" And we sat down to supper.

On one side of me sat the host's son, and on the other Karp Dement'ich seated his young daughter-in-law.

[*107] Let us interrupt the story, dear reader. Give me a pencil and a small sheet of paper. For your amusement I will sketch the whole honorable company, and so make you a participant in the marriage feast, even if you are trapping beavers in the Aleutian Islands.[8] If I do not give you exact portraits, I shall content myself with silhouettes. Lavater[9] has taught us how to tell from them who is clever and who is stupid.

Karp Dement'ich has a gray beard, extending fourteen inches downward from his lower lip. His nose is a knob, his eyes are deep-set, his eyebrows pitch-black; he greets everyone with a handshake, strokes his beard, calls everybody his benefactor. Aksin'ya Parfent'evna is his beloved spouse. At sixty she is white as snow and red as a poppy; she constantly compresses her lips in a circle. She drinks no wine, only half a cup before dinner to keep the guests company, and a glass of vodka in the pantry. Her husband's clerk keeps a record of it for his master. [*108] At Aksin'ya Parfent'evna's order they buy an annual supply of three poods of face powder from Rzhev[10] and thirty pounds of rouge. Her husband's clerks are her lackeys. Aleksey Karpovich is my neighbor at the table. He has neither moustache nor beard, but his nose is already crimson; he blinks, his hair is clipped in a circle, he bows like a goose, shakes his head, and smoothes his hair. He had once been a clerk in a liquor shop in Petersburg. When he measures goods, he measures some two inches short on each yard: that's why his father loves him like himself. When he was fifteen, he boxed his mother's ears. Praskov'ya Denisovna, his bride, is white and red. Her teeth are black as coal. Her eyebrows are thin as thread and blacker than soot. In company she sits with downcast eyes, but all day long she never leaves the window, where she stares at all the men. In the evening she stands at the gate. She has one black eye — a first-day present from her beloved [*109] bridegroom; if you are quick-witted, you will know what for.

But, dear reader, you are already yawning. I had better stop making silhouettes. You are right, there will be nothing but nose after nose, lips and still more lips. And I don't know how you will be able to tell face powder from rouge on a silhouette.

"Karp Dement'ich, what are you dealing in nowadays? You don't go to Petersburg, don't haul flax, nor buy sugar, coffee, or dyes. I had thought your business was not unprofitable."

"I was almost ruined by it, but God just saved me. One year I made a tolerable profit and built my wife this house here. Next year the flax crop was a failure and I couldn't deliver what I had contracted to. That's why I went out of business."

"I remember, Karp Dement'ich, in payment for thirty thousand rubles advanced to you, you sent your creditors one thousand poods of flax to divide up [*110] among themselves."

"Believe me, on my conscience, I couldn't do any better."

"Of course, that was the year when there was a shortage of foreign goods, too. You had received advances of twenty thousand —. Yes, I remember; then came the headache."

"Truly, my benefactor, my head hurt me so badly that it almost cracked. How can my creditors complain? I gave them all my property."

"Three kopeks on the ruble." [11]

"Not at all: fifteen."

"And your wife's house?"

"How could I touch it? It is not mine."

"But tell me, what business are you engaged in?"

"None, really none. Ever since I went bankrupt, my son has been carrying on the business. This summer, thank God, he has delivered twenty thousand rubles' worth of flax."

"Next year, of course, he will contract for fifty thousand, have half the money advanced to him, and build a house for his young wife."

Aleksey Karpovich just smiled.

"My benefactor, you are an old joker. [*111] We've talked enough nonsense. Let us fall to." [12]

"You know I do not drink."

"At least a sip."

"A sip, a sip!" I felt that my cheeks were beginning to glow, and before the end of the feast I would have been as drunk as the rest. But fortunately one cannot sit forever at the table, just as one cannot always be wise. And for the same reason that I sometimes play the fool and wander in my mind, I remained sober at the wedding feast.

When I left my friend Karp Dement'ich I fell to musing. The commercial law, now universally established, that is, the law imposing severe and swift punishment for defaulting on commercial obligations, I had until now considered as a piece of legislation which upheld confidence. I had considered it a happy invention of modern times for the promotion of trade, an invention which had never occurred to the ancients. But why, if a man who gives a promissory note [*112] is dishonest, is it only a worthless scrap of paper? Would trade disappear, if there were no stern punishment for defaulting on notes? Should not the creditor know whom he can trust? For whom should the law be more concerned, the creditor or the debtor? Who deserves more consideration in the eyes of humanity, the creditor who lost his capital because he did not know his borrower, or the debtor in chains, in prison? On the one side, credulity; on the other, almost theft. The former lent money, depending on the sternness of the law, and the latter —. But if the punishment for defaulting on notes were not so severe? Then there would be no place for credulity, and there would perhaps be no cheating in transactions concerning notes. . . . I began to think again, the old system went to the Devil, and I went to bed with an empty head.

[*113] BRONNITSY

While they were changing the horses for my carriage, I decided to visit the high hill near Bronnitsy, on which they say — in ancient times, I think before the coming of the Slavs — there stood a temple famous for its oracles, which many northern rulers came to hear. It is said that in the place where the village of Bronnitsy now stands, there stood the city of Kholmograd, which was renowned in the ancient history of the North.[1] Now a small church is built on the site of the famous ancient fane.

As I climbed the hill, I imagined that I was transported into antiquity, and that I had come to have the future revealed to me by the Almighty, and to find peace from my perplexity. Divine awe [*114] seized my limbs, my breast began to heave, my eyes grew dull, their light was darkened. I heard a voice like thunder proclaiming: "Fool! Wherefore dost thou desire to pierce through the mystery which I have hid from mortals behind the impenetrable shroud of the unknown? Wherefore, audacious one, wilt thou learn that which only eternal thought can grasp? Know that thine ignorance of the future is in accord with the frailty of thy nature. Know that foreknown bliss loses its sweetness through long expectation, that the charm of present joy, when it comes upon exhausted senses, can never produce in the soul the delightful flutter that unexpected joy produces. Know that foreknown sorrow prematurely robs one of peace, and poisons the pleasures which one might have enjoyed if one had not known when they would end. What seekest [*115] thou, foolish child? My wisdom has implanted in thy mind and heart all that thou needest. Appeal to them in the day of sorrow, and thou wilt find comforters. Appeal to them in the day of gladness, and thou wilt find restraints upon thy presumptuous happiness. Return to thy home, return to thy family; quiet thy troubled thoughts, enter into thine innermost soul, and there thou wilt find my Godhead, there thou wilt hear my prophecy."

The peal of a mighty thunderbolt hurled by Perun [2] resounded down the valley. I regained my senses. As I reached the top of the hill and beheld the church, I raised my hands to heaven. "O Lord," I cried, "this is Thy temple, a temple, they say, of the one, true God. In this place, which is now Thy house, they say there once stood a temple of error. But I cannot believe, Almighty God, that man ever addressed his soul's prayers to any other being but Thee. Thy mighty right hand [*116] extends invisibly in all directions and compels even him who denies Thy all-powerful will, to recognize the architect and preserver of nature. If a mortal in his error calls Thee by strange, unbecoming, and bestial names, his worship nonetheless aspires to Thee, Ever-living Lord, and he trembles before Thy might. Jehovah, Jupiter, Brahma, God of Abraham, God of Moses, God of Confucius, God of Zoroaster, God of Socrates, God of Marcus Aurelius, God of the Christians, O my God! Thou art everywhere the same, the One. [3]

When mortals in their error seemed to be worshiping not Thee alone, they were deifying Thine incomparable forces, Thine inimitable deeds. Thy almighty power, felt everywhere and in everything, has everywhere and in everything been worshiped. The atheist who denies Thee, but recognizes the immutable law of nature, thereby proclaims Thy glory, [*117] lauding Thee even more than our songs of praise. For, moved to the depths of his soul by Thy wondrous works, he stands trembling before them. Most gracious Father, Thou seekest a true heart and spotless soul; they are open everywhere for Thy coming. Descend, O Lord, and enthrone Thyself in them."

I stood for a few moments, removed from the objects around me, lost in profound contemplation. Then, raising my eyes and glancing at the nearby dwellings, I cried, "Behold the miserable hovels of the downfallen, in the place where once a great city reared its proud walls. Not even the smallest trace of them remains. Reason, demanding conclusive and palpable evidence, refuses even to believe the story. And all that we see will pass away; all will fall to ruins; all will become dust. But a certain mysterious voice says to me, 'Something will forever live.' "

> [*118] The stars shall fade away, the sun himself
> Grow dim with age, and nature sink in years;
> But thou shalt flourish in immortal youth,
> Unhurt amidst the wars of elements,
> The wrecks of matter, and the crush of worlds.*

[*119] ZAYTSOVO

In the post station at Zaytsovo I found my old friend Mr. Krestyankin. I had known him since childhood. We were not often in the same town, but our conversations, although infrequent, had been frank. Mr. Krestyankin had long been

---

* *The Death of Cato* [sic], a tragedy by Addison. Act V, Scene I.[4]

in the Military Service, but becoming disgusted with its cruelties, especially in time of war, when great violence is justified in the name of military necessity, had had himself transferred to the Civil Service. Unfortunately for him, even in the Civil Service he did not escape what he had sought to avoid in leaving the Military. He had a very sensitive soul and a humane heart. His admittedly excellent qualities procured for him the position of presiding judge in a criminal court. At first he had not wanted to accept this post, but after some reflection he had said [*120] to me: "My friend, what a vast field is opened up to me for the satisfaction of my heart's desire! What an exercise for a gentle heart! We will break the scepter of cruelty, which so often oppresses the shoulders of innocence. Let the prisons be opened, and may awkward weakness and careless inexperience never see them, and may accident nevermore be accounted a crime! O my friend! In the execution of my duty I will wring tears from parents for their children and sighs from husbands and wives for their mates, but these tears will be blessed tears of regeneration. And the tears of suffering innocence and simplicity of soul will dry up. How this thought delights me! Come, let us hasten my departure. Maybe my immediate presence is needed there. By procrastination I may become a murderer, if I fail to anticipate an imprisonment or an accusation by a pardon or a release from chains."

[*121] With such thoughts my friend had started out for the scene of his labors. How surprised I was to learn from him that he had resigned from the service and intended to live the rest of his life in retirement. "My friend, I had imagined," Mr. Krestyankin said to me, "that in the execution of my duties I would reap a rich harvest of spiritual satisfaction. Instead of that I found in it only gall and thorns. Now, having grown sick of it and no longer being able to do any good, I have abandoned my place to a truly rapacious beast. In a brief time he has won praise by his speedy decision of long-

delayed cases, while I was considered a procrastinator. Sometimes they even considered me venal because I did not hasten to aggravate the lot of those unfortunates who are frequently driven into crime against their will. Before I entered the Civil Service, I had won the flattering name of a humane commanding officer. Now the very quality [*122] of which my heart was so proud is called weakness or intolerable indulgence. I saw my decisions ridiculed for the very thing which made them valuable; I saw them rendered nugatory. I observed with contempt that in order to release a real evildoer and dangerous member of society, or to punish alleged crimes with the forfeiture of property, honor, and life, my superior, who was unable to move me to an illegal acquittal of crime or to a sentence against innocence, persuaded my associates to do what he wanted; and frequently I saw my well-meant dispositions of cases go up like smoke. But my associates, as a reward for their disgraceful subserviency, received honors, as tainted in my sight as they were speciously enticing in theirs. In troublesome cases, when my belief in [*123] the innocence of the accused inclined me to mercy, I often had recourse to the law, hoping to find in it support in my uncertainty; but instead of mercy I frequently found in it cruelty, which had its origin not in the law itself but in its obsoleteness. The disproportion between punishment and crime often moved me to tears. I saw (could it be otherwise?) that the law judges deeds and does not concern itself with their causes. And the last case that involved considerations of this sort compelled me to resign from the service. For, being unable to save miserable offenders who had been dragged into crime by the mighty hand of fate, I did not want to become a guilty participant in their destruction. Unable to alleviate their lot, I sought escape from cruelty and washed my hands in my innocence.

"In our province there lived a nobleman who several years before [*124] had resigned from the service. Here is his service record. He began at Court as a stoker, and was promoted to lackey, chamber lackey, then butler. I do not know what virtues are required for advancement in the Court Service.[1] But I do know that he was passionately fond of wine. After he had been a butler for some fifteen years, he was sent to the Heralds' College to establish his rank. But feeling his unfitness for affairs, he petitioned for retirement, and was rewarded with the rank of Collegiate Assessor,[2] with which he came, six years ago, to his birthplace, that is, to our province. Such particular attachment to one's native place often has its source in vanity. A man of low estate who has been raised to the peerage, or a poor man who has acquired wealth, after shaking off all restraint of modesty, the last and weakest [*125] root of virtue, prefers to display his pomp and conceit in the place of his birth.[3] There the assessor soon had a chance to buy a village,[4] in which he settled down with his not inconsiderable family. If a Hogarth [5] were born in our country, he would find a fertile field for his caricatures in Mr. Assessor's family. But I am a poor artist. If I were able, with Lavater's [6] penetration, to read a man's innermost thoughts in his features, then I could make the picture of the assessor's family worthy of attention. Since I lack these qualities, I will make their actions speak for themselves, for actions are always the best indices of spiritual development.

"Being of very lowly origin himself, Mr. Assessor now saw himself as master of several hundred of his own kind. This turned his head. He is not the only one who might justly complain that the possession of power had turned his head. [*126] He considered himself an exalted being, and the peasants — cattle given to him (he almost thought his power over them proceeded from God) to be used for work at his arbitrary will. He was avaricious, miserly, cruel by nature, irritable, and hence overbearing with the weak. From this you can imagine how he treated his peasants. They had paid a commutation tax to their old master, but their new one made them work on his fields, took away all their land, bought all their cattle at a price which he determined, compelled them to work seven days a week for him, and, lest they starve, fed them in the yard of the manor, and only once a day, at that; though he gave a monthly allowance to a few as a special grace. If he thought anyone was lazy, he flogged him with switches, whips, sticks, or cat-o'-nine-tails, according to the degree of laziness. In regard to real [*127] crimes, such as robbery, not of him but of others, he said not a word. It looked as though he wanted to resurrect in his village the customs of ancient Lacedaemon or the Zaporog Sech.[7] It so happened that his peasants, to obtain food, robbed one traveler and killed another. He did not surrender them to the court, but hid them, and declared to the Government that they had run away. He felt that it would be no profit to him to have them flogged and sent off to hard labor for their crime. If one of his peasants stole something from him, he had him beaten just as for laziness or for a daring or witty answer; and in addition, he put fetters on their feet and a yoke on their neck. I could tell you of many more of his wise arrangements, but this will do for the description of my hero. His spouse had full power over the village women. Her sons and daughters were her aides in the execution of her commands, [*128] as they were also of their father's. For they made it their rule not to take the peasants from their work for any reason. For manorial servants they had a boy they had bought in Moscow, a hairdresser for their daughters, and an old woman who served as cook. They had no coachman and no horses; the master always drove the plough horses. The sons flogged the peasants with whips and cat-o'-nine-tails. The daughters struck the faces of the women and girls and pulled their hair. The sons in their free time disported themselves in the village and in the fields, flirting and carrying on with girls and women, not one of whom escaped violation. The daughters, not having any suitors, took out their boredom on the spinning women, many of whom they seriously injured. Judge for yourself, my friend, what must be the end of such behavior. I have observed from a great many examples that the Russian people are very patient and long-suffering, [*129] but when they reach the end of their patience, nothing can restrain them from terrible cruelty. This is just what happened in the case of the assessor. The occasion for it was provided by the brutal and dissolute, or say rather the beastly act of one of his sons.

"In his village there was a good-looking peasant girl who was betrothed to a young peasant of the same village. The assessor's middle son took a liking to her and used every possible means to win her love for himself; but the girl remained true to the promise she had made to her sweetheart, a steadfastness rare but still possible among the peasantry. The wedding was to have taken place on a Sunday. In accordance with the custom current on many landed estates, the bridegroom's father went with his son to the manor house and brought two poods of bridal honey to his master. The young 'nobleman' decided to use this last moment [*130] for the gratification of his lust. He took both his brothers with him and, having summoned the bride to the courtyard by a strange boy, gagged her and carried her off to a shed. Unable to utter a sound, she struggled with all her strength against her young master's beastly purpose. At last, overcome by the three of them, she had to yield to force, and the vile monster was just about to carry out his long-cherished purpose when the bridegroom, returning from the manor, entered the yard, saw one of the young masters near the shed, and guessed their evil intention. He called his father to help him and flew faster than lightning to the shed. What a spectacle presented itself to him! Just as he got there they closed the doors of the shed, but the combined strength of the two brothers could not stem the onrush of the maddened bridegroom. Nearby he picked up [*131] a stake, ran into the shed, and hit the ravisher of his bride over the back with it.

The others wanted to seize the bridegroom, but, seeing his father running with a stake to his assistance, they abandoned their prey, jumped out of the shed, and ran away. But the bridegroom caught up with one of them and broke his head with a blow of the stake. Bent on revenge for this injury, these evildoers went straight to their father and told him that they had met the bride while passing through the village and had jested with her, and that the bridegroom, seeing this, had straightway fallen upon them and beaten them, with the help of his father. As proof they showed him the one brother's wounded head. Infuriated by the wounding of his son, the father burst into a rage. He ordered the three evildoers — as he called the bridegroom, the bride, and the bridegroom's father — to be brought before him without delay. When they appeared before him, the first question [*132] he asked them was who had broken his son's head. The bridegroom did not deny that he had done it, and told him everything that had happened. 'How did you dare,' said the old assessor, 'to raise your hand against your master? Even if he had spent the night with your bride on the eve of your wedding, you should have been grateful to him. You shall not marry her. She shall be attached to my house, and you shall all be punished.' After this judgment, he turned the bridegroom over to his sons, and ordered them to flog him mercilessly with the cat-o'-nine-tails. He stood the scourging manfully and watched with indomitable fortitude as they began to subject his father to the same torture. But he could not endure it when he saw his master's children starting to take his bride into the house. The punishment was taking place in the yard. In an instant he snatched her from the hands of her abductors, and the two lovers, now free, ran away from the yard. Seeing this, the master's [*133] sons stopped beating the old man and started to pursue them. Seeing that they were catching up with him, the bridegroom snatched a rail out of the fence and prepared to defend himself. Meanwhile the noise attracted other peasants to the manor yard. They sympathized with the young peasant and, infuriated against their masters, they gathered around their fellow to defend him. Seeing all this, the assessor himself ran up, began to curse them, and struck the first man he met so violently with his cane that he fell senseless to the ground. This was the signal for a general attack. They surrounded their four masters and, in short, beat them to death on the spot. They hated them so much that not one wanted to miss the chance to take part in murdering them, as they themselves later confessed. Just at this time the chief of the country police of that district happened to come by with a detachment of soldiers. He [*134] was an eyewitness of part of what happened. He had the guilty persons — that is, half the village — put under guard, and instituted an investigation which ultimately reached the criminal court. The case was clearly established, and the guilty persons confessed everything, pleading in their defense only the barbarous acts of their masters, of which the whole province had been cognizant. In the course of my official duty it was incumbent upon me to pass the final sentence of death upon the guilty persons and to commute it to confiscation of property and lifelong penal servitude.

"Upon reviewing the case, I found no sufficient or convincing reason to condemn the offenders. The peasants who had killed their master were guilty of murder. But was it not forced upon them? Was not the murdered assessor himself the cause of it? If in arithmetic a third number follows invariably from two given ones, [*135] the consequence was equally inevitable in this case. The innocence of the defendants was, at least for me, a mathematical certainty. If I am going on my way and an evildoer falls upon me and raises a dagger over my head to strike me down, am I to be considered a murderer if I forestall him in his evil deed and strike him down lifeless at my feet? If a Mohock today, having won the universal contempt he deserves, wants to revenge himself for it on me, and, meeting me in a solitary place, attacks me with drawn sword to deprive me of life or at least to wound me, am I guilty if I draw my sword in self-defense and deliver society from a member who disturbs its peace? Can an act be considered prejudicial to the inviolable human rights of a fellow being if I do it to save myself, if [*136] it prevents my destruction, if without it my well-being would be forever undone? [8]

"Full as I was of such thoughts, you may imagine the torment of my soul when I reviewed this case. With my customary frankness I communicated my thoughts to my associates. They unanimously rose up against me. Mercy and charity seemed to them a culpable defense of crime; they called me an abettor of murder, an accomplice of murderers. In their opinion, the safety of the home would disappear with the dissemination of my subversive opinions. 'Can a nobleman,' they said, 'live safely on his estate from henceforth? If those who oppose their master's will, or, even worse, his murderers, are declared innocent, then obedience will vanish, domestic bonds will be severed, and the chaos of [*137] primitive societies will come again. Agriculture will die, its implements will be destroyed, the fields will become deserts, overgrown with useless weeds. Not having any authority over them, the peasants will wander about in idleness and indolence, and finally will scatter. Cities will soon feel the imperious hand of destruction. The citizens will lose their stomach for work, handicraft will lose its diligence and ambition, trade will run dry at its source, wealth will give way to misery, the most magnificent buildings will crumble, the laws will become incomprehensible and inoperative. Then the mighty structure of society will begin to fall to pieces and each part of it will breathe its last, separate from the whole. Then the Imperial throne, on which the strength and cohesion of society are now based, will decay and crumble into dust. Then the ruler of nations will be accounted merely an ordinary citizen, and society [*138] will behold its end.' My associates tried to paint this picture, worthy of the brush of Satan, for the eyes of all who knew anything of this case. 'Our presiding judge,' they cried, 'thinks it right to justify murder committed by the peasants. Ask of what origin he is! If we are not mistaken, he used to follow the plough himself in his youth. These newly created noblemen always have strange conceptions of the natural rights of noblemen over their peasants. If he had his way, he would make us all peasant proprietors, in order to equalize his descent with ours.' With such words my associates intended to insult me and to make me hateful to all society. But they were not satisfied with that. They said that I had received a bribe from the widow of the murdered assessor so that she would not be deprived of her peasants by sentencing them to hard labor in exile, and that this was the real reason [*139] for my strange and dangerous opinions which were so prejudicial to all the rights of the whole gentry. The fools thought that their ridicule would cut me to the quick, that their slander would insult me, that their false representation of my good intention would distract me from it. They did not know my heart. They did not know that I have always faced the court of my own conscience without trembling, that my cheeks have never burned with the crimson blush of a guilty conscience.

"Their notion that I had been bribed, they based upon the fact that the assessor's widow did not want to avenge her husband's death, but, prompted by her avarice and following her husband's rule, wanted the peasants to be freed from punishment, in order that, as she said, she might not lose her property. She came to me with such a petition. I agreed with her as to the remission of punishment for the murder of her husband, but we differed as to the motive. She assured me that she [*140] would give them adequate punishment herself, and I assured her that if the murderers of her husband were acquitted, they must never again be driven to such desperate extremities, lest they become in very truth the criminals they had been wrongly called.

"Soon the governor was informed of my views in this matter — that I had been trying to convert my associates to my way of looking at it, and that they were beginning to waver in their opinions. They were influenced, however, not by the strength and persuasiveness of my reasoning, but by the money of the assessor's widow. Since the governor himself had been brought up under the principle of the absolute authority of the gentry over the peasants, he could not accept my views, and he became indignant when he saw that they were beginning to prevail in the judgment of this case, albeit for very divers reasons. He sent for my associates, admonished them, and urged upon them the wickedness of my views, [*141] maintaining that they were an insult to the gentry and an insult to the supreme power, in that they violated its fundamental laws. He promised a reward to those who obeyed the law and threatened with punishment those who did not. And soon he prevailed upon these weak judges, who followed no principles in their decisions and had no firmness of spirit, to return to their earlier opinions. I was no more surprised at this, their second change, than I had been at their first. It is characteristic of weak, craven, and base souls to cower before the threats of the powers that be and to rejoice at their gracious nod.

"Our governor, having converted my associates, apparently flattered himself with the conviction that he could also convert me. For this purpose he summoned me, as it happened, on the morning of a holiday. He was obliged to summon me, because I never waited upon him with those meaningless expressions of respect and forced flattery which pride [*142] regards as a duty in subordinates and which a wise man considers contemptible and disgraceful to humanity.[9] He purposely chose a festal day, when there was a large gathering of people at his house; he purposely chose to address me at a public assembly, because he hoped in that way to persuade me more readily. He hoped to find me either cowardly in soul or weak in mind. He directed his speech against both weaknesses. I do not think it necessary to recount to you everything to which conceit, the sense of power, and the belief in his own penetration and erudition inspired his eloquence. His conceit I met with equanimity and calm; his show of power, with steadfastness; his arguments with my own; and for a long time I spoke in a cool and collected manner. But finally my agitated heart poured out all that was pent up in it. The more subservience I saw in those who were standing around, the more impulsive my speech [*143] became. With a firm voice, loud and clear, I finally exclaimed:

" 'Every man is born into the world equal to all others All have the same bodily parts, all have reason and will. Consequently, apart from his relation to society, man is a being that depends on no one in his actions. But he puts limits to his own freedom of action, he agrees not to follow only his own will in everything, he subjects himself to the commands of his equals; in a word, he becomes a citizen. For what reason does he control his passions? Why does he set up a governing authority over himself? Why, though free to seek fulfillment of his will, does he confine himself within the bounds of obedience? For his own advantage, reason will say; for his own advantage, inner feeling will say; for his own advantage, wise legislation will say. Consequently, wherever being a citizen is not to his advantage, he is [*144] not a citizen. Consequently, whoever seeks to rob him of the advantages of citizenship is his enemy. Against his enemy he seeks protection and satisfaction in the law. If the law is unable or unwilling to protect him, or if its power cannot furnish him immediate aid in the face of clear and present danger, then the citizen has recourse to the natural law of self-defense, self-preservation, and well-being. For the citizen, in becoming a citizen, does not cease to be a man, whose first obligation, arising from his very nature, is his own preservation, defense, and welfare. By his bestial cruelty the assessor who was murdered by the peasants had violated their rights as citizens. At the moment when he abetted the violence of his sons, when he added insult to the heartfelt injury of the bridal pair, when he, seeing their opposition to his devilish tyranny, moved to punish them, [*145] then the law that protects a citizen fell into abeyance and its efficacy disappeared; then the law of nature was reborn, and the power of the wronged citizen, which the positive law cannot take from him when he has been wronged, comes into operation, and the peasants who killed the beastly assessor are not guilty before the law. On rational grounds my heart finds them not guilty, and the death of the assessor, although violent, is just. Let no one presume to seek in reasons of state or in the maintenance of public peace grounds for condemning the murderers of the assessor, who expired in the midst of his wickedness. No matter in what estate heaven may have decreed a citizen's birth, he is and will always remain a man; and so long as he is a man, the law of nature, as an abundant wellspring of goodness, will never run dry in him, and whosoever dares [*146] wound him in his natural and inviolable right is a criminal. Woe to him, if the civil law does not punish him. He will be marked as a pariah by his fellow citizens, and may whosoever has sufficient power exact vengeance against him for his evildoing.'

"I fell silent. The governor said not a word to me. Now and then he gave me lowering glances charged with the fury of impotence and the malice of vengeance. Everyone was silent, expecting that I, the profaner of all laws, would be put under arrest. Every now and then a murmur of disapproval could be heard on their servile lips. Everyone turned his eyes away from me. It looked as though terror had seized those who stood near me. Imperceptibly they withdrew from me, as from one infected with a deadly plague. Weary of the spectacle of this mixture of arrogance and basest servility, I left this assembly of flatterers.[10]

[*147] "Unable to find any means to save the innocent

homicides whom my heart acquitted, I did not want to be an accomplice in or a witness of their execution. I petitioned for my retirement and, having been granted it, I am now on my way home to bewail the lamentable fate of the peasant class, and to relieve my weariness in association with my friends." [11] As he said this, we took leave of one another, and each went his own way.

That day my journey was not successful. The horses were poor, and had to be changed every minute. Finally, as we were going down a low hill, the carriage axle broke, and we could not drive any farther. I am in the habit of taking walks. I picked up my cane and started off for the post station. But a stroll on the highway is not very pleasant for a Petersburger, for it is not like a promenade in the Summer Garden or in Baba; [12] it soon tired me, and I had to sit down.

[*148] While I was sitting on a rock, drawing all sorts of crooked figures in the sand and thinking of this and that, a carriage rushed past me. The passenger saw me and ordered his driver to stop — and I recognized an old acquaintance of mine.

"What are you doing here?" he said to me.

"I am just thinking. I have plenty of time for thinking; my axle is broken. What's the news?"

"The same old rot: the weather changes with the wind, now there's slush, now sunshine —. But wait! Here's news for you: Duryndin [13] got married."

"Impossible! He's almost eighty."

"True enough. Well, here's a letter for you. Read it at your leisure. I've got to be on my way. Good-bye!" And we parted.

The letter was from a friend of mine. He dearly loved gossip and had promised to keep me supplied with it while I was away, and he had kept his word. Meanwhile they had fitted the carriage with a spare axle which by good luck we had in reserve. As we drove off again, I read:

[*149] "Petersburg.

"My dear friend,

"The other day there took place here the marriage of a seventy-eight year old lad and a sixty-two year old lass. You would find it hard to guess the reason for such a belated coupling, if I didn't tell you. Open your ears wide, my friend, and listen. Mme. Sh., sixty-two years old and not the last heroine of her kind, had been a widow since her twenty-fifth year. She had been married to a merchant who had had bad luck in business. She had a rather pretty face, and, being left a poor orphan after her husband's death and knowing of the hardheartedness of his associates, she did not wish to beg them for alms, and was determined to support herself by her own labors. As long as the comeliness of youth shone in her face, she was constantly employed and received generous pay from her customers. But as soon as she noticed that her beauty was beginning [*150] to fade, and her amorous duties were giving way to boredom and loneliness, she took thought and, not finding any more purchasers for her antiquated charms, began to trade in the charms of others, who, if they did not always have the advantage of beauty, had at least that of novelty. Having in this manner accumulated some thousands, she took her honorable discharge from the despised society of procurers and began to loan out on interest the money she had acquired by her shamelessness and that of others. In time her old profession was forgotten, and the former madam became an indispensable personage in the society of spendthrifts. When she had peacefully reached her sixty-second year, the Devil prompted her to get married. All her acquaintances were amazed. Her closest friend, N., came to see her. 'It is rumoured, my dear,' she said to the gray-haired bride, 'that you are about to get married. I think it must be a lie. Some joker has invented this fairy tale.'

[*151] "Sh. — 'It's the gospel truth. To-morrow will be the betrothal. Come and celebrate with us.'

"N. — 'You've lost your mind! Is your old blood hot again, or has some milksop come to look for shelter under your wing?'

"Sh. — 'O my dear, you do me wrong to put me on a level with flighty young things. I'm taking a suitable husband —'

"N. — 'Yes, I know he'll suit you. But remember, no one ever falls in love with the likes of us, except for money.'

"Sh. — 'I'm not taking anybody who could be false to me. My bridegroom is sixteen years older than I am.'

"N. — 'You're joking!'

"Sh. — 'On my word of honor: Baron Duryndin.'

"N. — 'It can't be!'

"Sh. — 'Come to-morrow evening. You'll see for yourself that I'm not lying.'

[*152] "N. — 'And if it is so, he's not marrying you, but your money.'

"Sh. — 'But who's going to give it to him? I shan't so lose my head the first night as to give him all my possessions; that time is past long since. A gold snuffbox, some silver buckles, and such like rubbish, which were pawned with me and are hard to dispose of — that's all the dowry my beloved bridegroom will get. And if he snores, I'll kick him out of bed.'

"N. — 'At least he gets a snuffbox out of it. But what do you get?'

"Sh. — 'How is that, my dear? Nowadays it's not a bad thing to have a noble title, to have them call you "Your Ladyship," and the stupid ones even "Your Excellency." Besides, I'll have someone to play cribbage with on long winter evenings. But now I sit here all alone; I don't even have the [*153] pleasure of hearing anyone say "God bless you!" when I sneeze. But once I have my man, every time I catch cold I'll hear him say, "God bless you, my pet; God bless you, my darling!" '

"N. — 'Good-bye, my dear.'

"Sh. — 'Tomorrow's the betrothal, and a week from tomorrow's the wedding.'

"N. — (Departs.)

"Sh. — (Sneezes.) 'She'll not be coming back. How different it will be when I'm married!'

"Do not marvel, my friend! In this world, the wheel comes full circle. Today the sensible is in fashion, tomorrow the stupid. I hope you get to see a lot of Duryndins. If they do not always distinguish themselves by their marriages, they do it in some other way. Without its Duryndins the world would not last three days."

[*154] KRESTTSY

At Kresttsy I witnessed the parting of a father from his children. It moved me the more deeply because I am myself a father and may soon be parting from my own children. An unfortunate prejudice of the gentry impels them to go into the service. The very mention of this word makes my blood boil! One may safely bet a thousand to one that out of a hundred young noblemen who enter the service, ninety-eight will become good-for-nothing scoundrels, and two, in their old age, or, more correctly, in their decrepitude, although they are not old in years, will become good men. The rest advance in rank, squander or acquire property, and so on. Now and then, when I look at my eldest son and realize that he will soon be going into the service, or, in other [*155] words, that the little bird will soon be leaving the nest, my hair stands on end. Not because the service in itself corrupts morals, but because one should not enter the service until one's morals are already maturely developed. Someone will say, "But who pushes the milksops into it?" "Who? The common example. Staff officer at seventeen, colonel at twenty, general at twenty, gentleman of the chamber, senator, governor, commander of an army. What father would not wish his children, although still in their youth, to attain high rank, in the wake of which come wealth, honor, and wisdom?" As I look at my son, I can see this in my mind's eye: he has begun to serve and has made the acquaintance of spendthrifts, libertines, gamblers, dandies. He has learned to dress sprucely, to play cards, to gain a livelihood by playing cards, to talk about everything without knowing anything, to run after [*156] wenches, or to talk nonsense to the ladies. Fickle fortune, twirling on her spindleshanks,[1] has somehow smiled on him, and my young son has become a famous man even before he has started to shave his beard. He imagines he is wiser than all the world. What good can one expect from such a military commander or municipal governor? Tell me frankly, O father who lovest thy son; tell me, O honest citizen, would you not rather choke your son to death than let him go into the service? Does it not make your heart ache, that your son, a famous man, has nothing but contempt for men of real worth, because it is their fate to trail behind on the road to high rank, because they scorn to use underhanded methods? Will you not weep to see that your beloved son with a pleasant smile on his face will rob people of their property and honor, and poison and slaughter them, not always with his own aristocratic hands but with the paws of his favorites?

[*157] The Kresttsy nobleman looked as though he were about fifty years old. Here and there streaks of gray showed through his blond hair. His settled features betokened a spiritual calm invulnerable to the passions. A gentle smile of untroubled content, born of benevolence, had marked his face with dimples, which are so charming in women. As I entered the room where he was sitting, he was looking at his two sons. His eyes, eyes of kindly reasonableness, seemed to be veiled with a light film of sadness, but sparks of sturdy confidence and faith flashed from them. Before him stood two youths of almost equal age, for there was but one year's difference between them, while they were equal in maturity of mind

and heart. For the father's eagerness had hastened the mental growth of the younger, while brotherly love had led the elder to delay somewhat his progress in learning. [*158] The two brothers had an equal comprehension of things and of the rules of life, but nature had endowed them with different degrees of intellect and sensitiveness of heart. In the elder the eyes were firm, and his imperturbable features bore witness to an intrepid soul that would not waver in its undertakings. The eyes of the younger were sharp, his features restless and changeable. But the youths' frank and engaging animation was a sure sign of their father's beneficent teaching. They looked at their father with unaccustomed constraint, due to grief at their imminent parting and not to any imposition of power or authority upon them. Now and then teardrops fell from their eyes. "My friends," said the father, "today we must part," and, embracing them, he pressed them sobbing to his breast. Standing motionless at the door, I had been a witness to this spectacle for some minutes, when the father turned to me and said:

[*159] "Be my witness, kind traveler, be my witness before the world, with what a heavy heart I obey the sovereign will of custom. In letting my children range beyond the watchful care of the parental eye, my one motive is that they may gain experience, learn to know man from his acts, and, weary of the turmoil of worldly life, may joyfully abandon it. But they should have a refuge from persecution, and their daily bread, if they are in need. For this reason I am remaining on my land. Most gracious Lord, do not let them have to wander about seeking alms from the mighty and finding consolation in them! Let their hearts be their comforters, and their minds be their givers of alms! Be seated, and hearken to my words, which should abide in your innermost souls. I repeat to you, today we must part. With inexpressible joy [*160] I behold the tears that water your cheeks. May this agitation of your

souls carry my counsel to their sanctuary, so that they may be stirred at the thought of me, and may I in my absence be your defense from evils and sorrows![2]

"From the time that I received you from your mother's body into my embrace, I willed that no one else should be responsible for all the things concerned with your care. Never did a hired nurse touch your bodies, never did a hired tutor touch your hearts and minds. My vigilant and zealous eye watched over you day and night lest anything harmful should come near you; and I consider myself fortunate indeed to have guided you up to this hour of parting from me. But do not imagine that I want to extort from your lips any thanks for the care I have taken of you, or any acknowledgment, however feeble, for anything I have done for you. I was moved by the impulse of my own [*161] interest, and whatever I did for you, I did for my own satisfaction. Therefore put away the thought that you are subject to my power. You owe me nothing. Not in reason, and much less in law, do I want to look for the strong foundation of our union. It is grounded in your hearts. Woe to you if you ever forget it! My image will pursue the violator of our union of friendship, will seek him out in his hiding place, and will cause him unbearable torture until he returns to the union. Once more I say to you, you owe me nothing. Look upon me as a transient and pilgrim, and if your heart feels any tender inclination towards me, we shall live in friendship, that greatest blessing on earth. If, however, your heart is not stirred, may we forget each other as though we had never been born. — Most gracious Father, let me never see that day, [*162] take me back to Thy lap before that! — You owe me nothing for your food, nor for your instruction, and least of all for your birth. For your birth? Wherein were you responsible? Were you asked whether you wanted to be born? Were you to be born for your good or for your harm? Does the father or mother, in begetting a son, know whether he will be happy or unhappy in life? Who will say that, in entering into wedlock, he thought of his heirs and descendants? And if he did have them in mind, did he want to bring them into existence for the sake of their happiness, or for the perpetuation of his name? How can I wish good things to him whom I do not know, and what is good? Can an indefinite wish, born in uncertainty, be called good? The urge toward marriage explains why parents bring children into the world. Attracted more by your mother's spiritual goodness than by the beauty of her face, I used a sure means to kindle our mutual passion, namely, true [*163] love. I won your mother for my wife. But what incited our love? Mutual desire, satisfaction of the flesh and of the spirit. In partaking of the joy decreed by nature, we did not think of you. Your birth was a pleasure for us, but not for you. The reproduction of our kind flattered our vanity; your birth was a new and, so to speak, a sensuous union, confirming our spiritual union. This is the source of the initial love of parents for their children; it is strengthened by habit, by the sense of one's power, and by the honor reflected upon the father by the praises earned by his son. Your mother shared my opinion that you owed us nothing for your birth. She did not pride herself on having carried you in her womb, did not demand any recognition for having nourished you with her blood, did not want any filial reverence for her pain in giving you birth, nor for the weariness of having nursed you [*164] at her breasts. She sought to give you a good soul, like her own, and she wished to implant friendship in it, not duty, obligation, or servile obedience. Fate did not permit her to see the fruit of her planting. She left us with firmness of spirit, but she did not want to die so soon, seeing your youth and my love. In emulating her, we shall not lose her entirely. She will live with us until we join her. You must know that my favorite conversation with you is about her who gave you birth. Then it seems as though her soul were holding converse with us, then she is present with us, then she appears within us, then she is still alive." Saying this, he wiped off the tears of his soul's abiding grief.

"Little as you owe me for your birth, you owe me just as little for your sustenance. When I entertain a stranger, when I feed little birds, [*165] when I give food to a dog who licks my hand, do I do it for their sakes? In all that I find my own personal joy, amusement, or profit. The same motives lead people to foster their children. When you were born into the world, you became citizens of the society in which you live. It was my duty to nurture you, for, if I had let you starve, I would have been a murderer. If I took better care of you than many do, I simply followed the dictates of my heart. It was in my power to care well for you or to neglect you, to save your days or to squander them, to keep you alive or let you perish; and this proves clearly that you are not indebted to me for being still alive. If you had died from my neglect, as so many die, the vengeance of the law would not have pursued me. But some may say that you are indebted [*166] to me for your training and education. Did I not seek my own profit in your virtue? The praises bestowed upon your good behavior, judgment, knowledge, and ability, falling upon you, are reflected upon me, as the sun's rays are from a mirror. In praising you, they praise me. What would it have profited me if you had abandoned yourselves to vice, had been estranged from learning, dull in mind, malicious, and lacking in fineness of feeling? Not only should I have become a fellow sufferer in your aberrations but, perhaps, a victim of your madness. As it is, I can remain calm upon your departure; your minds are sound, your hearts are strong, and I live in them. O friends, sons of my heart! In begetting you, I incurred many obligations toward you, but you owe me nothing. I seek your friendship and love, and if you bestow it upon me, I shall blissfully return to the Source of life, and, in dying, I will not rebel against [*167] leaving you forever, since I shall live in your memories.

"But if I have done my duty in your education, I must now tell you the reason why I brought you up thus and not otherwise, and why I taught you one thing and not another; therefore listen to the story of your education, that you may know the reason for all the things which I have done for you.

"From your childhood on you have never experienced any compulsion. Although you were guided in your actions by my hand, you were never conscious of its direction. Your actions were predetermined and anticipated, but I did not want timidity or abject obedience to make you feel so much as the weight of its finger. Hence your spirit, impatient with any unreasonable command, is amenable to the counsels of friendship. If in your childhood I found that, diverted by some accidental force, you departed from the path I had prepared for you, [*168] I stopped you, or, better, imperceptibly led you back into the old path, even as a stream that breaks through its dikes is turned back within its banks by a skillful hand.[3]

"There was no timid tenderness in me when, as it seemed, I did not protect you from the inclemency of the elements and the weather. I preferred that your bodies be hardened by momentary pain rather than that you grow soft and fat in adult life. Therefore you often went barefooted and bareheaded, and lay down to rest in dust and dirt, on a bench or a stone. No less did I try to keep you from deleterious food and drink. Work was the best seasoning for our dinner. Remember how joyfully we dined in a strange village when we could not find our way [*169] home. How good the rye bread and rustic kvas tasted to us then!

"Do not be angry with me if you are sometimes ridiculed because you have no courtly bearing, because you stand as is most comfortable for your body, and not as fashion or custom prescribes, because you do not dress according to fashionable taste, because your hair is curled by the hand of nature, not of the hairdresser. Do not be angry if you are neglected in society, especially by women, because you do not know how to flatter their beauty. But remember that you know how to run fast, how to swim without tiring, that you can lift weights without straining, lead a plough, dig up a garden bed, that you have learned how to handle a scythe, axe, plane, and chisel, that you know how to ride and shoot. Do not grieve because you cannot leap about like clowns. You must know that even the finest dancing represents nothing majestic, and that, if you are ever moved by the sight of it, lust is its [*170] real root, and the rest merely incidental. But you know how to portray animate and inanimate nature, and nature's king, man. In painting you will find true pleasure, not only for the senses, but for the mind. I have taught you music, that the string, vibrating in harmony with your nerves, may awaken your slumbering heart, for music, by bringing our innermost spirit into motion, makes tenderness of heart a habit. I have also taught you the barbarous art of fighting with the sword. But may this art remain dormant within you, unless you are provoked to self-defense. I trust it will not make you arrogant, for you have a firm spirit and will not consider it an insult if an ass kicks at you or a pig touches you with its smelly snout. Do not be afraid to tell anyone that you know how to milk a cow, how to cook cabbage soup and porridge, or that you can roast a piece [*171] of meat and make it taste good. He who knows how to do something himself will know how to order others to do it, and will be lenient toward others' mistakes, since he knows the difficulties of doing things.

"In your childhood and boyhood I did not burden your mind with ready-made deductions and other people's thoughts; I did not burden your memory with useless facts. After I had shown you the way to knowledge, you yourselves, as soon as you became conscious of your power of reasoning, proceeded on the road that was opened to you. Your knowledge is all the better grounded because you have not acquired it by rote, chattering, as the proverb says, like Jacob's magpie.[4] In accord with this principle, so long as your reasoning power was inactive, I did not lay before you the concept of the Supreme Being, much less that of Revelation. For what you would have learned before you learned to reason would only have been prejudice, and would have hindered independent thought. [*172] But when I saw that in your judgment you were guided by reason, I presented to you a sequence of concepts which lead to the recognition of God, for I was most deeply convinced that the ever-loving Father preferred to see two uncorrupted souls in whom the lamp of heavenly knowledge was not lighted by prejudice but who themselves ascended to the Source of fire to light their lamps. Then I also put before you the law of Revelation, without hiding from you all that many men had said in denying it. For I wanted you to choose yourselves between the milk and the gall, and I rejoiced to see that you unhesitatingly lifted up the vessel of consolation.

"In giving you scientific information, I did not neglect to acquaint you with various nations by teaching you foreign languages. But my first concern was that you should learn your own language, that you should be able [*173] to express your thoughts orally and in writing, without strain and without bringing sweat to your brow. Above all, I tried to impart to you the English,[5] and then the Latin language. For the elasticity of the spirit of freedom, passing over into the representation of speech, trains the mind in firm conceptions, which are so necessary in all governments. But in leaving your reason free to guide your steps in the paths of learning, I was even more anxiously concerned for your morals. I tried to temper your momentary anger, and subjected to reason the lasting anger which leads to vengeance. Vengeance! — your soul abhors it. Of this natural impulse of sensient beings you have retained only the desire for self-preservation, and have put away the desire to return insults.[6]

[*174] "Now the time has arrived when your senses, having reached the peak of susceptibility but not yet the highest

understanding of its causes, are beginning to be disturbed by every external stimulus and to produce a dangerous agitation in your innermost being. You have now arrived at the time when, as they say, reason becomes the determiner of action or nonaction; or, to put it better, when the senses, hitherto untroubled during the happy reign of childhood, begin to feel a stirring; or when the vital humors, having filled the vessel of youth, begin to overflow its sides, seeking a path appropriate for their movement. Until now I have guarded you against harmful sensual shocks, but I did not hide from you under cover of ignorance the destructive consequences of departing from the path of moderation in sensual enjoyments. You saw for yourselves the shamefulness of unbridled sensual enjoyment, [*175] and you were disgusted; you were witnesses of the horrible tumult of the passions when they went beyond their natural bounds; you saw the terrible devastation caused by them, and you were horrified. My experience, hovering over you like a new aegis,[7] preserved you from untoward injury. Now you will be your own guides, and, although my counsels will always be a guiding light for your actions, since your hearts and souls are open to me, still, as light illuminates an object less the farther it recedes from it, so you, deprived of my presence, will feel the warmth of my friendship but faintly. Hence I will now lay before you the rules of individual and social life, so that, after mastering your passions, you may not be ashamed of the acts committed under their pressure, and may not learn what repentance is.

"The rules of individual life, insofar as they apply to you, are concerned with your physical and [*176] moral being. Never forget to make use of your bodily powers and sensations. Moderate exercise will strengthen without exhausting them, and will help give you health and a long life. To this end keep in practice the skills, arts, and crafts you have learned. Perfection in them may some day be invaluable. The future is unknown to us. If an unfriendly fate should rob you of everything it has given you, you can remain rich in the moderation of your desires, while supporting yourselves by the labor of your hands. But if you neglect everything in the day of prosperity, it will be too late to think about it in the day of adversity. Effeminacy, idleness, and incontinence ruin both body and spirit. For he who weakens his body by unrestrained indulgence also exhausts the strength of his spirit. But the rightful exercise of one's powers strengthens body and spirit alike. If your food palls on you and sickness knocks at your door, jump up [*177] from the couch on which you are pampering your senses, exercise your torpid muscles, and you will feel an immediate renewal of your strength; go without food needed in health, and hunger will sweeten your food which had palled on you from satiety. Always remember that a piece of bread and a dipper of water will suffice to satisfy hunger. If the beneficent loss of external consciousness, sleep, departs from your pillow, and you are unable to renew your mental and bodily powers, run from your chambers, and, having tired your limbs to the point of exhaustion, lie down upon your couch, and you will enjoy sweet sleep.

"Be cleanly in your clothing, and keep your body clean, for cleanliness is conducive to health, while dirtiness and stench often imperceptibly open the way to shameful vices. But even in this you must not be immoderate. Do not be above [*178] lending a helping hand to raise a carriage out of a ditch where it is stuck in the mud, or to lift up one who has fallen; you will soil your hands, feet, and body, but will cleanse your heart. Go into the huts of the humble, console him who is languishing in poverty, partake of his food, and it will do your heart good to have brought comfort to the sorrowful. I repeat, you have now reached that terrible time when the passions begin to stir, but reason is still too weak to bridle them. For on the balance of the will, the scale of reason without experience will rise, while the scale of the passions will at once go far down. Equipoise can be reached only by patient labor. Work with your body, and your passions will not be so easily stirred up; work with your heart by practicing meekness, gentleness, compassion, generosity, forgiveness, and your passions will be directed to a good end. Work with your mind [*179] in the practice of reading, meditation, and the quest for truth or facts, and reason will rule your will and passions. But do not imagine, in the elation of your mind, that one can crush the roots of the passions, that one ought to be entirely without passion. The root of the passions is good and is planted by nature itself in our sensuous organism. When our external and internal senses grow weak and dull, our passions, too, are weakened. They arouse a wholesome energy in man, without which he would fall into lazy sleep. A completely passionless man is a fool and a lifeless block, incapable of doing either good or evil. It is no merit to abstain from evil thoughts when one is unable to conceive them. An armless man cannot hurt anyone, but neither can he help a drowning man, nor can be hold back on the shore one who is about to cast himself into the raging sea. Hence moderation in [*180] passion is wise; the safest way to travel is in the middle of the road.[8] Excess in passion is destructive; absence of passion is moral death. As the traveler who deviates from the middle of the road is in danger of falling into one ditch or the other, so it is also in the path of morality. But if your passions are directed toward a good end by experience, reason, and affection, you may drop the reins of anxious prudence, and let them soar at will; their goal will always be greatness, and there only will they be able to rest.

"But though I urge you not to be passionless, your youth needs above all moderation in the passion of love. It has been implanted in our hearts by nature, for our good. Hence it can never err in its awakening, but only in its object and through excess. Therefore you must take care not to be mistaken [*181] in the object of your love, and not to mistake false seeming for true love. With a worthy object for your love, excess in this passion will be unknown to you. Speaking of love, it would be natural to speak of marriage, that sacred body of society, the rules of which are not etched in the heart by nature, but whose sacredness arises from the basic principles of society. This would be incomprehensible — and the account of it, therefore, useless — both to your reason, which is barely beginning its progress, and to your heart, which has not yet experienced the selfish passion of love in society. If you wish to have a concept of what marriage is, think of the one who gave you birth. Think of me with her and you, remember our conversations and mutual caresses, and lay this picture to your heart. Then you will feel a delightful [*182] perturbation. What is it? You will understand in time, but for the present be satisfied with perceiving it.

"Let us now briefly examine the rules of social life. They cannot be prescribed exactly, because they are often determined by the circumstances of the moment. But in order to make the minimum of mistakes, consult your heart in everything you do. Do what it asks of you. If you follow your heart in your youth, you will not err, if you have a good heart. But whosoever pretends to follow reason before he has any beard betokening experience is a fool.

"The rules of social life refer to the observance of national customs and habits, or to observance of the law, or to the practice of virtue. If social customs and habits are not contrary to law, if the law sets up no obstacle to the progress of virtue, [*183] then the observance of the rules of social life is easy. But where does such a society exist? Every society we know of is full of many contradictions in manners, customs, laws, and virtue. Thence arises the difficulty of doing one's duties as a man and as a citizen, since they are often diametrically opposed to one another.

"Inasmuch as virtue is the highest end of human action, its practice should not be impeded by anything. Disregard customs and usages, disregard civil and ecclesiastical law, however sacred they may be in human society, whenever their observance keeps you from virtue. Do not presume to defend its violation on the ground of the timidity of prudence. Without virtue you may prosper outwardly but you can never be happy.

"By complying with the usages and customs imposed upon us, we shall gain [*184] the approval of those among whom we live. By carrying out the injunctions of the law, one may gain the reputation of being an honest man. But in practicing virtue, we shall gain universal trust, respect, and admiration, even from those who do not wish to have such feelings for us in their souls. When the treacherous Senate of Athens handed the poison cup to Socrates, they trembled inwardly before his virtue.[9]

"Never presume to comply with a custom that is contrary to the law. The law, however bad it is, is the bond that holds society together. Even if the Sovereign himself should command you to violate a law, do not obey him, for he is in error, to the detriment of himself and of society. Let him abolish the law which he orders you to violate; then obey him, for in Russia the Sovereign is the source of the laws.

"But if the law, or the Sovereign, or any power on earth should tempt you to falsehood or to depart [*185] from virtue, remain immovably true to it. Fear not ridicule, nor torture, nor sickness, nor exile, nor even death itself. Remain immovable in your soul, like a rock amidst tumultuous but impotent waves. The fury of your tormentors will be broken against your firmness; and if they give you over to death, they will be laughed to scorn, while you will live unto eternity in the memory of noble souls. First and last, beware of misnaming as 'prudence' any weakness in action, for weakness is the foremost enemy of virtue.[10] Today you will depart from virtue for one consideration or another, and tomorrow this departure will seem to you to be virtue itself; and thus vice will enthrone itself in your heart and will distort the features of innocence in your soul and upon your countenance.

"Virtues are either individual or social. Individual virtue grows out of gentleness, kindness, and compassion, and its root its always good. The impetus toward social [*186] virtue frequently arises from vanity and ambition. But this should not keep you from practicing the social virtues. The cause they serve is what makes them important. One thinks of Curtius,[11] who saved his country from destructive pestilence, not as a vainglorious or despairing man tired of life, but as a hero. When our striving toward the social virtues has its origin in a humane firmness of soul, then their luster is so much the brighter. Always practice individual virtues, so that you may be more worthy to practice the social virtues.[12]

"I will give you yet a few more rules of life for your guidance. This above all: strive in all your actions to maintain your self-respect, so that when, in solitude, you look inward, you need not repent for what you have done, [*187] but may look upon yourselves with honor.

"In following this rule you must, as far as possible, avoid even the appearance of servility. Once you have entered the world, you will soon learn that in society it is the custom to call upon distinguished personages on holiday mornings: a miserable, senseless custom which betrays a spirit of timidity in the caller, a spirit of conceit and a weak intellect in the personage visited. The Romans had a similar custom, which they called *ambitio*, that is, 'seeking,' or 'going around'; and from this the seeking of honors came to be called *ambitio*, because, in calling on great personages, ambitious young men sought for themselves a road to honors and preferment. The same thing is being done nowadays. But I doubt if the purpose of this custom — which was introduced among the Romans in order that young people might learn something from contacts with experienced men — has been honorably [*188] maintained. In our days no one calls upon the mighty to seek instruction; all come only to curry favor. Therefore let not your feet cross the threshold that separates servility from the performance of duty. Never visit the antechamber of a magnate except in the line of duty. In the thick of the contemptible mob who fawn upon him, he will then, however indignantly, distinguish you in his heart from the rest.

"If death should happen to cut off my days before you have gained strength on the path of virtue, and the passions, in your youth, should entice you away from the path of reason, do not despair if, betimes, you recognize your errors. In your very mistakes, in your self-forgetfulness, you may come to love goodness. A life of dissipation, vaulting ambition, arrogance, and all the vices of youth, need not be without hope of improvement, because these vices only glide [*189] over the surface of the heart, without wounding it. I would rather have you dissolute, prodigal, and rude in your early years than avaricious, stingy, or vain, with more concern for your outward appearance than anything else. A so-called systematic tendency toward dandyism always indicates a narrow intellect. If they tell you that Julius Caesar was a dandy, his dandyism had a purpose. Its driving power in his youth was his passion for women. But he would have changed instantly from gay attire to ill-smelling rags if they would have helped him get what he wanted.

"In a young man temporary dandyism, and indeed almost any foolishness, is pardonable. But even if you disguise trickery, lying, disloyalty, avarice, pride, [*190] vengefulness, and bestiality under the semblance of the noblest acts of life, so that you blind your contemporaries with the bright light of your external glamour, and even if you do not find anyone who loves you enough to place before you the mirror of truth, do not imagine that you can dim the All-seeing Eye. It will pierce through the shining mantle of your deceit, and virtue will lay bare the blackness of your soul. Your heart will hate it, and it will shrink from your touch like a sensitive plant — but only for a moment, for its arrows will soon begin to wound and torment you from afar.

"Farewell, my beloved ones, farewell, friends of my soul! Today with a favorable wind you will launch your untried boat from the shore. Venture forth on the waves of human life so that you may learn how to govern yourselves. Happy your fortune if, without suffering shipwreck, you reach the haven for which we all long. May you be happy in your voyage. This is my heartfelt [*191] wish. My vital powers, exhausted by life and action, will decline and die; I shall leave you forever, but this is my last will and testament. If outrageous fortune hurl upon you all its slings and arrows, if there is no refuge left on earth for your virtue, if, driven to extremes, you find no sanctuary from oppression, then remember that you are a man, call to mind your greatness, and seize the crown of bliss which they are trying to take from you. Die. As a legacy I leave you the words of the dying Cato.[13] But if you have learned how to die in virtue, you should also learn how to die in vice, and to be, as it were, virtuous even in evil. If, forgetting my advice, you rush headlong into wickedness, your soul, accustomed to virtue, will be troubled, and I shall appear to you in your dreams. Arise then from your bed and in spirit follow my apparition. If, then, a tear falls from your [*192] eye, go back to sleep, and you will wake up the better for it. But if, amidst your evil doings, your soul does not stir at the thought of me, and your eye remains dry — that is steel, that is poison. Deliver me from that grief; deliver the earth from that disgraceful burden! Be my son still! Die for virtue's sake!"

As the old man said this, a youthful blush covered his wrinkled cheeks, his eyes shone with hopeful joy, his countenance glowed with supernatural splendor. He kissed his children and, accompanying them to the carriage, remained firm to the last farewell. But scarcely had the sound of the post bell informed him that they had started, when his spirit's strong control gave way. Tears welled from his eyes, his breast heaved, he stretched his arms after his departing sons, as though he would have stopped the horses' forward movement. The youths, already some distance off, [*193] saw their father's sorrow, and sobbed so loud that the wind carried their pitiful cries to our ears. They, too, stretched out their arms toward their father and seemed to be calling him. The old man was unable to bear this spectacle, his strength gave way, and he fell into my arms. Meanwhile a hill on the road had hidden the young men from our view. On coming to, the old man knelt down and raised his hands and eyes to heaven. "O Lord," he cried, "I implore Thee, strengthen them in the path of virtue, I implore Thee to grant them happiness. Thou knowest, Ever-loving Father, I have never troubled Thee with bootless prayer. I know in my soul that Thou art good and just. The quality Thou lovest most in us is virtue; the acts of a pure heart are the best offering to Thee.[14] This day I have parted from my sons. O Lord, Thy blessing be upon [*194] them!" He returned home troubled but firm in hope.

I could not forget the words of the Kresttsy nobleman. His reasoning as to the invalidity of the power of parents over children seemed to me incontrovertible. Although in a well-ordered society it is necessary that young people respect their elders, and inexperience respect wisdom, yet there seems to be no reason for making parental power unlimited. If the bond between father and son is not based on tender feelings of the heart, it is certainly weak, and will remain weak in spite of all legislation. If the father regards his son as his slave and seeks the foundation of his power in legal enactments, and if the son honors his father only for the sake of his inheritance, what good is this to society? It means either a new slave on top of all the others, or a snake in the bosom. . . . [*195] A father must provide for and teach his son, and is responsible for his delinquencies until he comes of age, while a son must feel his obligations in his heart. If he feels none, it is the father's fault, because he had implanted none. The son has a right to expect assistance from his father so long as he is helpless and under age; but when he comes of age, this natural bond is severed. A fledgling does not seek further aid from its parents after it has begun to find its own food. The father and mother birds forget their young as soon as they are grown. Such is the law of nature. Whenever the civil laws depart from it, they beget a monstrosity. A child loves his father, mother, or teacher until his love is turned to another object. Let not thy heart be offended, O father who lovest thy children; [*196] nature demands it. Let this thought be your one consolation, that your son's son likewise will love his father only until he comes fully of age. After that it will depend on you to turn his love toward you. If you succeed in this, you will be deemed fortunate and worthy of all honor. With such thoughts I arrived at the post station.

[*197] YAZHELBITSY

Fate chose this day for my trial. I am a father and have a tender heart for my children. For this reason the words of the Kresttsy nobleman had moved me deeply. But while they stirred me to the depths of my heart, they also filled me with a certain comforting feeling of hope that our joy in our children depends largely on ourselves. At Yazhelbitsy, however, I was destined to witness a spectacle which sank a deep root of sorrow into my soul, with no hope of ever plucking it out. Listen, O youth, to my story! Recognize your error, refrain from willful ruin, and make future repentance unnecessary.

I was driving past the cemetery. The unearthly sobs of a man who was tearing his hair caused me [*198] to stop. As I approached, I saw that a funeral was in progress. They were about to lower the coffin into the grave, but the man whom I had seen from afar tearing his hair threw himself on the coffin and clung to it so firmly that they could not lower it into the earth. With great difficulty they took him from the coffin, lowered it into the grave, and hastily covered it with earth. Then the mourner cried to those about him: "Why have you snatched him from me? Why did you not bury me alive with him and thereby end my grief and repentance? Know, know that I am the murderer of my beloved son, whose dead body you have returned to the earth. Do not be amazed. I did not cut short his life with the sword or with poison. No, I did worse than that. I prepared the way for his death before he was born, by giving him a poisoned life. I am a murderer, like many others, but a murderer more savage than any other. I murdered my son before [*199] his birth. I, I alone, shortened his days by infusing slow poison into him at his conception. It prevented the development of his bodily powers. During his whole life he enjoyed not a single day of health, and the spread of the wasting poison cut off the flow of his life. No one, no one will punish me for my wickedness!" Despair was painted on his face, and they carried him away almost lifeless.

 A sudden chill coursed through my veins. I felt numb. It seemed to me that I heard my own sentence pronounced.[1] I thought of the days of my dissolute youth. I recalled all the times when my soul, stirred by my senses, chased after their gratification, falsely considering the hired partner of amorous satisfaction an object of true love. I recalled that incontinence in passion had brought upon my body a loathsome disease. Oh, if only it had not sent down its root more deeply! [*200] Oh, if only it had been cut off with the waning of passion! Having received this poison in enjoyment, we not only nourish it within us, but bequeath it to our descendants. O my beloved friends, O children of my soul! You do not know how I have sinned before you. Your pallid brow is my condemnation. I dread telling you about the disease of which you are sometimes aware. You will perhaps hate me, and your hatred will be justified. Who can assure you and me that you do not harbor in your blood the hidden sting destined to bring your days to an untimely end? ² Since I received that loathsome poison into my body when I was fully grown, the firmness of my members enabled me to resist its spread and struggle against its deadly effects. But you received it before your birth and have borne it within you as an integral part of your being; how, therefore, can you resist [*201] its fiery ravages? All your sicknesses are the consequence of this poisoning. O my beloved ones, weep for the error of my youth, appeal to medical art for aid, and, if possible, do not hate me!

But now the whole enormity of this amorous crime is revealed to me. I have sinned against myself by condemning myself, while still young, to premature old age and decrepitude. I have sinned before you, poisoning your vital humours before your birth and thereby preparing for you poor health, and, perhaps, untimely death. I have sinned (and may this be my punishment!), I have sinned in my love, by marrying your mother. Who can guarantee to me that I was not the cause of her death? The death-dealing poison, diffused in enjoyment, settled in her pure body and poisoned all her chaste being. It was the more deadly [*202] for being unsuspected. False shame kept me from informing her of it, while she took no precautions against her poisoner, in her love for him. The fever which carried her off may have been the fruit of the poison I implanted in her. — O my beloved ones, how you must hate me!

But who is to blame for the fact that this loathsome disease causes such great devastation in all countries, not only mowing down many of the present generation, but also shortening the days of those to come? Who is to blame, if not the government? In licensing prostitution it not only opens the way to many vices but also poisons the lives of its citizens. Public women have their defenders and in some countries are under the protection of the government. Some say that if the venal satisfaction of amorous [*203] passion were prohibited, violent upheavals would often be felt in society. Rape, violence, and murder would frequently take place as a result of unsatisfied lust. They might shake society to its very foundations. And so you prefer quiet and with it languishing disease and grief to agitation and with it health and manliness. Be silent, wicked teachers; you are the hirelings of tyranny; it always preaches peace and quiet — and casts into fetters those who have been lulled to sleep by flattery. It even fears agitation in others. Tyranny desires universal conformity in thought so that it may safely enjoy its power and wallow in voluptuousness — .[3] I am not surprised at your teachings. It is characteristic of slaves to want to see everyone in fetters. An equal fate for all alleviates their lot, while the superiority of others burdens their mind and spirit.

[*204] VALDAI

This new little town was settled, they say, in the reign of Tsar Aleksey Mikhaylovich, by Polish prisoners of war.[1] This town is famous for the amorous inclinations of its inhabitants, especially of its unmarried women.

Who has not been to Valdai, who does not know the Valdai doughnuts and painted wenches? The bold and shameless Valdai girls stop every traveler and try to kindle his passion in order to exploit his generosity at the cost of their chastity. In comparing the morals of the inhabitants of this village, which has been raised to the dignity of a city, with the morals of other Russian cities, one might think that it was the oldest of them all and that its lewdness was the only [*205] vestige of its antiquity. But since it has been settled for little more than a hundred years, one may judge how dissolute its first inhabitants must have been.

The baths have always been and still are the place for amorous celebrations. After arranging terms for his stay with an obliging old woman or young fellow, the traveler stops at the house whither he intends to bring his offering to the universally worshiped Lada.² Night falls. The bath is already prepared for him. The traveler disrobes and goes to the bath, where he is met by the hostess, if she is young, or by her daughter, or relative, or neighbor. They rub down his weary limbs and wash the dirt from his body. They do this after removing their own clothes to enkindle his desire, and he spends the night there, losing his money, his health, and his valuable traveling time. It has happened, they say, that a careless traveler, drowsy with amorous [*206] exploits and wine, has been murdered by these lustful monsters to enable them to possess themselves of his property. I do not know whether this is true, but I do know that the boldness of the Valdai girls has been checked. And although they do not even now refuse to satisfy the traveler's wishes, they no longer display their former brazenness.

Lake Valdai, on which this town is situated, will remain famous in story because of the monk who sacrificed his life for his sweetheart. About a verst and a half from the town, in the middle of the lake, on an island, stands the Iberian Monastery, founded by Nikon the famous Patriarch.³ One of the monks of this monastery, having visited Valdai, fell in love with the daughter of one of its citizens. Their love soon became mutual, and both soon strove to consummate their desire. Having once indulged in the delights of love, [*207] they were unable to resist their mutual desire. But their circumstances interposed a barrier to it. The lover could not often leave his monastery, nor could his paramour visit her gallant's cell. But love conquered all; it turned the lovesick monk into a fearless man and gave him almost supernatural strength. Daily, in order to enjoy the embrace of his sweetheart, this new Leander would softly leave his cell the moment night covered everything with its black mantle, and, taking off his cassock, he would swim across the lake to the opposite shore, where he was received into the arms of his sweetheart. The bath and the delights of love with it were waiting for him, and in them he forgot the danger and difficulty of the swim and the fear that his absence would be discovered. A few hours before dawn he would return [*208] to his cell. Thus he passed a long time in these dangerous swimming expeditions and dispelled with nighttime joys the tedium of his daytime imprisonment. But fate set a period to his amorous exploits. One night, as this dauntless lover was crossing the waves to visit his beloved, a contrary wind suddenly sprang up as he was in the middle of his course. His whole strength was insufficient to cope with the angry waves. In vain did he strain his muscles to the point of exhaustion; in vain did he raise his voice, hoping to make himself heard in his dangerous plight. When he saw that he would not be able to reach the shore, he decided to return to his monastery, which he hoped to reach more easily, since the wind would now be favorable. But he had barely turned back when the waves overcame his wearied muscles and pulled him down into a whirlpool. In the morning his body was found at a remote spot of the shore. If I were writing [*209] a poem on this subject, I would describe his sweetheart's despair for the delectation of my reader. But that would be superfluous here. Everyone knows that, at least in the first moment, a woman is grieved to hear of her lover's death. Besides, I do not know whether this new Hero threw herself into the lake, or whether she heated the bath for a traveler again the next night. The chronicle of love declares that the Valdai beauties do not die for love, save, perhaps, in the hospital.[4]

The customs of Valdai have also spread to the adjoining post station, Zimnogor'e. There the traveler gets the same reception as at Valdai. The first thing one sees are painted girls with doughnuts. But since my youthful days are over, I parted speedily from the painted sirens of Valdai and Zimnogor'e.

[*210] EDROVO [1]

When I reached this settlement, I got out of my carriage. Nor far from the highway, near the water, stood a crowd of women and girls. By force of habit, my lifelong master, passion, though now spent, drew my steps to the bevy of village beauties. The crowd consisted of more than thirty women. They were all in holiday attire, with their necks open, their legs bare, their arms akimbo, their dresses tucked up in front under their belts, their long shirts white, their faces happy, their cheeks glowing with health. Natural charm, although roughened by heat and cold, is delightful without any false front of sophistication. The beauty of youth was visible here in full splendor, on their lips smiles or hearty laughter, and behind them rows of teeth whiter than purest ivory. Teeth which would drive our [*211] fashionable ladies frantic. Come hither, my dear Moscow and Petersburg ladies, look at their teeth and learn from them how they keep them white. They have no dentists.[2] They do not scour away the gleam of their teeth every day with toothbrushes and powder. Stand mouth to mouth with any one of them you choose: not one of them will infect your lungs with her breath. While yours, yes, yours may infect them with the germ . . . of a disease . . . I am afraid to say what disease, because, though you may not blush, you will be infuriated. Am I not telling the truth? The husband of one of you runs after all the sluts, and, having caught a disease, goes right on drinking, eating, and sleeping with you; another one of you is pleased to have her own yearly, monthly, weekly, or, God forbid! daily lovers. Having made his acquaintance today and satisfied her desire, she does not know him tomorrow, nor [*212] does she know that she may already have been infected by his mere kiss. And you, my sweet maid of fifteen summers, you, perchance, are still pure; but I see on your brow that all your blood is poisoned. Your father of blessed memory never left the doctor's hands; and milady, your mother, guiding you upon her own estimable path, has already found a bridegroom for you, a deserving old general, and is in a hurry to get you married off, solely to avoid having to make a visit to an orphanage with you. And it's not bad to be the wife of an old man, for you do just as you please; and so long as you are married, the children are all his. He will be jealous? So much the better, for there will be a greater delight in stolen pleasures, and you can teach him from the first night not to follow the silly old custom of sleeping in the same room with his wife.

My dear city gossips, aunts, [*213] sisters, nieces, etc., I had not noticed how long you had detained me. Truly, you are not worth it. On your cheeks there is rouge, on your heart rouge, on your conscience rouge, on your sincerity — soot. Rouge or soot, it's all the same. I shall gallop away from you at full speed to my rustic beauties. True, there are some of them who resemble you, but there are others the likes of whom have not been heard or seen in the cities. See how all my beauties' limbs are round, well-developed, straight, and not contorted. You think it funny that their feet are over eight or even ten inches long. But, my dear niece with your five-inch feet, stand in a row with them and run a race: who will be the first to reach the tall birch tree that stands at the end of the field? Ah — but — you are not up to it! And you, my dear little sister, you, with your three-span[3] waist, you are pleased to make [*214] fun of my village nymph, because her abdomen has been allowed to grow naturally. Wait, my dear, I'll have my laugh at you. You have been married these ten months, and your three-span waist is all askew. When it comes to childbirth, you will pipe a different tune. God grant that nothing worse than laughter may ensue. My dear brother-in-law walks about downcast. He has already thrown all your lacings into the fire. He has pulled the stays out of all your dresses, but it is too late. Your distorted joints can't be straightened out now. Weep, my beloved brother-in-law, weep. Our mother, following the lamentable fashion which often leads to death in childbirth, has for many years been preparing sorrow for you, sickness for her daughter, and feeble bodies for your children. Even now this illness hovers like a deadly weapon over her head, and if it does not cut short your wife's days, thank your lucky stars, [*215] and, if you believe that God's Providence was concerned about the matter, thank Him, too, if you wish. But here I am still with the city ladies. That's what custom does: one doesn't feel like leaving them. Indeed I would not leave you if I could persuade you not to paint your faces and your sincerity. And now, good-bye!

While I was watching the village nymphs washing their clothes, my carriage drove off. I was about to start after it, when a girl who looked to be about twenty, but was really only seventeen, put her wet clothes on a yoke and started off the same way I was going. When I caught up with her, I spoke to her.

"Isn't it hard for you to carry such a heavy load, my dear — ? I don't know your name."

"My name is Anna, and my load isn't heavy. And even if it were, I would not ask you, sir, [*216] to help me."

"Why so stern, Annushka dear? I mean you no harm."

"All right, all right! We've seen gallants like you before. Please go your way!"

"Truly, Anyutushka, I'm not the man you take me for and not the sort you're talking about. I understand that they start by kissing a girl, not by talking with her; but if I were to kiss you, it would be just as though I were kissing my own sister."

"Don't sidle up to me, if you please. I've heard such talk before. If you really mean no harm, what is it you want of me?"

"Dear Annushka, I wanted to know whether your father

and mother are still alive, what your circumstances are, whether you're rich or poor, whether you're happy, whether you have a fiancé?"

"What's that to you, sir? This is the first time in my life I've heard such talk."

"From which you may judge, Anyuta, that I'm not a scoundrel and do not mean to insult or dishonor you. [*217] I love women because they embody my ideal of tenderness; but most of all I love village or peasant women, because they are innocent of hypocrisy, do not put on the mask of pretended love, and when they do love, love sincerely and with their whole hearts."

While I was saying this, the girl looked at me with eyes wide open with amazement. How, indeed, could it have been otherwise, for who does not know the impudence, the crude, unchaste, and offensive jests, with which the audacious gentry assail the village maidens? In the eyes of old and young nobles alike, they are simply creatures for their lordly pleasure. And they treat them accordingly, especially those unfortunate ones subject to their commands. During the recent Pugachev Rebellion, when all the serfs rose up in arms against their masters, some peasants (this story is not an invention) had tied up their master and started to carry [*218] him off to certain death. What was the reason for this? In everything else he was a good and charitable master, but neither the wives nor the daughters of his peasants were safe from him. Every night his emissaries brought him his chosen victim for that day's sacrifice to dishonor. It was known in the village that he had dishonored sixty maidens, robbing them of their purity. A detachment of soldiers that happened to pass by rescued this barbarian from the hands of those who were raging against him. Stupid peasants, you looked for justice from an impostor![4] But why did you not report your grievance to your rightful judges? They would have condemned the offender to civil death, and you would have remained innocent. But now this evildoer is saved. Happy he if the sight of imminent death has changed his way of thinking and given a new direction to his vital humours. But, we said, the peasant is dead to the law? No, no, he lives, he will live, if he wishes to! [5]

[*219] "If you are not jesting, sir," Anyuta said to me, "I will tell you. I have no father; he died two years ago. I have a mother and a little sister. Father left us five horses and three cows. And there are plenty of small animals and fowl, but there is no man in the house to do the farm work. They were going to marry me off into a rich house, to a ten-year-old lad, but I didn't want that.[6] What could I do with such a child? I could not love him. And by the time he was grown up, I would have been an old woman, and he would have been running after others. They say that his father sleeps with his young daughters-in-law until his sons grow up. That's why I didn't want to marry into his family. I want someone my own age. I shall love my husband, and he will love me; I've no doubt of that. I don't want to gallivant with the boys, but I do want to get married, sir. And do you know why?" Anyuta said, [*220] letting her eyes droop.

"Tell me, dear Anyutushka, don't be bashful; every word from the lips of innocence is pure."

"Well, then, I'll tell you. A year ago last summer our neighbor's son married my friend with whom I always used to go to quilting parties. Her husband loves her, and she loves him so much that in the tenth month after their wedding she bore him a little son. Every evening she takes him out by the gate to give him an airing. She can't get to see her fill of him. And it looks as though the little fellow already loves his mother. Whenever she says to him 'Agoo, agoo,' he laughs. Tears come to my eyes every day I see him; I should love to have a child like that myself."

At this point I could no longer refrain from embracing Anyuta, and kissed her with all my heart.

"See what a deceiver you are, sir! You are already playing with me," said Anyuta, bursting into tears. "Go away and leave a poor orphan alone. If [*221] my father were alive and saw this, he would give you a good beating in spite of your being a nobleman."

"Don't be offended, dear Anyutushka, don't be offended! My kiss does not sully your virtue, which is sacred in my eyes. My kiss is a token of my respect for you, and it was the joyous response of my deeply moved soul. Do not be afraid of me, dear Anyuta, for I am not a rapacious animal like our young noblemen who think nothing of robbing a maiden of her purity. If I had known that my kiss would offend you, I swear in God's name that I would not have dared to kiss you."

"You can see yourself, sir, that I could not help being offended by your kiss, since all mine are meant for another. I have promised them in advance, and I am not free to dispose of them."

"How charming! You have already learned how to love. You have found another heart for your own, a fitting mate. You will be happy. Nothing will [*222] sever your union. You will not be surrounded by busybodies who will be watching for a chance to lure you into the nets of destruction. Your true lover's ear will not be open to the voice of temptation, inciting him to violate his troth to you. But why, my dear Anyuta, are you deprived of the pleasure of enjoying happiness in your dear friend's arms?"

"O sir, because they won't let him off to come to us. They demand a hundred rubles. And my mother won't let me go, because I'm her only helper."

"But does he love you?"

"Indeed he does. Every evening he comes to our house and together we watch my friend's baby. He'd love to have a little fellow just like that one. It will be hard for me, but I shall have to stand it. My Vanyukha wants to go to Petersburg to work on the boats, and he will not come back until he has earned a hundred rubles to buy his release."

"Do not let him go, dear Anyutushka, [*223] do not let him go! He will be going to his ruin. There he will learn to drink, to waste his money, to eat dainties, despise farm work, and worst of all, he will stop loving you."

"O sir, don't frighten me," said Anyuta, almost in tears.

"And it would be even worse, Anyuta, if he should take service in a nobleman's house. The example of the masters infects the higher servants, these infect the lower, and from them the pestilence of debauchery spreads to the villages. The bad example is the real plague, for everybody does what he sees others do."

"Then what will become of me? I'll never be able to marry him. It's time for him to get married; he's not one to go running about with other girls. They won't let me go into his household; they'll marry him to someone else, and I, poor girl, shall die of grief." Saying this, she shed bitter tears.

"No, my dear Anyutushka, you shall marry him tomorrow. Take me to your mother."

[*224] "Here is our house," she said, as she stopped. "Please go away, for if Mother sees me with you, she'll think ill of me. Though she doesn't strike me, her mere words hurt me more than blows."

"No, Anyuta, I'll go with you." And, without waiting for her answer, I walked right through the gate, up the stairs, and into the hut. Anyuta cried after me, "Wait, sir, wait!" But I paid no attention to her. In the hut I found Anyuta's mother, who was kneading dough; near her, on a bench, sat her future son-in-law. I told her, without beating about the bush, that I wanted her daughter to marry Ivan, and that I had brought the means to remove the obstacle thereto.

"Thank you, sir," said the old woman, "but there is no longer any need for it. Vanyukha has just come to tell us that his father has agreed to let him off, to come to us. So we'll have the wedding on Sunday."

"Then let my promised gift [*225] be Anyuta's dowry."

"Thank you, no. Gentlemen do not give girls a dowry for nothing. If you have wronged my Anyuta and are giving her a dowry to make up for it, God will punish you for your misdeed, but I will not take the money. If you are a good man and do not hurt the poor, then malicious people would think the worst of me for taking money from you."

I could not sufficiently admire the noble dignity which I had found in these simple country people. Meanwhile Anyuta had come into the hut, and sang my praises to her mother. I tried again to give them the money, offering it to Ivan toward setting up his house, but he said to me: "I have two hands, sir, and with them I will set up my house." Seeing that my presence was not very pleasant for them, I left them and returned to my carriage.

As I drove on from Edrovo, I could not put Anyuta out of my mind. [*226] Her innocent sincerity pleased me beyond measure. Her mother's noble act enchanted me. I compared this noble mother, with her sleeves rolled up over the dough or over her milking pail near the cow, with urban mothers. The peasant woman refused to accept my honest, well-intended hundred rubles, which, in proportion to her means and status, would correspond to five, ten, fifteen thousand, or more, for the wife of a colonel, privy councilor, major, or general. Now if a distinguished magnate of the seventieth or — God forbid! — the seventy-second proof were to offer the wife of a colonel, major, privy councilor, or general, who has a pretty or merely virtuous daughter, five, ten, or fifteen thousand (which would be quite in proportion to my offer to the wife of the Edrovo coachman), or if he hinted that he would give her daughter a handsome dowry, or find her an official for her husband, or [*227] secure her an appointment as a lady-in-waiting — I ask you, city mothers, would not your heart give a leap? Would you not want to see your daughter in a gilt carriage, wearing diamonds, riding in a four-in-hand if she now goes on foot, or in a tandem of eight in place of the two sorry nags that draw her now? I grant that in order to preserve custom and decorum you would not give in as easily as chorus girls do. No, dear mothers, I give you one or two months' time, but no more. For if you leave the man of high estate sighing in vain, he, being very busy with affairs of state, will leave you so as not to waste on you the precious time which he can better employ for the public good. A thousand voices rise up against me and shower me with terms of abuse: swindler, cheat, canaille, beast, and so forth. [*228] My dear ones, calm yourselves, I am not casting aspersions on you. Are you really all like that? Look into this mirror: whosoever recognizes herself in it, let her scold me unmercifully.[7] I will not enter a complaint against her either, nor dispute her word through a lawsuit.

Anyuta, Anyuta, you have turned my head! Why did I not make your acquaintance fifteen years ago? Your frank innocence, which is proof against the audacity of passion, would have taught me to walk in the way of chastity. Why was not the first kiss of my life the one I pressed upon your cheek in my soul's ecstasy? The influence of your living virtue would have penetrated to the depths of my heart, and I would have escaped the shameful acts which have filled my life. I would have kept away from the loathsome hirelings of lust, would have honored the nuptial couch, would not have violated the domestic bond in my carnal insatiability; [*229] virginity would have been for me a holy of holies, and I would not have dared to lay violent hands on it. O my Anyutushka! Be ever near us and teach us by your unconstrained innocence. I know that you will lead back into the way of virtue him who has begun to turn aside, and strengthen him who is tending to go astray. Let not your heart be troubled if a man steeped in debauch and grown gray in shamelessness should pass by and scorn you; do not attempt to bar his way with the solace of your converse. His heart is already stone; his soul is encrusted with a layer of adamant. The beneficent sting of innocent virtue cannot make any real impression on him. Its point will glide over the smooth surface of vice. Beware lest your sharp weapon be blunted against it. But do not let the youth pass by who is allured by the dangerous charms of beauty; catch him in your net. He seems haughty, [*230] supercilious, impetuous, insolent, presumptuous, spiteful, and insulting. But his heart will yield to your influence and will respond to your wholesome example. Anyuta, I cannot part from you, although I can already see the fourteenth milestone dividing us.

But what of the custom Anyuta told me about? They wanted to marry her off to a ten-year-old boy. Who could sanction such a union? Why does not the hand that guards the law arm itself for the eradication of this evil custom?[8] In Christian law marriage is a sacrament, in civil law, an agreement or contract. What priest can bless an unequal marriage, and what judge can enter it upon his register? Where there is great disparity in ages, there can be no true marriage. It is forbidden by the law of nature, as a thing harmful [*231] to man, and it ought to be forbidden by the civil law, as injurious to society. Man and wife in society are two citizens who enter into an agreement, confirmed by law, whereby primarily they promise mutual satisfaction of their passion (let no one dare to deny this first law of cohabitation and the foundation of the marital bond, the source of the purest love, and the firmest foundation stone of conjugal concord), they promise to live together, to have and to hold their worldly goods in common, to bring up together the fruit of their passion, to live in peace, and to avoid offending one another. Can the terms of this agreement be satisfied if the ages are unequal? If the husband is ten years old, and the wife is twenty-five, as often happens among the peasantry, or if the husband is fifty and the wife fifteen or twenty, as is the case among the gentry, can there be any mutual satisfaction of desire? [*232] Tell me, you aged husbands, but tell me honestly, do you deserve the name of husband? You can kindle the fire of passion; you cannot put it out. By the inequality of years one of the first laws of nature is violated, and how can man-made law be firm, if it is not based on the law of nature? Let us answer unequivocally: it cannot. To bring up the fruits of their mutual passion. But can there be any mutuality where on one side there is a flame, and on the other, insensibility? Can there be any fruit, if the planted tree is deprived of beneficent rain and quickening dew? And if there ever is any fruit, it will be shriveled, unsightly, and liable to early decay. Do not offend one another. It is an eternally true principle that if passion is mutually satisfied through a blissful sympathy between husband and wife, [*233] the marital union is happy, and small domestic troubles subside with the approach of joy. And when the chill of old age draws an impenetrable, icy film over sensual enjoyment, the memory of former warmth will comfort dreary old age. One condition of the marriage contract can be fulfilled in inequality. That of living together. But will there be any mutuality in that? One will be an autocratic ruler who has absolute power in his hands, the other will be a feeble subject and a complete slave, capable only of carrying out the master's commands. These, Anyuta, are the virtuous thoughts with which you have inspired me. Good-bye, my dear Anyutushka! Your precepts will be deeply engraved in my heart forever, and my children's children shall inherit them.

The Khotilov post station was already in sight, but I was still thinking of the Edrovo lass, and, in the elation of my soul, [*234] I cried aloud: "O Anyuta! Anyuta!" The road was rough and the horses were going at a walk. The driver heard my exclamation and turned around. "It looks as though you've taken a liking to our Anyutka, sir," he said, smiling and adjusting his hat. "Yes, she's quite a girl. You're not the only one she's bewitched. She carries off the honors at everything. In our village there are a lot of beautiful girls, but they're not worth looking at beside her. How she can dance! She'll dance rings around any of them. And when she goes to reap in the field, you can't feast your eyes enough watching her. Well, brother Van'ka is a lucky dog!"

"Is Ivan your brother?"

"My cousin.[9] And a fine fellow he is! Three lads were courting Anyutka at the same time, but Ivan cut them all out. They tried one thing after another, but it was no good. Vanyukha hooked her right off." (Just then we entered the village.) "Yes, sir! Everybody dances, but not like a minstrel." And he drove up to the post station.

[*235] "Everybody dances, but not like a minstrel," I repeated, as I got out of the carriage. "Everybody dances, but not like a minstrel," I repeated again as I bent down, picked up, and unfolded —

[*236] KHOTILOV

A Project for the Future. We have brought our beloved country step by step to the flourishing condition in which it now stands; we see science, art, and industry carried to the highest degree of perfection which man can achieve; we see that in our realm human reason, spreading wide its wings, freely and unerringly soars everywhere to greatness, and has now become the sure guardian of public law. Our heart, too, under reason's sovereign protection, is free to ascend in prayer to the almighty Creator. With inexpressible joy we can say that our country is an abode pleasing to the Deity, because its order is not based on prejudice and superstition, [*237] but on our inward perception of the mercy of our common Father. Unknown to us are the hostilities which have so often separated people on account of their religious beliefs; unknown to us, also, is compulsion in them. Born in this freedom, we truly regard each other as brothers, belonging to the same family, and having one Father, God.

The torch of learning, enlightening our legislation, now distinguishes it from the legislation of many countries. The balanced separation of powers, the equality of property, destroy the root even of civil discord. Moderation in punishment causes the laws of the supreme power to be respected like the commands of tender parents to their children, and prevents even guileless misdeeds. Clarity in the ordinances concerning the acquisition and protection of property prevents the outbreak of family disputes. The boundary furrow that separates the possessions of one citizen [*238] from another is deep and plain to all and sacredly respected by all. Private offenses are rare among us, and are settled amicably. Popular education has taken pains to make us gentle, peace-loving citizens, but above all, to make us men.

Enjoying domestic tranquillity, having no external enemies, having brought society to the highest bliss of civic concord, shall we be so devoid of humane feeling, devoid of pity, devoid of the tenderness of noble hearts, devoid of brotherly love, that we endure under our eyes an eternal reproach to us, a disgrace to our remotest descendants — a whole third of our comrades, our equal fellow citizens, our beloved brothers in nature, in the heavy fetters of servitude and slavery? The bestial custom of enslaving one's fellow men, which originated in [*239] the hot regions of Asia, a custom worthy of savages, a custom that signifies a heart of stone and a total lack of soul, has quickly spread far and wide over the face of the earth. And we Slavs, sons of *slava* [i.e., "glory"], glorious [1] among earth-born generations, both in name and deed, benighted by the darkness of ignorance, have adopted this custom, and, to our shame, to the shame of past centuries, to the shame of this age of reason, we have kept it inviolate even to this day.

It is well known to you from the deeds of your fathers,

it is well known to all from our chronicles, that the wise rulers of our people, inspired by a sincere love of all men, and having come to understand the natural bond of civil society, tried to put an end to this hundred-headed evil. But their sovereign acts were nullified by that estate, then proud of its pre-eminent position in our realm [*240] but now superannuated and fallen into contempt, the hereditary nobility. Our royal ancestors were impotent, despite their scepter's might, to break the fetters of civil slavery. Not only were they unable to carry out their good intentions, but, by the machinations of the aforementioned highest estate of the realm, they were driven to enact laws contrary to their own judgment and inclinations. Our fathers, perhaps with heartfelt tears, beheld these oppressors tightening the fetters and making heavier the chains of the most useful members of society. The agriculturists are even to this day slaves among us; we do not recognize them as fellow citizens equal to ourselves, and we have forgotten that they are men. O beloved fellow citizens! O true sons of the fatherland! Look about you and see the error of your ways! The ministers of the everlasting God, moved by the same desire as ours for the good of society and the happiness of man, [*241] have, in their teachings in the name of the ever merciful God Whom they profess, explained to you how contrary to His wisdom and love it is to rule arbitrarily over your neighbor. They have sought with arguments drawn from nature and from our hearts to demonstrate to you your cruelty, injustice, and sinfulness. Their voice still calls out loud and solemnly in the temples of the living God: "Bethink yourselves, ye who have gone astray; be merciful, ye who are cruel of heart! Break the fetters of your brothers, open the prison of slavery, and give your fellow men a chance to taste the sweets of community life, for which they, like yourselves, have been destined by the All-Merciful. They enjoy the beneficent rays of the sun just as you do, they have the same limbs and the same senses as you, and they ought to have the same right to use them."

If the servants of the Godhead have made manifest to you [*242] the individual human iniquity of slavery, we consider it our duty to demonstrate to you what harm it does to society, and its injustice to the citizen. It would seem to be superfluous, since the spirit of philosophy has been abroad so long, to search out and repeat arguments in favor of the essential equality of man, and hence of citizens. To him who has grown up under the protection of liberty, who is filled with generous sentiments and not with prejudices, the normal emotions of his heart are proofs of this fundamental equality. But it is the misfortune of mortals on earth to go astray in the full light of day, to fail to see that which is right before their eyes.

When you were young, they taught you at school the foundations of natural and civil law. Natural law showed you men hypothetically outside of society, who had received from nature the same constitution, [*243] hence possessed the same rights, and consequently were equal in every way, no man being subject to any other. Civil law showed you men who had exchanged unlimited freedom for the right to enjoy freedom in peace. But though all have accepted restrictions upon their freedom and submitted their acts to regulation, yet all, because in a state of nature they would have been equal from birth, must still be equal in the limitations set to their natural freedom. And consequently no one is subject to any one else. The sovereign power in society is the law, because it is one and the same for all. But what was the impelling force that caused men to establish a social order and voluntarily restrict their freedom of action? Reason will say, "Their own good"; the heart will say, "Their own good"; the incorruptible civil law will say, "Their own good." We live in a society which has already passed through many stages of progress; therefore [*244] we have forgotten its original condition. But consider all new nations, and, if we may so put it, all societies in a state of nature. First, they regard enslavement as a crime; second, they subject only criminals or the enemy to the yoke of slavery. If we keep these concepts in mind, we will realize how far we have strayed from the aim of society, how far removed we still are from the ideal of social happiness. All that we have said is familiar to you; you have imbibed it with your mother's milk. Only the prejudice of the moment, only selfish greed (let not my words offend you!), only greed blinds us and makes us seem like madmen raving in darkness.

But who among us wears the fetters, who feels the burden of slavery? The agriculturist! The man who feeds us in our leanness and satisfies our hunger, who gives us health and prolongs our life, [*245] without having the right to dispose of what he cultivates nor of what he produces. But who has a greater right to a field than the man who cultivates it? Let us imagine that men have come into a wilderness to establish a community. Mindful of their need of sustenance, they divide up the uncultivated land. Who deserves a share in this division? Is it not he who knows how to plough the land, he who has the strength and determination requisite for the task? The land will be useless to a child, an old man, a weak, sick, or lazy man. It will remain a wilderness, and the wind will not rustle any grain growing upon it. If it is useless to the owner, it is equally useless to society, for the owner cannot render the surplus to society when he does not even have what he needs for himself. Hence, in primitive society, he who was able to cultivate his field had a proprietary right to it, and, by virtue of cultivating it, [*246] had the exclusive enjoyment of it. But how very far we have departed from the primitive social relation to property! With us, he who has the natural right to it is not only completely excluded from it, but, while working another's field, sees his sustenance dependent on another's power! To your enlightened minds these truths cannot be incomprehensible, but your acts, in the application of these truths, are impeded, as we have already said, by prejudice and self-interest. Even so, can your hearts, which are full of love for humanity, prefer self-interest to the sentiments that soothe the heart? But wherein does your profit consist? Can a country in which two thirds [2] of the citizens are deprived of their civil rights and to some extent are dead to the law to be called happy? Can the civic condition of the peasant in Russia be called happy? Only an insatiable bloodsucker will say that the peasant [*247] is happy, for he has no conception of a better state of affairs.

We shall now try to refute these brutal rules of the mighty, as our predecessors once unsuccessfully sought to do by their acts.

Civic happiness may present itself to us in various forms. A country is happy, they say, if peace and order reign in it.[3] It seems to be happy when the fields do not lie fallow and when proud buildings rise in the cities. It is said to be happy when it extends the sway of its arms and rules far and wide abroad, not only by force, but by its influence over the opinions of others. But all these manifestations of happiness may be called external, ephemeral, fleeting, partial, and imaginary.

Let us look at the valley which spreads out before our view. What do we see? [*248] A great military camp. Silence reigns everywhere in it. All the warriors stand in their places. The most precise order may be seen in their ranks. One order, one motion of the commander's hand, sets the whole camp in motion, and moves it in perfect order. But can we say the soldiers are happy? Having been turned into puppets by the strictness of military discipline, they are deprived even of the freedom of motion, the distinguishing characteristic of animate beings. They know only the commander's orders, think only what he wants them to think, and move where he orders them to. So all-powerful is the commander's control over the mightiest force in the country. United they can do anything, while disunited and as individuals they graze, like cattle, wherever the shepherd pleases. Organization at the expense of freedom is as inimical to our happiness as are fetters themselves. One hundred slaves, fettered to the benches of the ship [*249] which is propelled by their oars, live in peace and order; but look into their hearts and souls. There is torment, grief, despair. Often would they exchange life for death, but even that is denied them. To end their suffering would be happiness, but happiness and slavery do not belong together; hence they must live. Let us not, therefore, be blinded by the outward peace and order of a country; let us not consider it happy merely for these superficial reasons. Always look into the hearts of your fellow citizens. If you find calm and peace in them, then you may say in very truth that they are happy.

Having despoiled America, having fertilized its fields with the blood of its natives, the Europeans put a stop to their murders for the sake of new profit. The deserted fields of that hemisphere, newly created by the mighty convulsions of nature, felt the plough that racked its vitals. The grass that had grown on rich [*250] meadows and withered away unused felt its blades mowed down by sharp scythes. Down from the hills fell the proud trees that had shaded their summits from time immemorial. Barren forests and useless thickets were transformed into fruitful fields, covered with hundreds of plants native to America or successfully domesticated there. The rich meadows were trampled by innumerable cattle, destined for man's food and labor. Everywhere may be seen the cultivator's constructive hand, everywhere the appearance of well-being and external signs of order. But whose mighty arm is it that urges grudging, lazy nature to give her fruits in such abundance? Having massacred the Indians at a swoop, the raging Europeans, the preachers of peace in the name of the God of truth, the teachers of meekness and charity, by acquiring slaves through purchase have grafted the cold-blooded [*251] murder of slavery upon the root of the furious murder of conquest. These unfortunate victims from the torrid banks of the Niger and Senegal, torn from their homes and families, transported to foreign lands, groaning under the heavy yoke of authority, tear up the fertile fields of the America that scorns their labors. And we call this land of destruction happy because its meadows are not overgrown with thorns and its fields abound in plants of every variety. We call that country happy, where one hundred haughty citizens wallow in luxury, while thousands have no secure subsistence nor proper protection against heat and cold. Oh, that these prosperous lands might become wilderness again! Oh, that thorns and thistles might send their roots down deep and destroy all the precious products of America! Tremble, my beloved ones, lest they say of you: "Change the name, and the story may be told of you." [4]

[*252] Even now we marvel at the enormous size of the Egyptian buildings. The incomparable pyramids will for a long time bear witness to the daring architecture of the Egyptians. But why were these foolish heaps of stone erected? For the burial of the haughty Pharaohs. These vainglorious rulers, thirsting for immortality, wanted even after their demise to be externally distinguished from their people. Thus the immensity of these structures, useless as they were to the people, is palpable proof of their enslavement. In the ruins of decayed cities where the general welfare once ruled, we find the ruins of schools, hospitals, hostelries, aqueducts, theaters, and similar buildings; whereas in the cities where "I," and not "we," was supreme, we find the ruins of superb royal palaces, vast stables, and parks for animals. Let us compare the two: our choice will not be difficult.

[*253] What indeed do we discover in the glory of conquest? Sound, fury, boastfulness, and exhaustion. I would compare such glory with the balloons invented in the eighteenth century; [5] made of silk fabric and quickly filled with hot air, they ascend with the speed of sound to the extreme

limits of the ether. But what constituted their power is constantly seeping out through the fine interstices of the fabric, the weight which had been borne upward begins to sink again, and that which has taken whole months of labor, care, and expense to prepare can amuse the spectators for only a few hours.

But let us ask what the conqueror longs for, what he is seeking as he devastates populous countries or subjects wildernesses to his dominion. We may obtain an answer from the most savage of them all, from Alexander, called the Great, but in truth great, not in his deeds, [*254] but in the power of his spirit and in destruction. "O Athenians!" he exclaimed, "how greatly I deserve your praise!" Fool! Look at the road you have traveled. The fierce whirlwind of your progress, roaring over your realm, draws its inhabitants into its vortex, and, gathering up the whole power of the state in its onrush, leaves behind it only desert and dead void. You fail to realize, O savage boar, that when you have devastated your own land by your victories, you will find nothing in the conquered one to give you pleasure. If you have acquired a desert, it will become a grave for your fellow citizens, in which they will disappear; in settling the new desert, you will turn a fertile land into a sterile one. What shall it profit you to convert a desert into settlements, if in so doing you cause other settlements to be deserted? But if you have acquired an inhabited country, count your murders, and tremble with horror. You must root out [*255] all the hearts that have come to hate you in your terrible progress, for you must not expect to be loved by those who have been driven to fear you. After the destruction of the manly citizens, there will remain only timid souls, submissive to you and ready to accept the yoke of slavery; but even in them the hatred born of your crushing victory will take deep root. Do not deceive yourself: the fruit of your conquest will be murder and hatred. You will live in the memory of future generations as a scourge: [6] you yourself will be tortured by the thought that your new slaves detest you and pray for your death.

But, to return to our more immediate concern with the condition of the agriculturists, we find it most harmful to society. It is harmful because it prevents the increase of products and population, harmful by its example, and dangerous in the unrest it creates. Man, motivated by self-interest, [*256] undertakes that which may be to his immediate or later advantage, and avoids that from which he expects no present or future gain. Following this natural instinct, everything we do for our own sake, everything we do without compulsion, we do carefully, industriously, and well. On the other hand, all that we do not do freely, all that we do not do for our own advantage, we do carelessly, lazily, and all awry. Thus we find the agriculturists in our country. The field is not their own, the fruit thereof does not belong to them. Hence they cultivate the land lazily and do not care whether it goes to waste because of their poor work. Compare this field with the one the haughty proprietor gives the worker for his own meager sustenance. The worker is unsparing in the labors which he spends on it. Nothing distracts him from his work. The savagery of the weather [*257] he overcomes bravely; the hours intended for rest he spends at work; he shuns pleasure even on the days set aside for it. For he looks after his own interest, works for himself, is his own master. Thus his field will give him an abundant harvest; while all the fruits of the work done on the proprietor's demesne will die or bear no future harvest; whereas they would grow and be ample for the sustenance of the citizens. if the cultivation of the fields were done with loving care, if it were free.

But if forced labor brings smaller harvests, crops which fail to reach the goal of adequate production also stop the increase of the population. Where there is nothing to eat, there will soon be no eaters,[7] for all will die from exhaustion.

Thus the enslaved field, by giving an insufficient return, starves to death the citizens for whom nature had intended her superabundance. But this is not the only thing in slavery that interferes with abundant life. [*258] To insufficiency of food and clothing they have added work to the point of exhaustion. Add to this the spurns of arrogance and the abuse of power, even over man's tenderest sentiments, and you see with horror the pernicious effects of slavery, which differs from victory and conquest only by not allowing what victory cuts down to be born anew. But it causes even greater harm. It is easy to see that the one devastates accidentally and momentarily, the other destroys continuously over a long period of time; the one, when its onrush is over, puts an end to its ravages, the other only begins where the first ends, and cannot change except by upheavals which are always dangerous to its whole internal structure.

But nothing is more harmful than to see forever before one the partners in slavery, master and slave.[8] On the one side there is born conceit, on the other, servile fear. There can be no bond between them other than [*259] force. And this, concentrated in a small range, extends its oppressive autocratic power everywhere. But the champions of slavery, who, though they hold the sharp edge of power in their hands, are themselves cast into fetters, become its most fanatical preachers. It appears that the spirit of freedom is so dried up in the slaves that they not only have no desire to end their sufferings, but cannot bear to see others free. They love their fetters, if it is possible for man to love his own ruination.[9] I think I can see in them the serpent that wrought the fall of the first man. The examples of arbitrary power are infectious. We must confess that we ourselves, armed with the mace of courage and the law of nature for the crushing of the hundred-headed monster that gulps down the food prepared for the people's general sustenance — we ourselves, perhaps, have been misled into autocratic acts, and, although our intentions have always been good and [*260] have aimed at the general happiness, yet our arbitrary behavior cannot be justified by its usefulness. Therefore we now implore your forgiveness for our unintentional presumption.

Do you not know, dear fellow citizens, what destruction threatens us and in what peril we stand? All the hardened feelings of the slaves, not given vent by a kindly gesture of freedom, strengthen and intensify their inner longings. A stream that is barred in its course becomes more powerful in proportion to the opposition it meets. Once it has burst the dam, nothing can stem its flood. Such are our brothers whom we keep enchained. They are waiting for a favorable chance and time.[10] The alarum bell rings. And the destructive force of bestiality breaks loose with terrifying speed. Round about us we shall see sword and poison. Death and fiery desolation will be the meed [*261] for our harshness and inhumanity. And the more procrastinating and stubborn we have been about the loosening of their fetters, the more violent they will be in their vengefulness. Bring back to your memory the events of former times. Recall how deception roused the slaves to destroy their masters. Enticed by a crude pretender,[11] they hastened to follow him, and wished only to free themselves from the yoke of their masters; and in their ignorance they could think of no other means to do this than to kill their masters. They spared neither sex nor age. They sought more the joy of vengeance than the benefit of broken shackles.

This is what awaits us, this is what we must expect. Danger is steadily mounting, peril is already hovering over our heads. Time has already raised its scythe and is only awaiting an opportunity. The first demagogue or humanitarian who rises up [*262] to awaken the unfortunates will hasten the scythe's fierce sweep. Beware!

But if the terror of destruction and the danger of the loss of property can move those among you who are weak, shall we not be brave enough to overcome our prejudices, to suppress our selfishness, to free our brothers from the bonds of slavery, and to re-establish the natural equality of all? [12] Knowing the disposition of your hearts, I am sure that you will be convinced more readily by arguments drawn from the human heart than by the calculations of selfish reason, and still less by fears of danger. Go, my dear ones, go to the dwellings of your brothers and proclaim to them the change in their lot. Proclaim with deep feeling: "Moved to pity by your fate, sympathizing with our fellow men, having come to recognize your equality, and convinced that our interests are mutual, we have come to embrace [*263] our brothers. We have abandoned the haughty discrimination which for so long a time has separated us from you, we have forgotten the inequality that has existed between us, we rejoice now in our mutual victory, and this day on which the shackles of our fellow citizens are broken shall become the most famous day in our annals. Forget our former injustice to you, and let us sincerely love one another."

Such will be your utterance; deep down in your hearts you already hear it. Do not delay, my dear ones. Time flies; our days go by and we do nothing. Let us not end our lives merely fostering good intentions which we have not been able to carry out. Let not our posterity take advantage of this, win our rightful crown of glory, and say contemptuously of us: "They had their day."

That is what I read in the mud-stained paper which I [*264] picked up in front of the post hut as I left my carriage.

Upon entering the hut I asked who were the travelers who had stopped there immediately before me. "The last traveler," the postilion told me, "was a man about fifty years old; according to his traveling permit he was going to Petersburg. He forgot and left a bundle of papers here, and I'm forwarding them to him right now." I asked the postilion to let me look through the papers, and, unfolding them, I discovered that the piece I had found belonged with them. By means of a good tip I persuaded him to let me have the papers. Upon examining them I found that they belonged to a dear friend of mine; hence I did not consider their acquisition a theft. Up to the present, he has never asked me to return them, but has left me free to do with them what I pleased.

While they were changing my horses, I examined with great [*265] interest the papers I had acquired. I found a large number of articles in the same vein as the one I had read. Everywhere I recognized the spirit of a charitable man; everywhere I saw a citizen of the future. It was clear above all else that my friend was deeply disturbed by the inequality of the estates. A whole bundle of papers and drafts of laws referred to the abolition of serfdom in Russia. But my friend, realizing that the supreme power was not strong enough to cope with a sudden change of opinions, had outlined a program of temporary legislation leading to a gradual emancipation of the agriculturists in Russia. I will sketch here the main lines of his scheme. The first law provides for the distinction between rural and domestic serfdom. The latter is abolished first of all, and the landlords are forbidden to take into their houses any peasant or anybody registered in the last census as a village dweller. If a landlord [*266] takes a peasant into his house as a servant or artisan, he at once becomes free. Peasants are to be allowed to marry without asking their masters' permission. Marriage license fees are prohibited. The second law has to do with the property and protection of the peasants. They shall own individually the plot that they cultivate, for they shall pay the head tax themselves. Property acquired by a peasant shall belong to him, and no one shall arbitrarily deprive him of it. The peasant is to be reinstated as a citizen. He shall be judged by his peers, that is, in courts in which manorial peasants, among others, are to be chosen to serve. The peasant shall be permitted to acquire real estate, that is, to buy land. He may without hindrance obtain his freedom by paying his master [*267] a fixed sum to release him. Arbitrary punishment without due process of law is prohibited. "Avaunt, barbarous custom; perish, power of the tigers!" says our legislator. — Thereupon follows the complete abolition of serfdom.

Among the many decrees referring to the restoration of the highest possible degree of equality to all citizens, I found the Table of Ranks. How anomalous it is, how out of keeping with modern times, anyone may see for himself. But the bell in the harness bow of the shaft horse began to tinkle and called me for my departure; so I decided that it would be better to consider what is more profitable for a traveler by post — whether to let the horses go at a trot or at an amble, whether it is better for a post horse to trot or to gallop — than to occupy myself with that which does not exist.[13]

[*268] VYSHNY VOLOCHOK

I never pass this new town without stopping to look at the locks of its canal. The first man to whom it occurred to emulate nature in her benefactions and to put a river to work, thus bringing all the ends of a territory into closer communication, is worthy to be remembered by the most distant posterity. When the presently existing powers decay from natural and moral causes, when their golden fields are overgrown with thorns, when adders, serpents, and toads make their nests in the ruins of the magnificent palaces of their haughty rulers, then the curious traveler will find eloquent remains of their greatness in commerce. The Romans built great roads and aqueducts whose durability is justly admired even to the present day, [*269] but they had no conception of inland waterways such as we now have in Europe. Because of our long winters and hard frosts, we shall never have roads such as the Romans had, but our canals will not soon silt up, even without proper care.

It has been no small source of pleasure for me to watch the Vyshny Volochok Canal full of barges carrying grain and other goods as they got ready to pass through the locks for the rest of their voyage to Petersburg. Here one could see the true wealth of the soil and the agriculturist's superabundance, here one could see in its full glory the mighty mover of human actions, self-interest. But if at first glance my spirit was delighted at the sight of this prosperity, at second thoughts my joy soon waned. For I remembered that in Russia many agriculturists were not working for themselves, and that thus the abundance of the earth in many districts [*270] of Russia bears witness only to the heavy lot of its inhabitants. My satisfaction was transformed into indignation such as I feel when in summer time I walk down the customs pier and look at the ships that bring us the surplus of America and its precious products, such as sugar, coffee, dyes, and other things, not yet dry from the sweat, tears, and blood that bathed them in their production.

"Remember," my friend once said, "that the coffee in your cup, and the sugar dissolved in it, have deprived a man like yourself of his rest, that they have been the cause of labors surpassing his strength, the cause of tears, groans, blows, and abuse. Now dare to pamper your gullet, hard-hearted wretch!" The sight of his disgust as he said this shook me to the depths of my soul. My hand trembled, and I spilled the coffee.

[*271] But you, O inhabitants of Petersburg, who feed on the superabundance of the fertile districts of your country, whether at magnificent banquets, or at a friendly feast, or alone, as your hand raises the first piece of bread meant to nourish you, stop and think. Might I not say the same things to you about it that my friend said to me about the products of America? Have not the fields on which it grew been enriched by sweat, tears, and groans? You are fortunate if the piece of bread for which you hungered was made from grain grown on what is called crown land, or at least on a field that pays its proprietor a commutation tax. But woe to you if it is made of grain that comes from a nobleman's granary!

Upon it are grief and despair, upon it is made manifest the curse of the Almighty, who in His anger said: "Cursed be the earth in its fruits."[1] [*272] Beware lest ye be poisoned by the food ye covet. The bitter tears of the poor lie heavy on it. Put it away from your lips, and fast, for that may be a sincere and wholesome fast.

The story of a certain landed proprietor proves that man for the sake of his personal advantage forgets humanity towards his fellow man, and that to find an example of hardheartedness we need not go to far-off countries nor seek miracles through thrice-nine lands; they take place before our eyes in our own country.

A certain man who, as they say in the vernacular, did not make his mark in the government service, or who did not wish to make it there, left the capital, acquired a small village of one or two hundred souls, and determined to make his living by agriculture. He did not apply himself to the plough but intended most vigorously [*273] to make all possible use of the natural strength of his peasants by applying them to the cultivation of the land. To this end he thought it the surest method to make his peasants resemble tools that have neither will nor impulse; and to a certain extent he actually made them like the soldiers of the present time who are commanded in a mass, who move to battle in a mass, and who count for nothing when acting singly. To attain his end he took away from his peasants the small allotment of plough land and the hay meadows which noblemen usually give them for their bare maintenance, as a recompense for all the forced labor which they demand from them. In a word, this nobleman forced all his peasants and their wives and children to work every day of the year for him. Lest they should starve, he doled out to them a definite [*274] quantity of bread, known by the name of monthly doles. Those who had no families received no doles, but dined according to the Lacedaemonian custom, together, at the manor, receiving thin cabbage soup on meat days, and on fast days bread and kvas, to fill their stomachs. If there was any real meat, it was only in Easter Week.

These serfs also received clothing befitting their condition. Their winter boots, that is, bast shoes, they made for themselves; leggings they received from their master; while in summer they went barefooted. Naturally these serfs had no cows, horses, ewes, or rams. Their master did not withhold from these serfs the permission, but the means to have them. Whoever was a little better off and ate sparingly, kept a few chickens, which the master [*275] sometimes took for himself, paying for them as he pleased.

With such an arrangement it is not surprising that agriculture in Mr. So-and-So's village was in a flourishing condition. Where the crops were a failure elsewhere, his grain showed a fourfold return; when others had a good crop, his grain had a tenfold return or better. In a short time he added to his two hundred souls another two hundred as victims of his greed, and, proceeding with them just as with the first, he increased his holdings year after year, thus multiplying the number of those groaning in his fields. Now he counts them by the thousand and is praised as a famous agriculturist.

Barbarian! You do not deserve to bear the name of citizen. What good does it do the country that every year a few thousand more bushels of grain are grown, if those who produce it are valued on a par with the ox whose job it is [*276] to break the heavy furrow? Or do we think our citizens happy because our granaries are full and their stomachs empty? Or because one man blesses the government, rather than thousands? The wealth of this bloodsucker does not belong to him. It has been acquired by robbery and deserves severe punishment according to law. Yet there are people who, looking at the rich fields of this hangman, cite him as an example of perfection in agriculture. And you wish to be called merciful, and you bear the name of guardians of the public good! Instead of encouraging such violence, which you regard as the source of the country's wealth, direct your humane vengeance against this enemy of society. Destroy the tools of his agriculture, burn his barns, silos, and granaries, and scatter their ashes over the fields where he practiced his tortures; stigmatize [*277] him as a robber of the people, so that everyone who sees him may not only despise him but shun his approach to avoid infection from his example.

[*278] VYDROPUSK

Here I again took up my friend's papers. Into my hands fell a draft of a law for the abolition of court ranks.

A Project for the Future. In order to restore gradually the natural and civil equality which had been violated in society, our ancestors considered it by no means unimportant to curtail the rights of the nobility. Though at first useful to the country through its personal merits, its inherited rights subsequently weakened its achievements: the root, sweet in its planting, ultimately produced a bitter fruit. In place of bravery, conceit and selfishness were enthroned; instead of nobility of soul and generosity, servility and lack of self-confidence, those true devourers of greatness. Living among [*279] such small souls and impelled toward pettiness by their flattery of hereditary virtues and merits, many rulers imagined that they were gods, and that everything they touched became good and radiant. Such, indeed, ought to be the effect of our acts, but only for the public good. In such a delusion of grandeur, the rulers came to think that their slaves and attendants who constantly stood around in their presence took on something of their luster, that the royal radiance was refracted, so to speak, in these new crystals, and appeared magnified and even more brilliantly reflected. While their minds were thus gone astray, the rulers set up their court idols, who, like true little theatrical gods, obey the whistle or the rattle. Let us review the ranks of court offices, and with a smile of compassion turn away from those who boast about their services, though we should weep [*280] when we see them preferred to those of real merit. My lord steward, my master of the horse, and even my groom and coachman, my cook, cupbearer, falconer, and his subaltern hunters, my gentlemen of the bedchamber, he who shaves me, he who combs the hair on my head, he who wipes the dust and dirt from my shoes, not to mention many others, are made equal or even superior to those who serve their country with their spiritual and physical strength, sparing for its sake neither their health nor blood, happy even to die for the glory of their country. What good does it do you that cleanliness and neatness reign in my house? Will you satisfy your hunger the better because my food is prepared better than yours and because wine from all the corners of the universe flows in my goblets? Can you find shelter against the inclemency of the weather on your journey because my coach of state is gilded and my horses are sleek? [*281] Will your fields produce a better crop, will your meadows be greener if they are trampled over for my entertainment in the hunt? You will smile compassionately. But many another, in his just indignation, will say to us: "He who supervises your palace, he who heats it, he who blends the hot spiciness of southern plants with the cold viscosity of northern fats to please your weary stomach and jaded taste, he who makes the sweet juice of the African grape foam in your goblet, he who greases the wheels of your chariot and feeds and waters your horses, he who in your name wages bloody war against the beasts of the forest and the birds of the air — all these parasites, all these pamperers of your conceit, and many others of their ilk, rank above me, who have shed [*282] streams of blood on the battlefield, who have lost the most essential limbs of my body in defending your cities and palaces (where your cowardice was cloaked by a semblance of majesty and valor); above me, who have sacrificed the days of joy, of youth, and of pleasure in order to save the smallest farthing, so that, as far as possible, the common burden of taxation might be lightened; who have neglected my own estate, while working day and night to find means to promote the general welfare; who have slighted kindred, friends, and the union of heart and blood, in order to proclaim in court true justice in your name, that you might be loved. Our hair grows white in our exploits, our strength is exhausted in our undertakings, and at the brink of the grave we barely earn your good will, while these calves that are fatted at the udders of luxury and vice, these bastard sons of the fatherland, will inherit our property."

[*283] This and even more will many of you say, and justly so. What shall we, the lords of power, reply? We shall veil our humiliation in hard indifference, but our eyes will shoot forth flames of wrath against those who have said these things. Such frequently are our answers to proclamations of the truth. And let no one be surprised to see even the best among us dare to reply thus, for even the best of rulers lives with flatterers, converses with flatterers, sleeps in flattery, and walks in adulation. And flattery and adulation make him deaf, blind, and unfeeling.

But let no such reproach fall upon us. Having hated flattery from our childhood, we have turned our heart away from its poisonous sweetness even to this day, and now a new proof of our love and devotion to you shall be made manifest. We now abolish the equation of the Court Service to the Military and [*284] Civil Service. Let the custom that to our shame has existed for so many years now be expunged from memory. Only real worth and real merit, only work for the public good shall receive the rewards and distinctions of meritorious service.

In lifting from our heart this intolerable burden which has oppressed us for so long, we shall explain to you our reasons for abolishing the ranks that were so offensive to real service and merit. You have been told, and our ancestors held the same view, that the Imperial throne, whose strength is rooted in the opinion of the citizens, must be distinguished by external splendor, so that the thought of its grandeur may remain whole and inviolable. Hence the pompous external display of the rulers of nations, hence the herd of slaves that surround them. Everyone must admit that narrow minds and petty souls are impressed by external splendor. But the more enlightened a nation is, [*285] the greater the number of enlightened individuals, the less do appearances matter. Numa could convince the still rude Romans that the nymph Egeria guided him in his legislation.[1] The weak Peruvians readily believed Manco Capac when he told them that he was the son of the sun and that his laws came from heaven.[2] Mohammed was able to deceive the nomadic Arabs with his delirious dreams. All of them made use of appearances; even Moses received the tablets of the law upon a mountain amidst flashes of lightning. Nowadays, however, one who would beguilingly persuade needs not glittering outward show, but, so to speak, glittering argument, seeming conviction. Nowadays he who would strengthen his message from on high should seek to give it the appearance of utility, and thereby he will reach all. But of what use is external pomp to us, who direct all our powers toward the well-being of each and every one of our subjects? Is not our countenance radiant [*286] with the utility of our decrees issued for the good of the country? Everyone who looks at us will see our benevolence, will see his own advantage in our acts, and will bow to us not as to a tyrant striding in terror, but as to a sovereign enthroned in goodness. If the ancient Persians had always been ruled benevolently, they would not have invented Ahriman, the hateful principle of evil. But if ostentatious show is useless to us, how dangerous to the country its instruments can be! Their one duty in our service being our satisfaction, how inventive they will be in striving to please us. Our every wish will be anticipated; they will not allow us to conceive a wish — indeed, not a thought — without having it realized. Look with fear upon the effects of such servility. Shaken in its principles, the firmest soul [*287] will lend an ear to this enticing flattery, and will fall asleep. Thus the sweet sorcery enmeshes our mind and heart. Other people's sorrows and wrongs hardly seem to us as important as passing indispositions; we think it unseemly or disgusting to bewail them and indeed we forbid complaints about them. The most painful griefs and wounds, even death itself, will appear to us as inevitable results of the course of events; and, seen only, as it were, behind a dark curtain, will scarcely be able to arouse in us that momentary emotion which theatrical representations produce. For it is not into our breast that the dart of disease and the sting of evil have penetrated, and it is not in our breast that they are trembling.

This is a feeble picture of all the ruinous consequences of royal pomp. Are we not truly blessed if we have managed to protect ourselves from the perversion of our good intentions? Are we not truly blessed if we have blocked this infectious example? Firm in our good intentions, [*288] firm against temptation from without, firm in the moderation of our desires, we shall prosper anew and shall be an example to the most distant posterity of how power can be joined with liberty for mutual advantage.[3]

[*289] TORZHOK

At the post station here I met a man who was on his way to Petersburg to present a petition. It consisted of a request for permission to set up a free printing press in this town. I told him that no such permission was necessary, since this freedom had been granted to all.[1] But what he really wanted was freedom from censorship, and here are his reflections on the subject.

Everyone in our country is now permitted to own and operate a printing press, and the time has passed when they were afraid to grant this permission to private individuals, and when, because in free printing offices false statements might be printed, they renounced the general good and this useful institution. Now anybody may have the tools of printing, but that which may be printed is still under watch and ward. The censorship has become the nursemaid [*290] of reason, wit, imagination, of everything great and enlightened. But where there are nurses, there are babies and leading strings, which often lead to crooked legs; where there are guardians, there are minors and immature minds unable to take care of themselves. If there are always to be nurses and guardians, then the child will walk with leading strings for a long time and will grow up to be a cripple. Mitrofanushka [2] will always be a minor, will not take a step without his valet, and will not be able to manage his inheritance without a guardian. Everywhere these are the consequences of the usual censorship, and the sterner it is, the more disastrous are its consequences. Let us listen to Herder: [3]

The best means of promoting good is noninterference, permission to work for a good cause,[4] freedom of thought. Any inquisition is harmful to the realm of learning: it makes the air stifling and smothers [*291] the breath. A book that has to pass through ten censorships before it sees the light of day is no longer a book, but a creature of the Holy Inquisition, very often a mutilated unfortunate, beaten with rods, gagged, and always a slave. . . . In the province of truth, in the kingdom of thought and spirit, no earthly power can or should pass judgment; the government cannot do it, much less its hooded censor.[5] In the realm of truth he is not a judge, but a party, like the author. . . . All improvement can take place only through enlightenment; neither hand nor foot can move without head and brain. . . . The better grounded a state is in its principles, the better ordered and the brighter and stronger in itself, the less danger it incurs of being moved and swayed by the winds of shifting opinion, by any pasquinade of an overwrought [*292] writer; all the more readily, then, it will grant freedom of thought and (with some allowance for its situation and condition)[6] freedom of writing, through which truth will ultimately be victorious. Only tyrants are suspicious; only secret evildoers are fearful. An open-hearted man, who does good and is firm in his principles, lets anything be said about himself. He walks in the light of day and turns to his own advantage even the worst lies of his enemies. . . . All monopolies of thought are harmful. . . . The ruler of a state must be almost without any favorite opinion of his own in order that he may be able to embrace, tolerate, refine, and direct toward the general welfare the opinions of everyone in his state: hence great rulers are so rare.

Having recognized the usefulness of printing, the government has made it open to all; having further recognized that control of thought might invalidate its good intention in granting freedom to set up presses, it turned over the [*293] censorship or inspection of printed works to the Department of Public Morals. Its duty in this matter can only be the prohibition of the sale of objectionable works. But even this censorship is superfluous. A single stupid official in the Department of Public Morals may do the greatest harm to enlightenment and may for years hold back the progress of reason: he may prohibit a useful discovery, a new idea, and may rob everyone of something great. Here is an example on a small scale. A translation of a novel is brought to the Department of Public Morals for its imprimatur. The translator, following the author, in speaking of love calls it "the tricky god." The censor in uniform and in the fullness of piety strikes out the expression, saying, "It is improper to call a divinity tricky." He who does not understand should not interfere. If you want fresh air, remove the smoky brazier; if you want light, remove [*294] that which obscures it; if you do not want the child to be timid, throw the rod out of the school. In a house where whips and sticks are in fashion, the servants are drunkards, thieves, and worse.*

* They tell of a censor of this sort who would not permit any works to be published in which God was mentioned, saying, "I have no business with Him." If in any work the popular customs of this or that foreign country were criticized, he considered this inadmissible, saying, "Russia has a treaty

Let anyone print anything that enters his head. If anyone finds himself insulted in print, let him get his redress at law. I am not speaking in jest. Words are not always deeds, thoughts are not crimes. These are the rules in the *Instruction for a New Code of Laws*.[7] But [*295] an offense in words or in print is always an offense. Under the law no one is allowed to libel another, and everyone has the right to bring suit. But if one tells the truth about another, that cannot, according to the law, be considered a libel. What harm can there be if books are printed without a police stamp? Not only will there be no harm; there will be an advantage, an advantage from the first to the last, from the least to the greatest, from the Tsar to the last citizen.

The usual rules of the censorship are: to strike out, blot out, prohibit, tear, burn everything that is opposed to natural religion and Revelation, everything in opposition to the government, every personal reflection, everything contrary to public morality, order, and peace. Let us examine this more closely. When a fool in his raving saith, not only in his heart, but with a loud voice, "There is no God," there is heard upon the lips of all the fools a loud [*296] and fleeting echo, "There is no God, there is no God." But what of it? The echo is a sound that strikes the air, sets it vibrating, and disappears. It seldom leaves a mark upon the mind, and then only a faint one, and never any trace upon the heart. God will ever be God, perceived even by those who do not believe in Him. But if you think that the Supreme Being will be offended by blasphemy, can an official of the Department of Public Morals be His chosen attorney? The Almighty will not give a power of attorney to one who shakes a rattle or sounds the tocsin. The hurler of thunder and lightning, Whom all the elements obey, the agitator of hearts beyond the limits of the universe,

---

of friendship with that country." If a prince or count was mentioned anywhere, he did not permit that to be printed, saying, "That is a personal allusion, for we have princes and counts among our distinguished personages."

will disdain to be avenged even by the king himself, who imagines himself to be His vicegerent upon earth. Who can be the judge in an offense against the Eternal Father? The real offender against God is he who imagines that he can sit in judgment on an offense against Him. It is he who will be answerable before Him.

[*297] The dissenters from the revealed religion have so far done more harm in Russia than those who do not acknowledge the existence of God, the atheists. There are not many of the latter among us, because few among us are concerned about metaphysics. The atheist errs in metaphysics; the dissenter in crossing himself with only two fingers.[8] Dissenters or *raskol'niki* is our name for all those Russians who in any manner depart from the common doctrine of the Greek Church. There are many of them in Russia; hence they are allowed to hold divine services. But why should not every aberration be permitted to be out in the open? The more open it is, the quicker it will break down. Persecutions have only made martyrs; cruelty has been the support of the Christian religion itself. The consequences of schisms are sometimes harmful. Prohibit them. They are propagated by example. Destroy the example. A printed book will not cause a *raskol'nik* to throw himself into the fire, but a moving example will.[9] To prohibit foolishness is to encourage it. Give it [*298] free rein; everyone will see what is foolish and what is wise. What is prohibited is coveted. We are all Eve's children.

But in prohibiting freedom of the press, timid governments are not afraid of blasphemy, but of criticism of themselves. He who in moments of madness does not spare God, will not in moments of lucidity and reason spare unjust power. He who does not fear the thunders of the Almighty laughs at the gallows. Hence freedom of thought is terrifying to governments. The freethinker who has been stirred to his depths will stretch forth his audacious but mighty and fearless arm against the idol of power, will tear off its mask and veil, and lay bare its true character. Everyone will see its feet of clay; everyone will withdraw the support which he had given it; power will return to its source; the idol will fall. But if power is not seated in the fog of contending opinions, if its throne is founded on sincerity and true love of the common weal, [*299] will it not rather be strengthened when its foundation is revealed? And will not the true lover be loved more truly? Mutuality is a natural sentiment, and this instinct is deeply implanted in our nature. A solid and firm building needs only its own foundation; it has no need of supports and buttresses. Only when it is weakened by old age does it have need of lateral support. Let the government be honest and its leaders free from hypocrisy; then all the spittle and vomit will return their stench upon him who has belched them forth; but the truth will always remain pure and immaculate. He whose words incite to revolt (in deference to the government, let us so denominate all firm utterances which are based on truth but opposed to the ruling powers) is just as much a fool as he who blasphemes God. Let the government proceed on its appointed path; then it will not be troubled by the empty sound of calumny, even as the Lord of Hosts [*300] is not disturbed by blasphemy. But woe to it if in its lust for power it offends against truth. Then even a thought shakes its foundations; a word of truth will destroy it; a manly act will scatter it to the winds.

A personal attack, if it is unjustly offensive, is a libel. A personal attack which states the truth is as admissible as truth itself. If a blinded judge judges unjustly, and a defender of innocence publicizes his unjust decision and shows up his wiles and injustice, that will be a personal attack, but one that is permissible; if he calls him a venal, false, stupid judge, that is a personal attack, but it is admissible. But if he begins to call him dirty names and slanders him with offensive words such as one hears in the marketplace, that is a personal attack, but it is offensive and inadmissible. But it is not the business of the government to defend [*301] the judge, even though he may have been criticized unjustly. Not the judge, but the *person*, offended, should appear as plaintiff in this case. Let the judge justify himself, before the world and before those who appointed him, by his deeds alone.* Thus one must judge of a personal attack. It deserves punishment, but in print it will do more good [*302] than harm. If everything were in order, if decisions were always rendered in accordance with the law, if the law were founded on truth, and all oppression were barred, then perhaps, and only then, a personal attack might be injurious to the state. Let us now say something about public morals and how words may harm them.

Pornographic works, full of suggestive descriptions, breathing forth vice, whose every page and line gapes with provocative nudity, are injurious to youth and to the emotionally immature. By fanning an already inflamed imagination, by rousing dormant sensations and wakening a peacefully slumbering heart, they lead to premature sexual ripening, deceiving the youthful senses as to their powers of endurance and leading them to early decrepitude. Such works may be harmful, but they are not the real root of vice. If young people who read them are incited to an unrestrained indulgence of their desire, they would still [*303] have been estopped if there were not those who offered their beauty for sale. In Russia such writings have not yet appeared, but we see these painted harlots in every street in both the capitals. Deeds cor-

* Mr. Dickinson, who took part in the recent revolution in America and thus achieved fame, and later became President of Pennsylvania, did not disdain to do battle with those who attacked him. The most heinous accusations against him were published. The first officer of the state went into the arena, published his defense, justified himself, overthrew the contentions of his opponents, and put them to shame. . . .[10] This is an example worth imitating, of the way one ought to take revenge when publicly attacked by another in print. If one rages against the printed word, one only leads others to conclude that what is printed is true, and that he who seeks revenge is precisely such a man as he is described in print.

rupt more than words, but example most of all. The streetwalkers, offering their hearts in public auction to the highest bidder, infect with the plague a thousand youths and all the posterity of these thousand, whereas no book has yet caused disease. Thus, though censorship of venal girls should be instituted, censorship should not concern itself with productions of the mind, however dissolute. I will close with this: the censorship of what is printed belongs properly to society, which gives the author a laurel wreath or uses his sheets for wrapping paper. Just so, it is the public that gives its approval to a theatrical production, and not the director of the theater. Similarly the censor can give neither glory nor dishonor to the publication of a work. The curtain rises, and everyone [*304] eagerly watches the performance. If they like it, they applaud; if not, they stamp and hiss. Leave what is stupid to the judgment of public opinion; stupidity will find a thousand censors. The most vigilant police cannot check worthless ideas as well as a disgusted public. They will be heard just once; then they will die, never to rise again. But once we have recognized the uselessness of the censorship, or, rather, its harmfulness in the realm of knowledge, we must also recognize the vast and boundless usefulness of freedom of the press.

It would seem that no proof of this is necessary. If everyone is free to think and to proclaim his thoughts to all without hindrance, then naturally everything that is thought out and discovered will become known: what is great will be great, and truth will not be obscured. The rulers of nations will not dare to depart from the way of truth, lest their policy, their wickedness, and their fraud [*305] be exposed. The judge will tremble when about to sign an unjust sentence, and will tear it up. He who has power will be ashamed to use it only for the gratification of his lusts. Secret extortion will be called extortion, and clandestine murder — murder. All evil men will fear the stern glance of truth. Peace will be real, for there will be no ferment in it. Nowadays only the surface is smooth, but the ooze that lies at the bottom is growing turbid and dims the transparency of the water.

As he bade me good-bye, the critic of the censorship handed me a small copybook. Reader, if you are not afraid of being bored, read what lies before you. But if by any chance you yourself belong to the Censorship Committee, turn the page and hurry past.

[*306] *A Brief Account of the Origin of the Censorship.*[11] If we state — and confirm our statement with clear proofs — that the censorship springs from the same root as the Inquisition, and that the founders of the Inquisition invented the censorship, that is, the official examination of books before their publication, we are, to be sure, saying nothing new, but we are extracting from the darkness of ages past a clear proof, to add to many other proofs, that priests have always been the inventors of fetters with which they have at various times burdened the human mind, that they have clipped its wings lest it should soar aloft to greatness and freedom.

As we survey times past and bygone ages, we observe everywhere the ruinous aspects of brute power; everywhere we see might rising up against truth, and sometimes superstition arrayed against superstition. [*307] Egged on by priests, the Athenian people proscribed the writings of Protagoras and ordered that all copies of them be collected and burned.[12] Was it not the same people that in its madness, and to its eternal and inexpiable shame, condemned to death incarnate truth, Socrates? In Rome we find still more examples of this fury. Livy reports that the writings found in Numa's grave were burned by order of the Senate.[13] It happened at various times that prophetic books were ordered to be taken to the praetor. Suetonius relates that Caesar Augustus ordered such books, to the number of two thousand, to be burned.[14] Another example of the vacuity of human reason! Did these rulers really think that by prohibiting superstitious writings they would eradicate superstition itself?[15] All private individuals were forbidden to have recourse to the oracles, which were often consulted only for the momentary relief of gnawing sorrow; [*308] but the public oracles of the augurs and haruspices were left in peace. But if in these days of enlightenment one were to undertake to forbid or burn books that deal with divination or preach superstition, would it not be ridiculous for truth to lift the cudgel of persecution against superstition? Need truth seek the support of tyrannic might and the sword to overcome error, when the very sight of it is the most cruel scourge of error?

Caesar Augustus extended his persecution not only to the oracles, but also ordered the books of Titus Labienus to be burned. "His enemies," says Seneca the Rhetorician,[16] "invented this new kind of punishment for him. It is an unheard of and extraordinary thing to draw from a man's writings the justification for punishing him. Fortunately for the country, this assault on reason was not invented until after Cicero's time. What might have happened if the triumvirs had thought it expedient to condemn the writings of Cicero?" But the tyrant soon avenged Labienus against [*309] the man who had brought about the burning of Labienus' works. This man lived to see his own writings consigned to the fire.* "It was not a bad example that was followed here," says Seneca, "but his own." ** God grant that evil may always redound upon its perpetrator, and that anyone who undertakes to persecute ideas may always see his own ideas ridiculed and condemned to contempt and destruction! If revenge can ever be excusable, it is in this case.

---

* The works of Arias Montano, who published the first register of prohibited books in the Netherlands, were placed on that register.[17]
** Cassius Severus, the friend of Labienus, seeing his writings in the fire, said: "Now I should be burned, for I know them by heart." This gave occasion, in the reign of Augustus, for legislation against libelous works, which, thanks to man's apish inclination, was adopted in England and other countries.[18]

[*310] In the time of the popular government in Rome such persecutions were directed only against superstition, but under the emperors they were extended to combat all independent thought. Cremutius Cordus, in his history, described Cassius — who dared to ridicule Augustus' persecution of the writings of Labienus — as the last Roman. The Roman Senate, crawling before Tiberius, for his gratification ordered that Cremutius' book be burned. But many copies of it survived. "So much the more," says Tacitus, "must we laugh at the solicitude of those who think that by their omnipotence they can blot out the following generation's memory of the past. Power may rage against ideas, but in its fury it is preparing shame and disgrace for itself, and glory for them."[19]

Under Antiochus Epiphanes, the king of Syria, the Jewish books did not escape burning.[20] The books of the Christians [*311] were subjected to the same fate. The Emperor Diocletian ordered that the books of Holy Writ be consigned to the flames.[21] But the Christian religion was victorious over persecution, conquered the persecutors themselves, and is now an incontrovertible proof of the fact that the persecution of ideas and opinions is not only impotent to destroy them but is also effective in confirming and disseminating them. Arnobius justly protests against such persecution and tyranny. "Some claim," says he, "that it would benefit the country for the Senate to order the destruction of the writings which serve as a proof of the Christian profession of faith and which deny the importance of the ancient religion. But to proscribe writings and to try to destroy what has been published is not to defend the gods, but to show fear of the truth of the evidence."[22] After the spread of the Christian faith, however, its priests became just as [*312] hostile to writings which were opposed to them or were of no advantage to them. They had but recently criticized this severity in the pagans and considered it a sign of lack of faith in what they were defending, but now they quickly armed themselves with omnipotence.

The Greek emperors, who busied themselves more with church disputes than with affairs of state and who therefore were ruled by clerics, persecuted all those who differed from them in their interpretation of the acts and teachings of Jesus. In the same way they persecuted the productions of understanding and reason. The tyrant Constantine, called the Great, following the decree of the Council of Nicaea which anathematized the doctrine of Arius, prohibited his books, consigned them to the fire, and condemned to death anyone who should possess these books. The Emperor Theodosius II ordered all the condemned books of Nestorius to be collected and burned. At the Council of Chalcedon the same decree was promulgated against [*313] the writings of Eutyches. In the Pandects of Justinian some of these enactments are preserved.[23] Fools! They did not know that in persecuting a perverse or stupid exposition of Christian doctrine and in forbidding the mind to exercise itself in the investigation of any and all opinions whatsoever, they were arresting its progress. They deprived truth of a strong support, namely, of diversity in opinions, the struggle between ideas, and the unchecked utterance thereof. Who can guarantee that Nestorius, Arius, Eutyches, and other heretics might not have been predecessors of Luther, and that, if the Oecumenical Councils had not been convoked, Descartes might not have been born ten centuries earlier? What a great step backwards into darkness and ignorance was taken there!

After the fall of the Roman Empire, the monks were the preservers of learning and science in Europe. But no one denied their freedom to write what they pleased. In the year 768 Ambrosius Autpertus, a Benedictine monk, in sending his [*314] exposition of the Apocalypse to Pope Stephen III and asking his permission to continue his work and publish it, says that he is the first author to ask such a permission. "But," he continues, "let not the freedom of writing disappear because humility has bowed voluntarily."[24] The Council of Sens in

1140 proscribed the opinions of Abelard, and the Pope ordered his writings to be burned.²⁵

But not in Greece nor in Rome nor anywhere do we find an instance of the appointment of a judge of thought who would dare to say: "Ask my permission, if you wish to open your lips to speak; we put the stamp of approval on reason, science, and enlightenment; and everything which is published without our stamp we will declare in advance to be stupid, abominable, and worthless." This shameful invention remained for the Christian priesthood; the Censorship was a contemporary of the Inquisition.

[*315] Frequently, in turning the pages of history, we find reason coexisting with superstition, and the most useful inventions with the rudest ignorance. At the same time that a timid distrust of expressed opinion led the monks to institute the censorship and thereby to stifle thought at its birth, at that very moment Columbus ventured into the uncertainty of the seas in search of America. Kepler surmised the existence of the gravitational force in nature, later proved by Newton. At the same time, Copernicus, who delineated the path of the heavenly bodies in space, was born. We must admit, however, with the deepest regret at the fate of human thought, that a great idea has sometimes brought forth folly. Printing gave birth to the censorship; philosophic reason in the eighteenth century produced the Illuminati.²⁶

In 1479 we find the oldest hitherto-known permission to print a book. At the end of a book [*316] entitled *Know Thyself*, printed in 1480, the following is attached: "We, Maffeo Gerardo, by the grace of God, Patriarch of Venice and Primate of Dalmatia, taking cognizance of the testimony of the gentlemen above named in approval of the above-mentioned work, and in accord with their decision and attached authorization, do certify that this book is orthodox and God-fearing." ²⁷ The oldest monument of censorship, but not the oldest of folly!

The oldest ordinance on censorship thus far known appeared in the year 1486, enacted in the very city where printing was invented. The monastic authorities had a premonition that it would become a tool for the destruction of their power, that it would hasten the dissemination of general knowledge, and that power based on opinion and not on general usefulness would come to an end through printing. We may be permitted [*317] to subjoin here a document which is still in existence to the ruination of freedom of thought and the disgrace of enlightenment.

"Decree against the publication of Greek, Latin, and other books, in the vernacular tongue, without previous approval of the learned. 1486.*

" 'Berthold, by the grace of God, Archbishop of the Holy Province of Mainz, Archchancellor in Germany,[29] and Electoral Prince. Although for the acquisition of human knowledge it is possible through the divine art of printing to produce in greater number and more easily books touching upon the various sciences, it has come to our knowledge that certain men, impelled by the desire for vain glory or wealth, have abused this art and have turned that which was given for man's instruction in wise living into destruction and evil-speaking.

[*318] " 'We have seen books on the sacred offices and rites of our faith translated from Latin into German, and, without proper regard for the sacred law, circulated among the common people. What, finally, shall be said about the precepts of the sacred canons and laws? Although they are written very wisely and carefully by men learned in theology, by very wise and eloquent men, yet this science is in itself so complex that the whole life of even the most eloquent and wisest man is barely sufficient for mastering it.

" 'Certain foolish, rash, and ignorant men have had the audacity to translate such books into the vulgar language. Many

---

* *Codex diplomaticus*, edited by Gudenus. Volume IV.[28]

learned men who have read these translations have certified that because of their great awkwardness and misuse of words they are less intelligible than the originals. What shall we say about works treating of the other sciences, into which [*319] they frequently introduce falsehoods, which they inscribe with false titles, and in which they the more readily attribute the figments of their own imaginations to famous authors in order to find purchasers more easily?

" 'Let such translators declare, if they love the truth, with what intention, whether good or bad, they do it; let them say whether or not the German language is suitable for the rendering of that which the distinguished Greek and Latin writers have treated most learnedly and most wisely in their masterly disquisitions on the Christian faith and on the sciences? We must confess that because of its poverty our language is not at all sufficient for this purpose, since they must either concoct unknown designations for things, or, if they use the old ones, they distort the true meaning, which we fear most in the sacred writings, in view of their importance.[30] For who [*320] will expound the true meaning to rude and ignorant men, and to the feminine sex, into whose hands these sacred books may fall? Examine the text of the Holy Gospel or the epistles of the Apostle [31] Paul: every learned man recognizes that there are many scribal additions and corrections in them.

" 'What we have said is sufficiently well known. Why should we dwell on matters which have already been subjected to the most penetrating consideration by the writers of the Catholic Church? We might adduce many examples, but what we have already said is sufficient for our purpose.

" 'Since the beginning of this art was, to use the true expression, divinely manifested in our glorious city of Mainz,[32] and continues therein much corrected and improved, it is only just that on account of its importance we should take this art under our protection. For it is our duty to preserve the sacred writings in immaculate [*321] purity. Having spoken of the errors and presumption of impudent and wicked men, and desiring as much as we can, with the help of the Lord, Whose affair this is, to forestall and bridle them, we herewith command each and every person, clerical and lay, subject to our jurisdiction, and those trading beyond [33] our borders, of whatsoever calling or estate they may be,[34] that no work whatsoever, in any science, art, or field of knowledge, shall be translated from the Greek, Latin, or any other language into German, nor shall any work already translated with a mere change of title or the like be distributed or sold, openly or secretly, directly or indirectly, unless before its printing or, if it has already been printed, then unless before its publication it has the definite permission of our beloved, [*322] illustrious, and noble doctors and masters of the University, to wit, in our city of Mainz, Johannes Bertram von Naumburg in works of theology, Alexander Diethrich in jurisprudence, Theoderich von Meschede in medicine, and Andreas Oehler in arts and letters, doctors and masters appointed for this purpose in our city of Erfurt. But in the city of Frankfurt [no book shall be sold] [35] unless such books offered for sale be inspected and approved by one honorable master of theology, acceptable to us, and by one or two doctors and licentiates, who are to be maintained by an annual salary paid by the said city council.

" 'If anyone shall violate this our precautionary decree, or shall give advice, aid, or comfort, either in his own person or through others, against this our order, [*323] he shall ipso facto be subject to excommunication, and besides, shall forfeit such books and shall pay a fine of one hundred florins into our treasury. And let no one dare, without special authorization from us, to violate this decree.[36] Given in the Castle of St. Martin, in our City of Mainz, and sealed with our seal, the 4th day of January in the year of our Lord 1486.' "

"From the same, as to the manner of exercising the censorship. 1486.

" 'Berthold, etc., to the most honored, learned, and beloved in Christ J. Bertram, Doctor of Theology; A. Dietherich, Doctor of Jurisprudence; Th. von Meschede, Doctor of Medicine; and A. Oehler, Master of Arts, greeting and request to take notice of the following.

" 'Having learned of the scandals and frauds practiced by certain translators and printers of learned books, and wishing as far as possible [*324] to prevent this and to check their evil course, we command that no one in our Archdiocese or under our jurisdiction presume to [37] translate books into German, to print them, or, if they are already printed, to distribute them, until such works or books, in our city of Mainz, have been examined by you, and, as regards the subject matter itself, until it has been specifically approved by you for sale as translated, in accordance with the above instructions.

" 'Firmly relying on your prudence and discretion, we charge you: when treatises or books intended for translation, printing, or sale, are brought to you, examine their contents, and if it is not easy to grasp their true meaning, or if they might give rise to errors and mischief, or offend against chastity, you must reject them; but those which you approve, two of you must sign in person, at the end, [*325] so that it shall be clear that these books have been examined and approved by you. Do this your duty, which will be pleasing and useful to our God and country. Given in the Castle of St. Martin, the 10th day of January 1486.' "

Upon examining this decree, which was new for that time, we find that its main tendency is the restriction of the printing of books in the German language; in other words, the desire to keep the people forever in ignorance. It does not appear that the censorship extended to works written in Latin. For those who were already skilled in Latin were deemed to be fortified and impregnable against error and to understand clearly and correctly what they read.* [*326] Hence the priests wanted only the adherents of their power to be enlightened, and the people to consider learning as of divine origin and above their comprehension, and not to dare to touch it. Thus that which was invented for the purpose of confining truth and enlightenment within the narrowest limits, that which was invented by a power distrustful to its own strength, that which was invented for the purpose of perpetuating ignorance and darkness, now, in the day of science and philosophy, when reason has thrown off the uncongenial shackles of superstition, when truth gleams in a hundred forms, ever more and more, when the stream of learning flows to the remotest branches of society, when governments are earnestly endeavoring to stamp out ignorance and to open up for reason unobstructed ways to truth — this disgraceful monastic invention of a trembling power is now accepted everywhere, deep-rooted, and considered a beneficent protection against error. [*327] Madmen, look about you! You are trying to support truth with falsehood, you seek to enlighten the peoples with error. Beware lest darkness be reborn. What advantage will it be to you to rule over ignoramuses who have become the more coarsened because they have persisted in ignorance of nature or, rather, in natural ignorance, not for lack of aids toward enlightenment, but because, having taken a step toward enlightenment, they have been arrested in their progress and driven back into darkness? What advantage is it to you to struggle against yourselves and pull up with your left hand what your right hand has planted? Look at the priesthood rejoicing over this. You have already become its slaves.

* This may be compared with a situation in which one is allowed to possess foreign books of every kind, and forbidden to possess versions in the native language.

Spread the darkness and then feel your fetters, if not always the fetters of clerical superstition, then those of political superstition, which is not so ridiculous, but equally disastrous.

[*328] Fortunately for society, printing has not yet been banished from your regions. As a tree planted in eternal spring does not lose its verdure, so the tools of printing may be hindered in their working, but cannot be destroyed.

The popes, recognizing the danger to their power which might arise from freedom of the press, did not fail to decree censorship ordinances, and their decrees received the force of universal law at a council held in Rome soon afterwards. In the year 1501,[38] the clerical Tiberius, Pope Alexander VI, became the first of the popes to issue a decree on censorship. Himself steeped in evil, he was unblushingly concerned for the purity of the Christian doctrine. But when did tyranny ever blush? He begins his bull with a complaint against the Devil, who sows tares among the wheat, and says: "Having learned that through the said art many books and tracts printed [*329] in divers parts of the world, especially in Cologne, Mainz, Trier, and Magdeburg, contain various errors and pernicious teachings hostile to the Christian religion, and that such works are still being printed in some places, and wishing without delay to put an end to this detestable plague,[39] [we forbid] each and all masters of said art, and all under their charge, and everyone who has anything to do with the business of printing in the above-mentioned territories, under penalty of excommunication and a monetary fine — to be determined and collected by our honorable brethren the Archbishops of Cologne, Mainz, Trier, and Magdeburg or their representatives [40] in their territories, in favor of the Apostolic Chamber — by virtue of our Apostolic power, we most sternly forbid any of them to dare to print or cause to be printed any book, tract, or writing, without first reporting to the above-named Archbishops or their [*330] representatives and without having first obtained their special and express permission, for which they shall apply without fee; and we lay it upon their conscience that, before they give such permission to print, they first diligently examine, or have learned and orthodox [41] men examine the works and take proper precautions that nothing contrary to the orthodox faith, nothing godless, or provocative of error be printed." And lest old books cause more trouble, it was ordered that all the registers of books and all printed books be examined, and that those containing anything contrary to the Catholic faith be burned.

O ye who introduce the censorship, remember that ye may be compared to Alexander VI, and burn with shame!

In 1515 the Lateran Council issued a dogmatic decree on the censorship, prohibiting the printing of any book without permission of the clergy.[42]

[*331] From the foregoing we see that the censorship was invented by the clergy, and was their exclusive prerogative. Accompanied by excommunication and monetary fines, it could in those days appear truly terrible to him who violated the decrees pertaining to it. But Luther's denial of the papal power, the separation of various confessions of faith from the Roman Church, and the quarrels of various powers during the Thirty Years' War produced a multitude of books which appeared without the usual censor's stamp. Still the clergy everywhere arrogated to itself the right to exercise censorship over the press, and when in 1650 the civil censorship was established in France, the Theological Faculty of the University of Paris protested against the new establishment on the ground that it had enjoyed this privilege for two hundred years.[43]

[*332] Soon after the introduction * of printing in England, the censorship was established. The Star Chamber,[44] in

---

* William Caxton, a London merchant, introduced the art of printing into England in the reign of Edward IV, in 1474. The first book printed in the English language was *The Game and Playe of Chesse*, translated from the French. The second, *The Dictes or Sayengis of the Philosophres*, was translated by Lord Rivers.[45]

its time no less terrible in England than the Inquisition in Spain or the Secret Chancellery [46] in Russia, determined the number of printers and printing presses and established a licenser without whose permission nothing was allowed to be printed. There were countless acts of cruelty against those who attacked the Government, and history is full of them. Thus if in England clerical superstition was not able to subject reason to the heavy yoke of censorship, it was imposed by political superstition. But the latter, like the former, saw to it that Power remained intact, that the eyes [*333] of Enlightenment should be forever veiled by a mist of Illusion, and that Violence should reign in place of Reason.

With the death of the Earl of Strafford, the Star Chamber collapsed, but neither its abolition nor the judicial execution of Charles I was able to establish freedom of the press in England.[47] The Long Parliament renewed the old decrees against it.[48] Under Charles II and James II [49] they were again renewed. Even after the achievement of the Revolution, this legislation was confirmed, in 1692, but only for two years.[50] On the expiration of these laws in 1694, freedom of the press was fully established in England, and the censorship, drawing its last breath, gave up the ghost.*

[*334] The American states provided for freedom of the press among their very first laws establishing civil liberty. The State of Pennsylvania, in its constitution, part I, "A Declaration [52] of the Rights of the Inhabitants of the Commonwealth, or State of Pennsylvania," section 12, says: "That the people have a right to freedom of speech, and of writing, and publishing their sentiments; therefore the freedom of the press ought not to be restrained." In part II, "Plan or Frame of Government for the Commonwealth or State of Pennsylvania," [53] section 35: "The printing presses shall be free to

---

* In Denmark freedom of the press was of brief duration. Voltaire's verses to the King of Denmark on this occasion remain as proof that one should not be in a hurry to praise even wise legislation.[51]

every person who undertakes to examine the proceedings of the legislature, or any part of government." In "A Project of a form of Government for the State of Pennsylvania, printed in order to put the inhabitants in a position to communicate their remarks (July 1776)," section 35: [54] "The freedom of the press shall be open to every person who undertakes to examine [*335] the proceedings of the legislature; and the General Assembly shall not attaint it by any act. No printer shall be reprehensible for having published remarks, censures, or observations on the proceedings of the General Assembly, on any part of the Government, on any public affair, or on the conduct of any officer, in so far as they refer only to the exercise of his functions." The State of Delaware, in its Declaration of Rights, section 23, says: "That the liberty of the press ought to be inviolably preserved." [55] The State of Maryland, in section 38, uses the same language.[56] That of Virginia, in section 14,[57] says: "That the freedom of the press is the greatest bulwark of liberty." [58]

Nowhere had the press been so persecuted as in France up to the Revolution of 1789. [*336] A hundred-eyed Argus, a hundred-handed Briareus,[59] the Paris Police, raged against writings and writers. In the dungeons of the Bastille languished the unfortunates who had dared to criticize the avarice and vice of ministers. If the French language had not been so generally known and used in Europe, France, which was groaning under the scourge of censorship, would not have attained the greatness of thought which many of her writers have manifested. But the general use of the French language led to the setting up of printing presses in Holland, England, Switzerland, and the German lands, and whatever was not allowed to appear in France was freely published in other places. Thus the brute power that bragged of its muscles was ridiculed and made harmless; thus the jaws that foamed with rage remained empty, and fearless truth escaped being swallowed by them.

[*337] But marvel at the inconsistency of the human mind!

Nowadays, when everyone in France is talking about liberty, when license and anarchy have reached the utmost possible limits, the censorship in France is not abolished. And although everything is now printed there without prohibition, it is all done secretly. We have recently read — let the French, and with them all mankind, lament their fate! — we have recently read that the National Assembly, proceeding just as autocratically as the King before it, laid violent hands upon a printed book and delivered its author to the courts for having dared to write against the National Assembly.[60] Lafayette was the executor of this sentence. O France, thou art still hovering over the abysses of the Bastille!

The wide dispersion of printing establishments throughout the German lands protected their tools from the authorities and deprived them of the chance of raging against reason [*338] and enlightenment. The small German states have, indeed, tried to put obstacles in the way of freedom of the press, but in vain. Wekhrlin was imprisoned by vengeful power, but *The Gray Monster* remained in everyone's hands.[61] The late Frederick II, King of Prussia, had almost freed the press in his lands, not by any specific legislation, but by a tacit permission and his own manner of thinking. Why wonder that he did not abolish the censorship? He was an autocrat whose favorite passion was omnipotence. But restrain your laughter. He learned that someone intended to publish his collected decrees. Even for this enterprise he appointed two censors, or, more accurately, expurgators.[62] O tyranny, O despotism, you do not trust your own muscles! You fear your own accusation, you fear that your own tongue may put you to shame, [*339] that your own hand may box your ears! But what good could these autocratic censors do? No good: only evil. They hid from the eyes of posterity some foolish piece of legislation which the ruler was ashamed to leave to the judgment of future generations; which, had it been published, might have served as a bridle to power so that it would not have dared to commit the monstrosities of despotism. The Emperor Joseph II partly destroyed the barrier to enlightenment which had oppressed reason in the Austrian realm in the reign of Maria Theresa; but he could not throw off the yoke of prejudice and issued a very long decree on the censorship.[63] If he is to be praised for not having forbidden criticism of his enactments, or of his conduct, and the publication of such criticism in the press, we must blame him for having left a bridle on the free expression of thought. How easy it is [*340] to use this for evil! — * But why wonder? We repeat: he was an emperor. Tell me, in whose head can there be more inconsistencies than in an emperor's?

In Russia —. You will find out some other time what happened to the censorship in Russia. But now I hastily resumed my journey, without setting up a censorship over the post horses.

[*341] MEDNOE

"In the field a birch-tree stood, in the field a fluffy birch, oh lyuli, lyuli, lyuli, lyuli." — "A chorus of young women and girls — they're singing and dancing — let's look closer," I said to myself, as I unfolded my friend's papers that I had found. But I read what follows. I could not go nearer the chorus. Sorrow sealed my ears, and the joyous voice of innocent merriment did not penetrate to my heart. O my friend,[1] wherever you may be, listen and judge.

Twice every week the whole Russian Empire is notified that N. N. or B. B. is unable or unwilling to pay what he has borrowed or taken or what is demanded of him. The borrowed money has been spent in gambling, traveling, carousing, eating, drinking, etc., — or has been given away, lost in fire or water, or N. N. or B. B. [*342] has in some other way

---

* We read in the latest news that the successor of Joseph II intends to re-establish the Censorship Commission which had been abolished by his predecessor.

gone into debt or incurred an obligation. Whatever the circumstances, the same story is published in the newspapers. It runs like this: "At ten o'clock this morning, by order of the County Court, or the Municipal Magistrate, will be sold at public auction the real estate of Captain G., Retired, viz., a house located in — Ward, No. —, and with it six souls, male and female. The sale will take place at said house. Interested parties may examine the property before the auction."

There are always a lot of customers for a bargain. The day and hour of the auction have come. Prospective buyers are gathering. In the hall where it is to take place, those who are condemned to be sold stand immovable. An old man, seventy-five years of age, leaning on an elmwood cane, is anxious to find out into whose hands fate will deliver him, and who will close his eyes. He had been with his master's father in the Crimean Campaign, under [*343] Field Marshal Münnich.[2] In the Battle of Frankfurt[3] he had carried his wounded master on his shoulders from the field. On returning home he had become the tutor of his young master. In childhood he had saved him from drowning, for, jumping after him into the river into which he had fallen from a ferry, he had saved him at the risk of his own life. In youth he had ransomed him from prison, whither he had been cast for debts incurred while he was a subaltern of the Guards. The old woman, his wife, is eighty years of age. She had been the wet-nurse of the young master's mother; later she became his nurse and had the supervision of the house up to the very hour when she was brought out to this auction. During all the time of her service she had never wasted anything belonging to her masters, had never considered her personal advantage, never lied, and if she had ever annoyed them, she had done so by her scrupulous honesty. The forty-year-old woman is a widow, the young master's wet-nurse. To this very day she [*344] feels a certain tenderness for him. Her blood flows in his veins. She is his second mother, and he owes his life more to her than to his natural mother. The latter had conceived him in lust and did not take care of him in his childhood. His nurses had really brought him up. They part from him as from a son. The eighteen-year-old girl is her daughter and the old man's granddaughter. Beast, monster, outcast among men! Look at her, look at her crimson cheeks, at the tears flowing from her beautiful eyes. When you could neither ensnare her innocence with enticements and promises nor shake her steadfastness with threats and punishments, did you not finally use deception, and, having married her to the companion of your abominations, did you not in his guise enjoy the pleasures she scorned to share with you? She discovered your deception. Her bridegroom did not touch her couch again, and since you were thus deprived of the object of your lust, [*345] you employed force. Four evildoers, your henchmen, holding her arms and legs — let us not go on with this. On her brow is sorrow, in her eyes despair. She is holding a little one, the lamentable fruit of deception or violence, but the living image of his lascivious father. Having given birth to him, she forgot his father's beastliness and her heart began to feel a tenderness for him. But now she fears that she may fall into the hands of another like his father. The little one — . Thy son, barbarian, thy blood! Or do you think that where there was no church rite, there was no obligation? Or do you think that a blessing given at your command by a hired preacher of the word of God has established their union? Or do you think that a forced wedding in God's temple can be called marriage? The Almighty hates compulsion; He rejoices at the wishes of the heart. They alone are pure. Oh, how many acts of adultery and violation [*346] are committed among us in the name of the Father of joys and the Comforter of sorrows, in the presence of His witnesses, who are unworthy of their calling! The lad of twenty-five, her wedded husband, the companion and intimate of his master. Savagery and vengeance are in his eyes. He repents the service he did his master. In his pocket is a knife; he clutches it firmly; it is not difficult to guess his thought — . A hopeless fancy! You will become the property of another. The master's hand, constantly raised over his slave's head, will bend your neck to his every pleasure. Hunger, cold, heat, punishment, everything will be against you. Noble thoughts are foreign to your mind. You do not know how to die. You will bow down and be a slave in spirit as in estate. And if you should try to offer resistance, you would die a languishing death in fetters. There is no judge between you. If your tormentor does not wish to punish you himself, he will become your accuser. He will hand [*347] you over to the governmental justice. Justice! Where the accused has almost no chance to justify himself! Let us pass by the other unfortunates who have been brought out for sale.

Scarcely had the dreadful hammer come down with its dull thud, and the four [4] unfortunates learned their fate, when tears, sobs, and groans pierced the ears of the whole gathering. The most stolid were touched. Stony hearts! Of what use is fruitless compassion? O ye Quakers! If we had your souls, we would take up a collection, buy these unfortunates, and set them free.[5] Having lived together for many years heart to heart, these unfortunates in consequence of this abominable auction will feel the anguish of parting. But if the law, or rather, the barbarous custom, for nothing is said about it in the law, permits such contempt for humanity, what right have you to sell this child? He is an illegitimate child. The law [*348] sets him free.[6] Stop! I will denounce this violation of the law; I will deliver him. If I could only save the others with him! O fortune! Why have you given me so miserably inadequate a portion? Today I long to enjoy your sweet favor, for the first time I begin to feel a passion for wealth. My heart was so troubled that, rushing away from the gathering and giving the last dime in my purse to the unfortunate people, I ran away. On the staircase I met a foreigner, a friend of mine.

"What's happened to you? You're weeping."

"Turn back," I said to him, "and do not be a witness to this shameful spectacle. You once cursed the barbarous custom of selling black slaves in the distant colonies of your country. Go away," I repeated, "and do not be a witness of our benightedness, lest, in talking to your fellow citizens about our customs, you have to report our shame."

"I cannot believe it," [*349] my friend replied. "It is impossible that in a land where everyone is allowed to think and to believe what he pleases, such a shameful custom should exist."

"Do not be amazed," I answered; "the establishment of religious freedom offends only the priests and monks, and even they would rather acquire a sheep for themselves than for Christ's flock. But freedom for the peasants offends, as they say, against the right of property. But all those who might be the champions of freedom are great landed proprietors, and freedom is not to be expected from their counsels, but from the heavy burden of slavery itself." [7]

[*350] TVER'

"Prosody with us," said my companion at dinner in the restaurant, "in the various senses in which it is understood, is still far from greatness. Poetry awoke, but has now gone back to sleep again, and versification took one step forward and then came to a standstill.

"Lomonosov recognized that our verses were ridiculous in Polish dress and stripped them of this unbecoming vestment.[1] He created good exemplars of the new verses and saddled his followers with his great example, and so far no one has dared to depart from it. Unfortunately, Sumarokov happened to live at the same time, and he was an excellent poet.[2] He wrote verses after the manner of Lomonosov, and now everyone, following in their wake, is unable to imagine that there could be any verses other than iambics [*351] such as both these famous men wrote. Although both these poets set forth the rules for other forms of versification, and Sumarokov left examples of poetry in all forms, they are so insignificant that they did not deserve any imitation. If Lomonosov had translated Job or the Psalms in dactyls, or if Sumarokov had written *Semira* or *Demetrius*[3] in trochees, Kheraskov would have realized that it is possible to write other verses than iambics, and he would have won greater glory from his labor of eight years by describing the conquest of Kazan' in a meter more appropriate to epic poetry.[4] I am not surprised that they have decked out Virgil in a three-cornered hat of the Lomonosov fashion,[5] but I do wish that Homer had not appeared among us in iambics, but in a meter corresponding to his own, in hexameter. Then Kostrov, although not an original poet but a translator, would have had an epoch-making effect on our versification; [*352] he would have advanced the progress of our poetry a whole generation.[6]

"But it is not only Lomonosov and Sumarokov who have arrested Russian versification. The tireless truck-horse Tredyakovsky contributed not a little to that end with his *Telemakhida*.[7] It is very difficult now to find an instance of a new kind of versification, because the old models of good and bad poetry have taken deep root. Parnassus is girded about with iambics, and rhymes stand guard everywhere. If anyone should think of writing in dactyls, Tredyakovsky will immediately be set up as a tutor over him, and the most beautiful child will be deemed a monster, until a Milton, Shakespeare, or Voltaire is born. Even then they will dig up Tredyakovsky from the oblivion of his moss-grown grave and find in the *Telemakhida* some good verses to cite as models.

"Wholesome change in prosody will long be hindered by [*353] the ear habitually accustomed to rhyme. When it has for a long time listened to the harmonious ending of verses, unrhymed verse will seem coarse, rough, and formless. Such it will indeed be, so long as the French language is employed more than any other in Russia. Our sentiments may grow straight or crooked, like a supple young tree, at our option. Besides, in poetry as in all things, fashion may prevail, and if it has anything natural about it, it will be accepted without gainsaying. But everything fashionable is ephemeral, especially in poetry. Superficial luster may grow dim, but true beauty will never fade. Homer, Virgil, Milton, Racine, Voltaire, Shakespeare, Tasso, and many others will be read until the human race is destroyed.

"I consider it superfluous to discuss with you the various meters [*354] congenial to the Russian language. Everyone who has the faintest idea about the rules of prosody knows what an iamb, trochee, dactyl, or anapest is. Even so, it would not be beside the point for me to give adequate illustrations of each kind. My strength and knowledge, however, are limited. If my advice is worth anything, I would say that Russian poetry, yes, and the Russian language itself would be greatly enriched if translations of poetic works were not always made in iambics. It would have been far more appropriate if the *Henriade*, as an epic poem, had not been translated in iambics,[8] and unrhymed iambics are worse than prose."

My table companion spouted all this in one breath and so glibly that I could not say anything in reply, although I had many things to say in defense of iambics and of those who had written in them.

[*355] "I myself," he continued, "have followed the infectious example and have written iambic verses, but that was in odes. Here is the only one that is left of the whole lot, for the rest were consumed in a fire, and the same fate that met its fellows awaits this one. In Moscow they did not want to print it for two reasons, first, because the meaning of the verses was not clear and many verses were clumsy; second, because the subject of the verses was not suitable for our country. Now I am on my way to Petersburg to petition for

its publication, and I flatter myself, as a tender father of my child, that just because of the second reason for which they did not want to print it in Moscow, they will indulgently overlook the first. If it isn't a bother to you to read a few stanzas — " he said as he handed me a paper. I unfolded it and read the following: *Liberty: An Ode*.[9] "The very title in itself caused them to forbid me to print the verses. [*356] But I well remember that the *Instruction for the Composition of a New Code of Laws* says of liberty: 'Liberty means that all obey the same laws.'[10] Hence it is permissible among us to speak of liberty."

1.[11]

O blessed gift of the heavens, source of all great deeds, O Liberty, Liberty, priceless gift! Permit a slave to sing of you. Fill my heart with your fire; with the stroke of your mighty arms, transform serfdom's night into light. Let Brutus and Tell wake once more, and let kings enthroned in [tyrannous] might[12] be dismayed at your voice.

"This stanza was condemned for two reasons: first, because the verse 'transform serfdom's night into light'[13] is very stiff and hard to pronounce on account of the frequent [*357] repetition of the letter 'T' and the piling up of too many consonants. In 'serfdom's night' there are ten consonants to three vowels, whereas it is possible to write as melodiously in Russian as in Italian — . Agreed — although some thought this verse successful, finding in the roughness of the verse an onomatopoetic expression of the very laboriousness of the action — . The second objection: 'Let kings be dismayed at your voice.' To wish a king dismay is to wish him evil, consequently — . But I do not want to tire you with all the remarks made about my verses. Many of them, I must confess, were justified. Let me read it to you.

2.

I came into the world and you with me. . . .
We shall omit this stanza. Its theme is: man is free in all things from birth —.

[*358] 3.

But what stands in the way of my freedom? Everywhere I behold a barrier to my yearnings; a communal power has arisen in the people, the source of power everywhere. Society obeys it in everything, and is everywhere of one accord with it. No limits are set to the general welfare. In the power of all I see my lot: in doing the will of all, I do my own: this is what law in society means.

4.

Amidst a fertile dale, amidst fields heavy with grain, where tender lilies bloom, in the shade of peaceful olive trees, whiter than Parian marble, brighter than the rays of the brightest day, stands a temple open to every view. There no false sacrifice swirls up in smoke, there the fiery inscription may be seen: 'Have done with the miseries of the innocent!"

[*359] 5.

Crowned with an olive branch, seated upon a hard stone, dispassionate and cold, a deaf divinity. . . .
And so forth. Law is represented in the form of a divinity within a temple whose guards are Truth and Justice.

6.

He lifts up his stern countenance, and spreads joy and terror around him; he looks with equanimity upon all persons, neither hating nor loving. He ignores flattery, subservience, high descent, eminence, wealth; and despises mortal offerings; he knows neither ties of blood nor of friendship, and distributes rewards and punishments impartially: he is the image of God on earth.

7.

Behold a horrible monster, hydra-like, with a hundred heads! [*360] It looks mild and its eyes are ever full of tears, but its jaws are full of venom. It tramples upon the earthly powers, and stretches its head up toward Heaven, which it claims as its native home. It sows false phantoms and darkness everywhere, it knows how to deceive and flatter, and commands all to believe blindly.

8.

It has enshrouded reason in darkness, and everywhere it spreads its creeping poison; . . .

The portrayal of religious superstition, robbing man of sensitiveness, enticing him into the yoke of slavery, and clothing him in the armor of error:[14]

It commands him to fear the truth. . . .

[Tyrannous] power calls this monster Revelation; reason calls it Deceit.

9.

Let us look into the vast regions where the tarnished throne of slavery stands;

[*361] In peace and quiet, religious and political superstition, each supporting the other,

join to oppress society. The one tries to fetter reason, the other strives to destroy the will: "For the common good," they say.

10.

In the shadow of slavish peace no golden fruit can

grow; where everything hinders the spirit's striving, nothing great can thrive.
And all the evil consequences of slavery, such as recklessness, idleness, trickery, hunger, and so forth.

11.

Raising his haughty brow and grasping his iron scepter, the king seats himself augustly on the throne of terror and sees his people only as base creatures. Holding life and death in his hands, he says: "At will I can spare the evildoer [*362] or delegate my power. When I laugh, all laugh; if I frown threateningly, all are confounded. You live only so long as I permit you to live."

12.

And we look on calmly. . .
as the ravenous dragon, reviling all, poisons their days of joy and happiness. But though all stand before your throne with bended knees, tremble, for, lo, the avenger comes, proclaiming liberty. . . .

13.

Everywhere martial hosts will arise, hope will arm all; everyone hastens to wash off his shame in the blood of the crowned tormentor. Everywhere I see the flash of the sharp sword; death, flying about in various forms, hovers over the proud head. Rejoice, fettered peoples! [*363] The avenging law of nature has brought the king to the block.

14.

Having rent the curtain of deceptive night with a mighty thunderbolt, having overthrown the enormous idol of haughty and stubborn power, having fettered the hundred-armed giant, it drags him to the throne, where the people now sit. "Violator of the power I granted you! Speak, villain whom I crowned, how dared you rise against me?

15.

"I clad you in the purple that you might preserve equality in society, watch over the widow and orphan, save innocence from calamity and be its loving father, but an implacable enemy of vice, the lie, and calumny; that you might reward merit with honor, forestall evil through order, and maintain purity of morals.

[*364] 16.

"I have covered the sea with ships. . . . I have provided means for achieving wealth and well-being. I desired that the peasant should not be a captive in his field, and that he should bless you. . . .

17.

"Ruthlessly, out of my own blood, I raised up a mighty host; I cast the brazen cannon with which to punish your external enemies. I commanded them to obey you and with you to strive for glory. For the common good, all things are permitted me. I tear up the bowels of the earth and extract the glittering metal for your adornment.

18.

"But you, forgetting the oath you swore to me, forgetting that I had chosen you, came to think that you had been crowned for your own pleasure, and that you were the master, not I. [*365] With the sword you destroyed my laws; you silenced all rights; you made truth blush with shame. You have opened the door to all abominations, you have begun to appeal not to me, but to God, and you thought you could scorn me.

19.

"Garnering with bloody sweat the fruit I planted for sustenance, dividing my crumbs with you, I did not spare my strength. But to you all treasures are insufficient! Tell me, what did you lack, to justify your tearing the rags off my back? To reward a sycophantic courtier or a woman lost to honor! Or have you made gold your god?

20.

"You gave to the arrogant the token of distinction established to reward the deserving; you brandished against the innocent my sword, sharpened against evildoers. [*366] The hosts brought together for the defense of the homeland — are you leading them into glorious battle to avenge suffering humanity? You fight in bloody fields so that tipsy Athenians, yawning, may call you a hero.[15]

21.

"O evildoer, worst of all evildoers. . .
You have combined all crimes in yourself and have directed your sting against me. . . .
Die, then, die a hundred deaths."
So spake the people. . . .

22.

O great man full of perfidy, hypocrite, flatterer, blasphemer! You alone might have given the world a great example of benevolence. I consider you, Cromwell, a criminal, because, having power in your hands, you destroyed the citadel of freedom. But you have taught generation after generation how nations can avenge themselves; you had Charles executed by due process of law.

[*367] 23.

The voice of freedom resounds on all sides. . . .
The whole nation streams to the assembly; it destroys the iron throne, and, as Samson did of yore, it pulls down the perfidious palace. It builds the citadel of nature on the foundation of the law. Thou art great, aye great indeed, Spirit of Liberty; creative as God Himself!

24.

The next eleven stanzas consist of an account of the kingdom of Liberty and its achievements, that is, security, peace, well-being, greatness. . . .

34.
But the passions that goad men to madness. . .
turn the civil peace into disaster. . . .
stir the father up against the son, tear asunder the bonds of marriage,
and bring all the dread consequences of boundless lust for power. . . .

[*368] 35. 36. 37.

Description of the ruinous consequences of luxury. Civil discord. Civil war. Marius, Sulla, Augustus. . . .
He put troublesome freedom to sleep, and wound flowers around the iron scepter. . . .
Thence came slavery. . . .

38. 39.

This is the law of nature: from tyranny, freedom is born; from freedom, slavery. . . .

40.

Why marvel at this, for man, too, is born to die. . . . The following eight stanzas contain prophecies about the future fate of our country, which will fall into separate parts — all the sooner, the greater it grows. But the time for that has not yet come. When it comes, then

The heavy fetters of night will break.

Even in its death throes, stubborn Power will set up a guard against free speech, and gather all its strength for its expiring [*369] effort to crush rising freedom. . . .

49.

But humanity will roar in its fetters, and, moved by the hope of freedom and the indestructible law of nature, will push on. . . . And tyranny will be dismayed. Then the united force of all despotism, of all oppressive power

Will in a moment be dispersed. O chosen day of days!

50.

Even now I hear the voice of nature, the primal voice, the voice of the Godhead.

The dark citadel totters, and liberty shines forth with a glorious radiance.

"That's the end," the newfangled poet said. I was very glad of it, and wanted to say something to him, perhaps raise an unpleasant objection to his verses, but the bell reminded me that in traveling it is better to make reasonable haste with post nags than to climb on Pegasus when he is mettlesome.

[*370] GORODNYA

As I drove into this village, my ears were assailed not by the melody of verse, but by a heart-rending lament of women, children, and old men. Getting out of my carriage, I sent it on to the post station, for I was curious to learn the cause of the disturbance I had noticed in the street.

Going up to one group of people, I learned that a levy of recruits was the cause of the sobs and tears of the people crowded together there. From many villages, both crown and manorial, those who were to be drafted into the army had come together here.

In one group an old woman fifty years of age, holding the head of a lad of twenty, was sobbing. "My dear child, to whose care are you committing me? To whom will you entrust the home of your parents? Our fields will be overgrown with grass, our hut with moss. I, your poor old mother, will have to wander [*371] about begging. Who will warm my decrepit body when it is cold, who will protect it from the heat? Who will give me food and drink? But all that does not weigh so heavily upon my heart as this: who will close my eyes when I die? Who will receive my maternal blessing? Who will return my body to our common mother, the moist earth? Who will come to remember me at my grave? Your warm tears will not fall upon it; I shall not have that consolation."

Near the old woman stood a grown-up girl. She, too, was sobbing. "Farewell, friend of my heart; farewell, my shining sun. I, your betrothed, will never know comfort or joy again. My friends will not envy me. The sun will not rise for me in joy. You are leaving me to pine away, neither a widow nor a wedded wife. If our inhuman village elders had only let us get married, if you, my darling, [*372] could have slept but one short night on my white breast. Perhaps God would have taken pity on me and given me a little son to comfort me."

The lad said to them: "Stop weeping, stop rending my heart. Our Sovereign calls us to service. The lot fell on me. It is the will of God. Those not fated to die will live. Perhaps I will come home to you with the regiment. I may even win rank and honors. Dear Mother, do not grieve. Take care of my Praskov'yushka." This recruit was drafted from an Economic village.[1]

From another group standing nearby I heard altogether different words. Amidst them I saw a man of about thirty, of medium size, standing erect and looking happily at the people around him. "The Lord has heard my prayers," he said. "The tears of an unfortunate man have reached the Comforter of all men. Now [*373] I shall at least know that my lot may depend on my own good or bad behavior. Heretofore it depended on the arbitrary whims of a woman. I am consoled by the thought that hereafter I shall not be flogged without a fair trial!"

Having gathered from what he said that he was a manorial serf, I was curious to learn the cause of his unusual joy. To my question he replied: "Dear sir, if a gallows were placed on one side of you and a deep river ran on the other, and you, standing between these two perils, could not possibly escape going either to the right or to the left, into the noose or into the water, which would you choose? Which would sense and impulse make you prefer? I think everyone would rather jump into the river, in the hope of escaping from peril by swimming to the other shore. No one would willingly investigate [*374] the strength of the noose by putting his neck into it. This was my situation. A soldier's life is a hard one, but better than the noose. Even that would be all right, if that were the end, but to die a lingering death under the cudgel, under the cat-o'-nine-tails, in chains, in a dungeon, naked, barefooted, hungry, thirsty, under constant abuse — my lord, although you look upon your peasants as your property, often less regarded than cattle, yet, unfortunately, they are not without feeling. You appear to be surprised to hear such words from the lips of a peasant; but why, when you hear them, are you not surprised at the cruelty of your brothers, the noblemen?"

And in very truth I had not expected such words from a man dressed in a gray caftan and with his head shaven.[2] But wishing to satisfy my curiosity, I asked him to tell me how, being of such a low estate, he had arrived at ideas which are [*375] frequently lacking in men improperly said to be nobly born.

"If it will not tire you to hear my story, I will tell you: I was born in slavery, the son of my master's former valet.³ How happy I am to think that they will never again call me Van'ka⁴ or any other offensive name, that they will never again call me like a dog by whistling. My old master, a kindhearted, reasonable, and virtuous man, who often lamented the fate of his slaves, wanted, on account of my father's long service, to do something special for me; so he gave me the same education as his son. There was hardly any difference between us, except that the cloth of his coat was perhaps better. Whatever they taught the young master, they taught me, too; our instruction was exactly the same, and I can say without boasting that in many things I did better than my young master.

[*376] "'Vanyusha,'⁵ the old master said to me, 'your happiness depends entirely on you. You have more of an inclination for learning and morality than my son. He will be rich by inheritance and will know no want, while you have known it from birth. So try to be worthy of the pains I have taken for you.' When my young master was in his seventeenth year, he and I were sent to travel abroad with a tutor, who was told to look upon me as a traveling companion, not a servant. As he sent me away, my old master said to me: 'I hope that you will return to give me and your parents joy. You are a slave within the borders of this country, but beyond them you are free. When you return, you will not find fetters imposed upon you because of your birth.' We were away for five years and then returned to Russia, my young master happy at the thought of seeing [*377] his father, and I, I must confess, flattering myself that I would obtain what I had been promised. My heart was atremble as I again entered the borders of my country. And indeed my foreboding was not false. In Riga my young master received the news of his

father's death. He was deeply moved by it; I was thrown into despair. For all my efforts to win his friendship and confidence had been in vain. Not only did he not love me, but — perhaps from envy, as is characteristic of small souls — he hated me.

"Observing the anxiety produced in me by the death of his father, he told me he would not forget the promise that had been made to me, if I would be worthy of it. It was the first time he had ventured to tell me so, for, having received control of his property through the death of his father, he had dismissed his tutor in Riga, paying him liberally for his labors. [*378] I must do justice to my former master: he has many good qualities, but timidity of spirit and thoughtlessness obscure them.

"A week after our arrival in Moscow, my master fell in love with a pretty girl, but one who with her bodily beauty combined a very ugly soul and a hard and cruel heart. Brought up in the conceit of her station, she respected only external show, rank, and wealth. In two months she became my master's wife, and I became her slave. Until then I had not experienced any change in my condition and had lived in my master's house as his companion. Although he never gave me any orders, I generally anticipated his wishes, as I was aware of his power and of my position. Scarcely had the young [*379] mistress crossed the threshold of the house, in which she was determined to rule, before I was made aware of my hard lot. On the first evening after the wedding and all next day, when I was introduced to her by her husband as his companion, she was occupied with the usual cares of a bride; but in the evening, when a fairly large company came to the table and sat down to the first supper with the newly married pair, and I sat down in my usual place at the lower end of the table, the new mistress said to her husband in a fairly loud voice that if he wished her to sit at the table with the guests, he must not permit any serfs to sit there. He looked at me and, at her instance, sent word to me that I should leave the table and eat my supper in my room. Imagine how deeply this humiliation hurt me! I suppressed the tears that came [*380] to my eyes, and withdrew. I did not dare to make my appearance the next day. They brought me my dinner and supper without saying anything to me. And so it went on succeeding days. One afternoon, a week after the wedding, the new mistress inspected the house, and, after apportioning the duties and living quarters to all the servants, entered my rooms also. They had been furnished for me by my old master. I was not at home. I will not repeat what she said there, to ridicule me, but when I returned home they gave me her order, whereby I was sent down to a corner on the ground floor with the unmarried servants, where my bed and my trunk, with my clothes and linens, had already been placed; all my other things she had left in my former rooms, in which she installed her serving maids.

"What took place in my soul when I heard this is easier to feel, if you can, than to describe. But [*381] so as not to detain you with superfluous details: my mistress, after taking control of the house and finding that I had no aptitude for service, made me a lackey and decked me out in livery. The least, imaginary remissness in my duties led to my ears being boxed, beatings, and the cat-o'-nine-tails. O, my lord, it would have been better if I had never been born! How many times did I complain against my dead benefactor for having fostered a responsive soul in me. It would have been better for me if I had grown up in ignorance and had never learned that I am a man, equal to all others. Long, long ago I would have freed myself from my hateful life, if I had not been held back by the prohibition of our Supreme Judge. I determined to bear my lot patiently. And I endured not only bodily wounds, but also those which she inflicted upon my soul. But I almost broke my vow and cut short the miserable remains [*382] of my woeful life as a result of a new blow to my soul.

"A nephew of my mistress, a youngster of eighteen years, a sergeant of the Guards, educated in the fashion of Moscow dandies, became enamored of a chambermaid of his aunt's, and, having quickly won her ready favors, made her a mother. Although he was usually quite unconcerned in his amours, in this case he was somewhat embarrassed. For his aunt, having learned about the affair, forbade the chambermaid her presence, and gently scolded her nephew. She intended, after the fashion of benevolent mistresses, to punish the one whom she had formerly favored by marrying her off to one of the stable boys. But since they were all married already, and since, for the honor of the house, there had to be a husband for the pregnant woman, she selected me as the worst of all the servants. In the presence of her husband, my mistress informed me of this as though it were a special favor. [*383] I could not stand this abuse any longer. 'Inhuman woman!' I cried. 'You have the power to torment me and to wound my body; you say the laws give you the right to do this. I hardly believe it, but I know full well that no one can be forced to marry.' She listened to my words in ominous silence. Then I turned to her husband and said: 'Ungrateful son of a generous father, you have forgotten his last will and testament, you have forgotten your own promise; but do not drive to despair a soul nobler than yours! Beware!' I could say no more, because, by command of my mistress, I was taken to the stable and whipped mercilessly with the cat-o'-nine-tails. The next day I could hardly get up out of bed from the beating; but I was brought before my mistress again. 'I will forgive you your impudence of yesterday,' she said; 'marry my Mavrushka; she begs you to, [*384] and I want to do this for her, because I love her even in her transgression.' 'You heard my answer yesterday,' I said; 'I have no other. I will only add that I will complain to the authorities against you for compelling me to do what you have no right to.' 'Then it's time for you to become a soldier!" my mistress screamed in a fury. — A traveler who has lost his way in a terrible desert will rejoice less when he finds it again than I did when I heard these words. 'Take him to be a soldier!' she repeated, and the next day it was done. Fool! She thought that being made a soldier would be a punishment for me, as it is for the peasants. For me it was a joy, and as soon as they had shaved my forehead, I felt like a new man. My strength was restored. My mind and spirit began to revive. O hope, sweet solace of the unfortunate, remain with me!" A heavy tear, but not [*385] a tear of grief and despair, fell from his eyes. I pressed him to my heart. His countenance was radiant with new joy. "All is not yet lost," he said; "you arm my soul against sorrow by making me feel that my misery is not endless."

From this unfortunate man I went to a group in which I saw three men fettered in the strongest irons. "It is amazing," I said to myself as I looked at these prisoners, "now they are downcast, weary, timid, and they not only do not want to become soldiers, but the greatest severity is required to force them into that status; but as soon as they become accustomed to the execution of their hard duty, they grow alert and spirited, and even look with scorn upon their former condition." I asked one of the bystanders who, to judge from his uniform, was a government clerk: [*386] "No doubt you have put them in such heavy fetters because you are afraid they will run away?"

"You guessed it. They belonged to a landed proprietor who needed money for a new carriage and got it by selling them to crown peasants, to be levied into the army."

I. — "My friend, you are mistaken. Crown peasants can't purchase their brothers."

He. — "It isn't done in the form of a sale. Having by agreement received the money, the master sets these unfortunates free; they are presumed to be 'voluntarily' registered as crown peasants of the commune which paid the money for them; and the commune, by common consent, sends them to be soldiers. They are now being taken with their emancipation papers to be registered in our commune."

Free men, who have committed no crime, are fettered, and sold like cattle! O laws! Your wisdom frequently resides only in your [*387] style! Is this not an open mockery? And, what is worse, a mockery of the sacred name of liberty. Oh, if the slaves weighted down with fetters, raging in their despair, would, with the iron that bars their freedom, crush our heads, the heads of their inhuman masters, and redden their fields with our blood! What would the country lose by that? Soon great men would arise from among them, to take the place of the murdered generation; but they would be of another mind and without the right to oppress others. This is no dream; my vision penetrates the dense curtain of time that veils the future from our eyes. I look through the space of a whole century. I left the crowd in disgust.

But the fettered prisoners are free now. If they had any fortitude, they could put to naught the oppressive intentions of their tyrants. Let us go back to them. — "My friends," I said [*388] to the captives, these prisoners of war in their own country, "do you know that if you do not freely wish to enter the army, no one can now compel you to do so?" "Stop making fun of poor wretches, sir. Even without your jesting, it was hard enough for us to part, one from his poor old father, another from his little sisters, a third from his young wife. We know that our master sold us as recruits for a thousand rubles."

"If you did not know it before, you must know now that it is against the law to sell men as recruits, that peasants cannot legally buy men, that your master has set you free, and that the purchasers intend to register you in their commune, as though of your own free will."

"O, sir, if that is really so, we do thank you. When they line us up for muster, we will all say that we do not want to become soldiers and that we are free men."

"Add to [*389] it that your master sold you at a time when such a sale was not legal, and that they are delivering you up as recruits in violation of the law." * One can easily imagine the joy that lighted up the faces of these unfortunates. Leaping up from their places and vigorously shaking their fetters, they seemed to be testing their strength, as though they would shake them off. But this conversation could have gotten me into serious trouble, for the recruiting officers, having heard what I said, rushed toward me in violent anger, and said, "Sir, don't meddle with other people's business, and get away while the getting's good!" When I resisted, they pushed me so violently that I was forced to leave this crowd as fast as I could.

As I approached the post station, I found another gathering of peasants, surrounding [*390] a man in a torn coat. He seemed to be somewhat drunk. He was making faces at the people, who laughed till the tears came, watching him. "What is it all about?" I asked a boy. "What are you laughing at?"

"Well, the recruit is a foreigner and can't speak a word of Russian." From the few words he spoke, I gathered that he was a Frenchman. That made me still more curious; I wanted to find out how a foreigner could be offered as a recruit by the peasants. I asked him in his native tongue: "My friend, by what fate did you get here?"

Frenchman. — "Fate wanted it so. Where things go well, there one should stay."

I. — "How did you become a recruit?"

Frenchman. — "I love a soldier's life. I've known it before, and I wanted it."

[*391] I. — "But how does it happen that you are sent

---

* During the time of a levying of recruits, it is against the law to make any contract for the sale of serfs.[6]

from a village? Usually they take only peasants, and Russians at that, as soldiers from the villages; but I see that you are neither a peasant nor a Russian."

Frenchman. — "It happened this way. As a child I was apprenticed to a hairdresser in Paris. I left for Russia with a gentleman whose hair I dressed for a whole year in Petersburg. He had no money to pay me; so I left him and almost starved to death, looking for a job. Luckily I got a berth as a sailor, on a ship flying the Russian flag. Before putting to sea, I had to take an oath as a Russian subject; then we set off for Lübeck. On the way the bosun often beat me with a rope's end for being lazy. Through my carelessness I fell from the rigging to the deck and broke three fingers, which ruined me for [*392] ever dressing hair again. When we got to Lübeck I fell in with Prussian recruiting officers and served in various regiments. They often took the stick to me for being lazy or drunk. When I was stationed in the garrison at Memel, I got drunk one day and stabbed a fellow; so I had to get out of there in a hurry. Remembering that I had taken my oath in Russia and that I was a faithful son of the fatherland, I started out for Riga, with two thalers in my pocket. On the way I lived on charity. In Riga my good luck and skill served me in good stead. I won some twenty rubles in a tavern, bought myself a good overcoat for ten, and went off with a Kazan' merchant as his lackey. As we were going along a street in Moscow, I met two of my countrymen, who advised me to leave my master and look for a teaching job in Moscow. I told them I could hardly read, but they said, 'You talk French [*393] — that's enough.' My master did not see me leaving him on the street, and kept on his way, while I stayed in Moscow. My countrymen soon found me a teaching job paying a hundred and fifty rubles a year, plus a pood of sugar, a pood of coffee, ten pounds [7] of tea, my board, a servant, and carriage. But I had to live in the country. So much the better. There they didn't find out for a whole year that I couldn't write. But some one of my master's in-laws, who was living at the same place, gave my secret away to him, and they took me back to Moscow. I couldn't find such another fool, I couldn't dress hair with my broken fingers, and I was afraid I'd starve to death; so I sold myself for two hundred rubles. They registered me as a peasant, and now they're sending me as a recruit. I hope," he said with an important air, "that as soon as a war comes along, I'll get to be a general; and if there isn't any war, I'll stuff my pockets (if possible), [*394] and, crowned with laurel, return to my country for a well-earned rest."

More than once I shrugged my shoulders as I listened to this rogue, and with a heavy heart I lay down in my carriage and continued on my journey.[8]

[*395] ZAVIDOVO

The horses were already hitched to the carriage, and I was getting ready to depart, when suddenly a great commotion arose in the street. People started running, from one end of the village to the other. In the street I saw a warrior in a grenadier's cap, strutting proudly, swinging a whip aloft, and shouting: "Horses! And be quick about it! Where's the elder? His Excellency will be here in a minute. Get me the elder!" — The elder, pulling his hat off while still a hundred steps away, was running full speed, in response to the call. "Horses! Quick!" "At once, sir! Your traveling permit, please?" "Here. But hurry, or I'll — " he said, as he raised the whip over the head of the trembling elder. His unfinished speech was as expressive as Virgil's speech of Aeolus to the winds in the *Aeneid*: [*396] "Quos ego! . . ."[1] Cringing at the sight of the imperious grenadier's whip, the elder felt the might of the threatening warrior's right hand as vividly as the riotous winds felt the power of the sharp Aeolian trident. As he returned the traveling permit to the latter-day Polkan,[2] the elder said: "His Excellency with his honorable family require fifty horses, but we have only thirty here present; the others are on the road."

"Produce them, old devil! If there are no horses, I'll mangle you."

"But where shall I take them from if there aren't any to take?"

"Still talking —. But I *will* have those horses" — and, seizing the old man by his beard, he began to lash his shoulders unmercifully with the whip. "Is that enough for you? Here are three fresh horses," said the stern judge of the post station, pointing to those that were hitched to my carriage. "Take these out for us."

"If the gentleman will give them up."

"How would he dare not [*397] to give them up? If he doesn't, he'll catch it from me just as you did. Who is he, anyway?"

"God only knows —." With what name he honored me I do not know.

Meanwhile I had gone into the street and prevented the brave forerunner of His Excellency from carrying out his intention of unhitching the horses from my carriage and thereby compelling me to pass the night at the post station.

My dispute with Polkan of the Guards was interrupted by the arrival of His Excellency. One could hear from afar the shouts of the drivers and the tramp of the horses galloping full speed. The rapid-fire clanging of hoofs and the whirling of wheels, too swift for the eye to follow, choked the air so much with the rising dust that His Excellency's carriage was veiled by an impenetrable cloud from the view of the drivers, who were awaiting his arrival as anxiously as that of a thundercloud. Don Quixote, of course, would have observed something marvelous here, for [*398] the dust cloud hovering about the august person of His Excellency suddenly stopped, split apart — and he burst upon us, gray with dust, like a son of darkness.

From my arrival at the post station to the time when the horses were hitched to my carriage again, at least a whole hour passed. But His Excellency's carriages were hitched up in no more than fifteen minutes — and away they flew, on the wings of the wind. But my nags, which seemed better than those which had been considered worthy to carry the person of His Excellency, not being afraid of the grenadier's whip, went at a moderate trot.

Blessed are the magnates in autocratic countries. Blessed are those who are decked out with ribbons and orders. All nature obeys them. Even the unreasoning brutes seek to please them, and, lest their yawning lordships find the journey too wearisome, the beasts gallop without sparing their legs and [*399] lungs, and often die of exhaustion. Blessed, I repeat, are they whose exterior fills all with awe. Of all those who tremble under the threatening whip, who knows that he in whose name they are threatened is categorized as "dumb" in the *Court Grammar*; that he never in all his life has been able to utter so much as "A" or "O"; * that he is ashamed to admit to whom he owes his high station; that in his soul he is a most vile creature; that deception, perfidy, treason, lechery, poisoning, robbery, extortion, and murder are no more to him than emptying a glass of water; that his cheeks have never blushed with shame, but often with anger or from a box on the ear; that he is a friend of every Court stoker and the slave of everybody, even the meanest creature, at Court? [*400] But he pretends to be a great lord and is contemptuous toward those who are not aware of his base and crawling servility. High dignity without true worth is like the sorcerers in our villages. All the peasants respect and fear them, thinking that they have supernatural powers. These cheats rule over them at will. But as soon as in their crowd of worshipers one turns up who has to some extent freed himself from the grossest superstition, their deception is laid bare, and they will not

---

* Compare the manuscript *Court Grammar* of Fon-Vizin.[3]

tolerate such clear-headed men in the place where they work their wonders. Similarly, let him beware who would dare to expose the sorcery of the magnates.

What would have been the use of chasing after His Excellency? He raised a column of dust which disappeared as soon as he was gone, and when I arrived at Klin, I found that even his memory had already vanished along with his noise.

[*401] KLIN

"It was in the city of Rome that Prince Euphemius lived — " Singing this folk song called "Aleksey the Man of God" [1] was a blind old man, sitting by the gate of the post station, surrounded by a crowd, mostly of children and young people. His silvery head, closed eyes, and the peaceful expression on his face caused the singer's audience to stand in awe before him. His song, artless but marked by touching sweetness of expression, moved the hearts of his listeners, who were more attentive to nature than the inhabitants of Moscow and Petersburg, accustomed to harmony, are to the elaborate melodies of Gabrielli, Marchesi, or Todi.[2] Not one of the bystanders was free from a deep inward agitation when the bard of Klin, [*402] having reached his hero's parting, was scarcely able to continue his tale in ever more broken accents. The hollows where his eyes had been were filled with tears proceeding from a soul made sensitive by misfortune, and they flowed down his cheeks in streams. O nature, how mighty thou art! As the women beheld the old man weeping, they burst into sobs; from the lips of youth flitted its customary smiles; on the face of childhood appeared timidity, a sure sign of painful but uncertain feeling; even adult manhood, so used to cruelty, assumed a serious expression. O nature! I cried again — .

How sweet is innocent sorrow! How it refreshes the heart and its responsive power. I wept in company with all the others at the post station, and my tears were as sweet to me as those which had once been called forth by Werther.³ O [*403] my friend, my friend!⁴ Why did you not see this picture? You would have shed tears with me, and the bliss of mutual feeling would have been even sweeter.

At the end of the song, all the bystanders gave him something, as though in reward for his labor. He accepted all the ha'pennies and farthings, all the slices and crusts of bread, quite calmly; but bowed with each expression of his thanks, made the sign of the cross, and said to the giver: "May God grant you health." I did not wish to leave without the prayer of this old man who was surely pleasing to Heaven. I wanted his blessing for the successful completion of my journey and the fulfillment of my desires. It seemed to me, and I have often dreamed this same thing, that the blessing of sensitive souls lightens the pains of travel and pulls out the thorns of doubt. I walked up to him and placed a ruble in his trembling hand, with my own hand trembling as much — from fear [*404] that I was doing it out of ostentation. He made the sign of the cross, but stopped before he could bestow his customary blessing upon the giver, for he was distracted by the unwonted feeling of what was lying in his hand. This stung my heart. "How much more pleasing to him," I said to myself, "is the gift of a farthing! In it he feels the usual sympathy of humanity for the suffering, while in my ruble it may be that he perceives my pride. He does not bestow his blessing upon it." O, how small I appeared to myself then, how I envied those who had given the old singer a farthing or a crust of bread!

"Is it a five-kopek piece?" he said, directing his speech, like all his words, to no one in particular.

"No, grandfather, a ruble," said a boy who was standing near him.

"Why such an alms?" said the blind man, letting drop the hollows of his eyes and apparently trying to see in his mind's eye what [*405] was lying in his palm. "What good is it to one who cannot use it? If I had not lost my eyesight, how grateful I would have been for it. If I had not needed it myself, I could have helped someone who had nothing. Oh, if I had only had it after the fire here not long ago! For at least a day it would have quieted the cries of my neighbor's hungry babes. But what shall I do with it now? I can't even see where to put it; it may be the cause of crime. It's hardly worth while to steal a farthing, but many would gladly stretch out their hands for a ruble. Take it back, good sir, for with your ruble you and I may change a man into a thief." O truth, how heavily you weigh upon a sensitive heart when you visit it reproachfully! "Take it back. Truly I do not need it, and I do not deserve it, for I have not served the sovereign represented on it. The Creator was pleased to deprive me [*406] of my two guides while I was still in my prime. I bear my affliction patiently. He has visited me for my sins. — I was a soldier, took part in many battles against my country's enemies, and always fought bravely. But one should ever be a soldier only so far as is necessary. My heart was always filled with fury at the beginning of a battle; I never spared an enemy who was lying at my feet, and I never gave quarter to one who asked it, even if he was disarmed. Elated by the victory of our arms, when I charged forward, thirsting for blood and booty, I fell, deprived of my sight and consciousness by a cannon ball that flew close by my eyes with all its force. O ye who come after me, be brave, but remember to be merciful!" He gave me back my ruble and calmly sat down again in his old place.

"Here's your holiday cake, grandfather," said a woman fifty years of age, as she went up to the blind man. With [*407] what delight he took it in both his hands. "This is true charity, true alms. For thirty years in a row, I've been eating this cake on holidays and Sundays. You've not forgotten the promise you made in your childhood. And does what I did for your father of blessed memory deserve that you should not forget me till I die? My friends, I saved her father from a beating such as passing soldiers often give to peasants. The soldiers wanted to take something from him; he resisted them. It happened back of the threshing-floor. The soldiers started to beat the peasant; I was sergeant of the soldiers' company, and happened to be near by; and when I heard the peasant cry out, I ran up and saved him from further blows — maybe from something worse, for there's no telling what might have happened. This is what my present benefactress remembered when she saw me here in my beggarly state. [*408] It is this that she does not forget on any day, on any holiday. My deed was not great, but good. And what is good is pleasing to the Lord; nothing is ever lost with Him."

"Will you really hurt me so much before all these people, good old man," I said to him, "by rejecting only my gift? Is my alms, then, the alms of a sinner? But even that may be for his good, if it serves to soften his hard heart."

"You are distressing a heart that has long been afflicted with a natural punishment," said the old man; "I did not know that I would offend you by not accepting a gift which might have led to crime. Forgive my sin, but if you want to give me something, give me something that will be useful —.We have had a cold spring, and my throat was sore. I had no scarf to tie around my neck, but God was merciful, and the sickness passed on —. Do you have an old scarf? [*409] I will tie it around me when I get a sore throat; it will warm my neck, and my throat will stop hurting. I will remember you, if you care about a beggar's remembrance." I took my scarf off and tied it around the blind man's neck. Then I parted from him.

When I came back through Klin, I did not see the blind singer again. He had died three days before my arrival. But the woman who had brought him cakes on holidays told me that he had put my scarf around his neck in his last illness, and that they had buried him with it. Oh, he who realizes the value of this scarf also realizes what moved within me when I heard this.[5]

[*410] PESHKI

However much I was in a hurry to finish my journey, hunger, which, according to the proverb, breaks stone walls,[1] compelled me to step into the post hut; and, since I could not get any ragout, fricassee, pâté, or other French food invented to bring on indigestion, I had to make a meal out of an old piece of roast beef which I carried with me for an emergency. After I had thus dined much worse than many a colonel (not to speak of generals) on distant campaigns, I followed the laudable popular custom and filled my cup with coffee freshly prepared for me, and thus satisfied my squeamish appetite with the fruit of the sweat of unfortunate African slaves.

Seeing the sugar in front of me, the landlady, who was mixing some dough, sent her little boy to me, to ask for a [*411] small piece of this lordly food. "Why lordly?" I said to her, as I gave the child what was left of my sugar; "can't you use it, too?"

"It is lordly because we have no money to buy it with, while the gentry use it because they do not have to earn the money for it. It's true that our bailiff buys it when he goes to Moscow, but he too pays for it with our tears."

"Then do you mean that anyone who uses sugar makes you weep?"

"Not all, but all the noblemen. Aren't you drinking your peasants' tears when they have to eat such bread as we eat?" Saying this, she showed me what her dough was made of. It consisted of three-fourths chaff and one-fourth of unsifted flour. "And with the crops failing this year, we can thank God even for this. Many of our neighbors have a worse time of it. What good does it do you noblemen to eat sugar when we are starving? [*412] The children are dying, and so are the grownups. But what can we do about it? You worry and worry, and then have to do what the master orders." And she began to put the bread into the oven.

This reproach, not uttered in anger or indignation, but with a profound feeling of sorrow in her soul, filled my heart with grief. For the first time I looked closely at all the household gear of a peasant hut. For the first time I turned my heart to things over which it had only glided heretofore. The upper half of the four walls, and the whole ceiling, were covered with soot; the floor was full of cracks and covered with dirt at least two inches thick; the oven without a smoke-stack, but their best protection against the cold; and smoke filling the hut every morning, winter and summer; window holes over which were stretched bladders which admitted a dim light at noon time; two or three pots (happy the hut if one of them each day contains some watery cabbage soup!). [*413] A wooden bowl and round trenchers called plates; a table, hewn with an axe, which they scrape clean on holidays. A trough to feed the pigs and calves, if there are any. They sleep together with them, swallowing the air in which a burning candle appears as though shrouded in mist or hidden behind a curtain. If they are lucky, a barrel of kvas that tastes like vinegar, and in the yard a bath house in which the cattle sleep if people are not steaming in it. A homespun shirt, the footwear given them by nature, and leggings and bast shoes when they go out. Here one justly looks for the source of the country's wealth, power, and might; but here are also seen the weakness, inadequacy, and abuse of the laws: their harsh side, so to speak. Here may be seen the greed of the gentry, our rapaciousness and tyranny; and the helplessness of the poor. Ravening beasts, insatiable leeches, what do we leave for the peasants? What [*414] we cannot take from them, the air. Yes, and nothing but the air. We frequently take from them not only the gifts of the earth, bread and water, but also the very light. The law forbids us to take their life — that is, to take it suddenly. But there are so many ways to take it from them by degrees! On one side there is almost unlimited power; on the other, helpless impotence. For the landlord is to the peasant at once legislator, judge, executor of his own judgments, and, if he so desires, a plaintiff against whom the defendant dare say nothing. It is the lot of one cast into fetters, of one thrown into a dismal dungeon: the lot of the ox under the yoke.

Hard-hearted landlord, look at the children of the peasants subject to you! They are almost naked. Why? Have you not imposed upon those who bore them — in pain and sorrow — a tax, in addition to all their work on your fields? Do you not [*415] appropriate the linen to your own use even before it is woven? And of what use to you are the stinking rags which your hand, accustomed to luxury, finds loathsome to touch? They will scarcely do for your servants to wipe your cattle with. You collect even that which you do not need, in spite of the fact that the unprotected nakedness of your peasants will be a heavy count against you. If there is no judge over you here, you will be answerable before the Judge Who is no respecter of persons, Who once gave you a good guide, conscience, whom, however, your perverse reason long ago drove from his dwelling place, your heart. But do not imagine that you will escape punishment. The sleepless watcher of your deeds will surprise you when you are alone, and you will feel his chastising strokes. Oh, if only they could be of some good to you and those subject to you! — Oh, if man would but look into his soul more frequently, and confess his deeds to his implacable judge, his conscience! [*416] Transformed by its thunderous voice into an immovable pillar, he would no longer dare to commit secret crimes; destruction and devastation would become rare — etc., etc., etc.

[*417] CHERNAYA GRYAZ'

Here I saw another fine example of a nobleman's arbitrary power over the peasants. A wedding was taking place. But instead of a joyous procession and the soft tears of a timid bride, soon to be changed to joy, one could see only grief and despondency on the brows of those who were about to enter into matrimony. They hate each other, and they are by order of their master dragged to their place of punishment, to the altar of the Father of all good, the Awakener of tender feelings and joys, the Author of true happiness, the Creator of the universe. And His minister will accept the vow exacted by tyranny, and will confirm the marriage! And this will be called a divinely sanctioned union! And this blasphemy will stand as an example for others! And this injustice will go unpunished by the law! — But why wonder at this? It is a hireling who is blessing [*418] the marriage; the commandant of the town, who is appointed to maintain the law, is a nobleman. Both profit by the transaction. The first is concerned for his fee; the second fears that, if he should root out this shameful violence to humanity, he might rob himself of the flattering privilege of ruling autocratically over his like. — O bitter fate of many millions! Thine end is hidden even from the view of my grandchildren. —

Dear reader, I forgot to tell you that the Parnassian judge with whom I dined in the restaurant at Tver' made me a present. His head had tried its strength on many things. How far his experiments were successful, you may judge for yourself, if you like, but whisper into my ear what you think of them. If the reading makes you want to sleep, put the book down, and sleep away. Keep it in reserve for a case of insomnia.

[*419] EULOGY ON LOMONOSOV [1]

The pleasant cool of evening after a hot summer day lured me from my cell. I made my way toward the Nevsky Monastery and strolled about for a long time in the grove beyond.* The sun had already hidden its face, but the light curtain of

* Ozerki.

night was still barely perceptible on the blue vault.* On my way home, I passed the Nevsky Cemetery. The gates were open. I stepped in. — In this place of eternal silence, where the most hardened brow cannot help frowning at the thought that here all brilliant deeds must come to an end; in this place of unruffled quiet and imperturbable equanimity, it would seem that there could be no room for boastfulness, vainglory, and conceit. But the magnificent tombstones? [*420] They are unmistakable signs of man's pride, but also signs of his desire to live forever. But is this the immortality for which man so yearns? — It is not a column erected above your mortal remains that will keep your memory alive for your most distant descendants. It is not a stone with your name carved upon it that will carry your fame into future centuries. Your word, living now and evermore in your works, the word of the Russian nation, regenerated by you in our tongue, will fly on the lips of the people beyond the illimitable horizon of the centuries. Let the elements in compound fury burst open the abysses of the earth and swallow up this magnificent city whence thy loud song was borne to the far corners of Russia; let some furious conqueror destroy even the name of your beloved country: so long as the Russian word shall strike an ear, you will live and will not die. When it is no longer heard, [*421] your fame will be extinguished. It is glorious, glorious thus to die. But if anyone knew how to calculate the measure of this influence, if the finger of prophecy could point to a limit for your name, would it not be eternity? . . . Thus I cried like one inspired, as I stood before the column erected above the mortal remains of Lomonosov. No, it is not this cold stone that tells us that you lived for the glory of the Russian name; it cannot tell what you were. Let your works tell us this, let your life say to us why you are famous.

Where are you, my beloved friend,[2] where are you? Come and let us talk together about this great man. Come and let

* It was in June.

us wind a wreath to the creator of Russian letters. Let others, in slavish adulation of Power, extol force and might. We will sing a paean to the service of society.

Mikhaylo Vasil'evich Lomonosov was born in Kholmogory.[3] The son [*422] of a man who could not give him an education by which his understanding might have been sharpened and adorned with useful and pleasant information; destined by his condition to pass his days among people whose circle of ideas did not extend beyond their occupations; compelled to divide his time between fishing and trying to get paid for his work, the mind of the young Lomonosov could not have attained that breadth which it acquired by the tireless study of nature, nor could his voice have attained that sweetness which it acquired from his intercourse with the chaste Muses. From his education in his parental home he received what might seem insignificant but is the key to learning, the ability to read and write, and from nature, he received curiosity. Nature, behold thy triumph! Eager curiosity, implanted by thee in our souls, strives after the knowledge of things, and the [*423] heart flaming with ambition cannot brook the fetters that would hold it captive. It roars, seethes, groans, and, breaking its bonds in an instant, flies headlong (nothing can stop it) toward its goal. Everything is forgotten, there is only one object in its mind; by it we breathe and live.

Never letting the object of his heart's desire out of his sight, the youth gathers the knowledge of things from the smallest rills that trickle down from the source of knowledge to the lowest layers of society. Being without guidance, which is so necessary for the quickening of understanding, he sharpens and adorns the first power of his mind, memory, with that which should have sharpened his reason. The narrow compass of information which he could obtain in the place of his birth could not slake his soul's thirst, but rather roused in the youth an unconquerable passion for learning. Fortunate was he that, at the age when, as we approach manhood, the stirring of the passions for the first time [*424] leads us out of insensibility, his striving was directed to the quest for knowledge.

Driven by hunger for knowledge, Lomonosov leaves his parents' home, makes his way to the capital, goes to the dwelling of the cloistered Muses, and is registered among the young people who devote themselves to the study of the liberal arts and the word of God.

The antechamber of learning is the knowledge of languages; but this looks like a field overgrown with thorns or like a mountain covered with sharp stones. The eye does not discover any pleasant landscape here, the traveler's feet find no soft resting place, the weary man finds no green retreat here. Thus the student, upon approaching an unknown language, is confused by strange sounds. His throat is exhausted by the unfamiliar rustling of air escaping from it, and his tongue, compelled to wag in a new way, [*425] grows lame. The mind grows stiff, reason is weakened by inactivity, imagination loses its wings; memory alone is wide awake and ever keener, filling all its convolutions and openings with hitherto unknown sounds. In learning languages, at first everything is repulsive and burdensome. If one were not encouraged by the hope that, after having accustomed his ear to the unusual sounds and having mastered the strange pronunciation, most delightful ways would be opened up to him, it is doubtful that one would want to enter upon so arduous a path. But when these obstacles are surmounted, how generous is the reward for perseverance in overcoming hardships! New aspects of nature, and a new chain of ideas then present themselves. By acquiring a foreign language we become citizens of the region where it is spoken, we converse wtih those who lived many thousand years ago, we adopt their [*426] ideas; and we unite and co-ordinate the inventions and the thought of all peoples and all times.

Untiring diligence in learning languages made Lomonosov a fellow citizen of the Athenians and Romans. And his perseverance was rewarded. Like a blind man who has not seen the light since he left his mother's womb and who suddenly perceives the glory of the light of day when his vision is restored by the skillful hand of the oculist: with a quick glance he surveys all the beauties of nature and admires its variety and simplicity. Everything charms him, eveything amazes him. He feels its splendor more vividly than those who have always been accustomed to see; he is delighted and goes into ecstasies. Just so Lomonosov, when he had acquired a knowledge of Latin and Greek, devoured the beauties of the ancient orators and poets. From them he learned to appreciate the loveliness of nature; from them he learned to understand all the rules of art which lie behind [*427] the forms inspired by poetry; from them he learned to express his feelings, to give a body to thought and a soul to what is lifeless.

If my powers were sufficient, I would show how the great man gradually adopted ideas of others, which, transformed in his mind and soul, appeared in a new form in his works, or gave rise to entirely new creations hitherto unknown to the human mind. I would present him seeking information in the ancient manuscripts of his school and constantly pursuing knowledge wherever he suspected it might be hiding. He was frequently deceived in his expectation, but by his continuous reading of the church books he laid the foundation for the elegance of his style, and therefore he counsels such reading to all who wish to achieve the mastery of the Russian word.[4]

[*428] Soon his curiosity received a rich reward. He became a student of the famous Wolff.[5] Rejecting the rules of scholasticism, or rather, the errors taught him in the monastic schools, he laid down firm and clear steps that lead up to the temple of philosophy. Logic taught him to reason; mathematics taught him to draw sound conclusions and to be convinced only by firsthand evidence; metaphysics instructed him in conjectural truths which often lead to error; physics and chemistry, to which he devoted himself eagerly, perhaps

because of their pleasant stimulus to the imagination, led him to the altar of nature and disclosed its mysteries to him; metallurgy and mineralogy, as corollaries of the preceding subjects, attracted his attention, and Lomonosov tried eagerly to learn the laws which govern these sciences.

An overabundance of crops and products compelled men to barter them [*429] for others that they needed. This led to trade. The great inconveniences in trade by barter led to the invention of tokens representing every kind of wealth and property. Money was invented. Gold and silver, the most costly because the most perfect metals, which had till then been used as ornaments, were transformed into tokens that represent all property. Only then, only then in truth there flamed up in the human heart that insatiable and abominable passion for riches, which, like an all-devouring conflagration, grows stronger the more food it receives. Then, abandoning his primitive simplicity and his natural employment, agriculture, man entrusted his life to the furious waves, or, undeterred by hunger and the heat of the deserts, made his way across them to unknown countries in search of wealth and treasures. Then, scorning the light of the sun, [*430] living man went down into the grave, and, tearing up the vitals of the earth, dug a burrow for himself like the mole that seeks its food by night. Thus man, burying himself in the depths of the earth, searched for the glittering metals and shortened the duration of his life by half through breathing in the poisonous vapours that rose from the earth. But even as a poison itself may become a habit and seeming necessity for man through constant use, so the mining of metals, although it shortens the lives of the miners, has not been rejected on account of its deadliness; on the contrary, methods have been devised for the extraction of the greatest possible quantity of metals in the easiest possible way.

It was precisely this that Lomonosov wanted to study directly, and for this purpose he set out for Freiberg. Methinks

I see him as he arrives at the opening through which flows the metal that is wrested from the vitals of the earth. [*431] He takes the dim lantern intended to illumine his way in the depths to which the sun's rays never penetrate. He has taken his first step. Reason cries out to him, "What are you doing? Has nature favored you with her gifts only that you may use them to harm your fellow men? What are you thinking of as you descend into this abyss? Are you trying to discover a better method of mining silver and gold? Do you not know what harm they have done in the world? Or have you forgotten the conquest of America? . . . But no, go down, learn the subterranean devices of man, and, when you return to your country, have enough firmness of spirit to advise the closing and leveling of these graves in which thousands are buried alive."

Tremblingly he descends into the opening and soon loses sight of the life-giving sun. I should have liked to follow him in his subterranean journey, [*432] to collect his thoughts, and to present them in the same connection and order in which they arose in his mind. The picture of his thoughts would be entertaining and instructive to us. As he passed the first stratum of earth, the source of all vegetation, the subterranean traveler found that it differed from the subsequent strata, being distinguished from them chiefly by its power of fertility. Perhaps he concluded from this that the earth's surface is composed of nothing but the decay of animal and plant matter; that its fertility, its sustaining and regenerative power had its origin in the indestructible and fundamental parts of each being, which, without changing their essence, change only their outward appearance, resulting from an accidental formation. As the subterranean traveler proceeded farther, he saw the earth always formed in strata. In these he [*433] occasionally found remains of marine animals and plants, from which he could conclude that the stratification of the earth had its origin in the flood and flux of the waters, and that, in streaming from one end of the globe to another, the waters gave the earth the form which it presents in its interior. In some places this uniform distribution disappeared from his view and showed him a mixture of many different strata. From this he concluded that the fierce element, fire, had penetrated into the bowels of the earth, and, meeting the hostile element, water, had razed, upset, shaken, overthrown, and hurled down everything that tried to oppose its action. Having confounded and mixed the various elements, it aroused with its hot breath the power of attraction in the primeval metallic matter and fused it. There Lomonosov saw these inert [*434] treasures in their natural form, and, recalling man's greed and misery, he left the gloomy abode of human insatiability with a sorrowful heart.

While he occupied himself with the study of nature, he did not abandon his favorite science of versification. Chance had shown him, while he was still in his own country, that nature had destined him for greatness, that he would not wander idly on the ordinary path of human existence. The Psalter, which had been rendered into verse by Simeon Polotsky,[6] had opened to him the secret of his nature and had revealed to him that he, too, was a poet. Long before, while holding converse with Horace, Virgil, and other ancient writers, he had convinced himself that Russian prosody was quite inadequate for the harmony and majesty of our language. In reading the German poets he found that their style was more fluent than the Russian, and that their meters were constructed to take account [*435] of the characteristics of their language. Hence he decided to experiment with a new kind of versification, first establishing rules of Russian prosody based on the harmony of our tongue. He accomplished this by writing an ode, which he sent from Marburg to the Academy of Sciences, on the victory gained by the Russian army over the Turks and Tatars and on the capture of Khotin.[7] The novelty of the style, the power of expression, the almost living pictures astonished the readers of this new production. And this first-born child of a pioneer imagination on an uncharted path served, together with other things, as a proof that once a nation is striving for perfection, it marches toward glory, not on one footpath, but on many highways at the same time.

Power of imagination and vividness of feeling do not exclude the investigation of details. While giving examples of poetic harmony, [*436] Lomonosov knew that elegance of style is based on rules that grow out of the nature of the language. He wanted to deduce them from speech itself, without forgetting, however, that custom always furnishes the first example in the concatenation of words, and that expressions based on rules become correct only through custom. Lomonosov composed his grammar [8] by sorting out all the parts of speech and analyzing them according to their usage. But not satisfied with merely teaching the rules of Russian speech, he gives an idea of human speech in general, as the noblest gift next to reason itself, given to man for the communication of his thoughts. Here is an epitome of his universal grammar: Speech expresses ideas; voice is the instrument of speech; the voice changes with cultivation or practice in speaking; various changes in voice express the variation of ideas; hence, speech is the representation of our ideas through [*437] the cultivation of the voice by means of the organs provided for it. Proceeding from this foundation, Lomonosov determines the indivisible parts of the word, which, being set forth in characters, are called letters. The combination of the indivisible parts of the word produces syllables, which differ, over and above the formative distinctions of the voice, in the so-called accents, on which prosody is based. The coalescence of syllables produces words, the significant parts of speech. These represent either a thing, or its action. The word which represents a thing is called a "noun"; the word which represents an action is called a "verb." Other parts of speech serve to represent the relationship of things to each other and to their whole. But the first are essential and may be called the main parts of speech, while the others are subordinate. Speaking of the different parts of speech, Lomonosov finds that some of them are subject to changes. [*438] A thing may stand in various relations to other things. The representation of such relationships is called "case." Every action occurs in time; hence verbs are conjugated according to tense, in order to represent the time in which their action takes place. Finally, Lomonosov speaks of the combination of significant parts of speech which produces sentences.

After this philosophic discussion of speech in general, based on the natural structure of the human body itself, Lomonosov sets forth the rules for the Russian language. And how could they be mediocre, since the mind which delineated them was guided through the grammatical thorns by the torch of wisdom? Great man, do not scorn this praise! It is not your grammar alone that has established your fame among your fellow citizens. Your services to the Russian language are [*439] manifold; and you are venerated for this your toilsome labor as the first founder of the true rules of our tongue, and as the discoverer of the natural order of all speech. Your grammar is the antechamber to the study of your rhetoric,[9] and both are guides for the appreciation of the beauty of expression in your works. By setting forth the rules of speech, Lomonosov intended to guide his fellow citizens along the thorny paths of Helicon — by showing them the way to eloquence and sketching the rules of rhetoric and poetry. But the brevity of his life allowed him to complete only one-half of his undertaking.

A man born with tender feelings, endowed with a powerful imagination, impelled by ambition, comes forth from amidst the people. He mounts the rostrum. All [*440] eyes are fixed on him, everyone impatiently awaits his utterance. Applause or ridicule worse than death awaits him. How can he be mediocre? Such a genius was Demosthenes; such was Cicero; such was Pitt; such now are Burke, Fox, Mirabeau, and others.[10] The rules of their oratory are drawn from the circumstances, their sweet eloquence of expression from their feelings, the force of their arguments from the sharpness of their wits. Admiring such great orators and analyzing their speeches, cold-blooded critics thought that rules might be prescribed for wit and imagination, that the road to beauty could be laid out by laborious precepts. This is the origin of rhetoric. Lomonosov, who, without observing it, was following the dictates of his imagination — improved by his converse with the ancient authors — also thought that he could impart to his fellow citizens the ardor which filled his soul. [*441] And although his labor to this end was in vain, the examples he cited to support and explain his rules may unquestionably serve as a guide to the seeker for fame in letters.

But even though he labored in vain to establish rules for that which must be felt rather than learned, Lomonosov nonetheless left in his own works the most dependable models for those who love Russian letters. In these works the lips that have sipped the sweetness of Cicero and Demosthenes speak most eloquently. In them every line, every sentence, every syllable (why may I not say every letter?) exhibits the harmonious consonance of that rare, inimitable elegance of speech which is so characteristic of him.

Endowed by nature with creative power, with the priceless right to influence his contemporaries, [*442] and thrown by nature into their crowded midst, the great man moves them to act, though not always in the same direction. Like the forces of nature which act from a center and extend their action to all the points of the periphery, making themselves steadily felt everywhere, so Lomonosov acted in various ways upon his fellow citizens, by opening up to the people's minds the various paths to learning. While he drew them along with him, unraveling the tangled language into eloquence and harmony, he did not abandon them at the thin wellspring of a literature without ideas. To fancy he cried: "Fly into the immeasurable space of dreams and possibilities, pluck the bright flowers of inspiration, and, guided by good taste, adorn with them even the incorporeal itself." And behold, Pindar's trumpet, which had sounded at the Olympic games, now proclaimed the glory of the Almighty [*443] in the manner of the Psalmist. By its means Lomonosov proclaimed the greatness of the Everlasting Who is enthroned on the wings of the wind, is preceded by thunder and lightning, and in the sun manifests to mortals His essence, life. Moderating the sound of Pindar's trumpet, he also sang upon it the transitoriness of man and the narrow limits of his understanding. Lost in the bottomless abyss of endless worlds, like the tiniest grain of sand in the waves of the sea, like a barely glimmering spark in never melting ice, like a speck of dust in the fiercest whirlwind, what is man's mind? — Such art thou, O Lomonosov, my cloak shall not conceal you.

I do not envy you because, following the common custom of flattering kings, who are frequently unworthy not only of an harmonious song of praise but even of a tinkling street song, you praised Elizabeth in fulsome verse.[11] If, without offending truth and posterity, it were possible to do so, I would forgive [*444] you because you thereby revealed your soul's gratitude for favors received. But the maker of odes who cannot follow in your footsteps will envy you, he will envy you your superb picture of national peace and quiet — that mighty protector of cities and villages and comforter of kingdoms and of kings; he will envy you the countless beauties of your diction, even if someone manages to attain the uninterrupted harmony of your verses, which no one so far has. Let them all surpass you in sweetness of song, let our descendants consider you uncouth in your thoughts and imperfect in the matter of your verses! . . . Behold, in the vast arena, the bounds of which the eye cannot see, amidst the crowding concourse, in the most prominent place, ahead of all, and opening the gate to the arena — it is you. Everyone may gain glory by his exploits, but you were the first. Not even [*445] the Almighty Himself can take away what He gave you. He created you before all others, He created you a leader, and your glory is the glory of a leader. O ye who heretofore have fruitlessly labored to understand the essence of the soul, and how it acts upon our corporeality, here is a difficult problem for you to solve. Tell us how one soul acts upon another, and what connection there is between minds. If we know how one body acts upon another by contact, inform us how the incorporeal acts upon the incorporeal and produces the corporeal, or what contact there is between the immaterial and the immaterial. You know that there is such. But if you know what influence the mind of a great man has upon the people's mind, then you must also know that a great man may bring forth another great man. And this is your crown of victory, O Lomonosov: you brought forth Sumarokov! [12]

[*446] But if the effect of Lomonosov's verses was to make a mighty advance in shaping the poetic concepts of his contemporaries, his eloquence made no perceptible or manifest impression. The flowers culled by him in Athens and in Rome, and so felicitously transplanted in his diction, the expressive strength of Demosthenes, the sweetness of Cicero's orations, he employed in vain: their effect is still veiled in the dim future. What man, surfeited with the superabundant eloquence of your songs of praise, though he does not thunder forth in your style, still shows himself to be your pupil? That time may be far or near: the wandering glance, lost in the uncertainty of the future, sees no support on which to rest. Although we find no direct progeny of Lomonosov's oratory, the effect of the harmony and melodious structure of his unrhythmic speech was none the less universal. If he had no [*447] successor in the art of public address, his achievement none the less influenced the general manner of writing. Compare what was written before Lomonosov with what was written after him, and the influence of his prose will become obvious to all.

But are we not mistaken in our conclusion? Long before Lomonosov we find in Russia eloquent shepherds of the Church who preached the word of God to their flocks in a style for which they are famous. True, there were such, but their style was not Russian. They wrote as one could write before the invasion of the Tatars, before the Russians came in contact with the European peoples. They wrote in [Old Church] Slavonic. But you, who saw Lomonosov himself and perhaps studied the art of eloquence in his works, you shall not be forgotten by me. When the Russian army defeated the proud Ottomans and thus surpassed the expectations of all who had watched its exploits with an [*448] indifferent or envious eye, and you were called on to give solemn thanks to the Lord of hosts, the Lord of power; when, standing before Peter's tomb, in the elation of your spirit you called him from his tomb to come and see the fruit of his planting, crying, "Arise, Peter, arise"; when the ear you had charmed, in its turn charmed the eye, when it appeared to all that you approached Peter's grave in order to raise him, being endowed therefor with strength from above — then I would have said to Lomonosov: "Behold, behold, here is the fruit of your planting." But although he might have taught you the words — still, in Platon was Plato's soul, and it was his own heart that taught him how to charm and enrapture us.[13]

Being a foe to servility not only in that which may rouse our awe, but even in our love, we want to do justice to the great man but not to imagine that he was God the Creator of all; let us not set him up as an idol to be worshiped [*449] by society nor contribute to the establishment of any prejudice or false conclusion. Truth is our highest divinity, and if the Almighty Himself should wish to change its aspect by no longer revealing Himself in it, we would turn our face away even from Him.

In pursuing the truth, we shall not try to discover a great historian in Lomonosov: we shall not compare him with Tacitus, Raynal, or Robertson;[14] nor will we place him on the same level with Marggraf or Rüdiger,[15] merely because he worked at chemistry. Though this science fascinated him, though he spent many days of his life in the investigation of the truths of nature, his course was that of a follower. He walked on trails previously opened up, and in the endless riches of nature he did not find the smallest blade of grass that better eyes than his had not seen, nor did he find any more primitive sources [*450] of matter than his predecessors had discovered.

Shall we place him near the one who was honored with the most flattering inscription any man could see beneath his portrait? It is an inscription not etched by flattery, but by truth attacking tyranny: "He has snatched the lightning from heaven and the scepter from the hand of tyrants."[16] Shall we place Lomonosov near him because, having investigated electricity in action, he was not turned away from this study even when he saw his teacher struck to death by this force?[17] Lomonosov knew how to generate electricity, he knew how to ward off the thunderbolt, but in this science Franklin is the architect, Lomonosov an artisan.

But if Lomonosov did not achieve greatness in the investigation of nature, he described its marvelous workings in a pure and understandable style. [*451] And although his works on natural science do not show him to have been a master scientist, we do find him to be a master of expression and always an example worthy of emulation.

In thus doing justice to a great man, by placing Lomonosov's name in the high light it deserves, we are not trying to ascribe to him honor for what he did not do or for that on which he produced no effect; we will not let blind admiration or prejudice lead us into unreasonable praise. That is not our purpose. We wish to show, with regard to Russian literature, that he who laid out the road to the temple of glory is the first cause for the attainment of that glory, even if he himself could not enter the temple. Is Bacon of Verulam not worthy to be remembered because he could only show how to advance learning? [18] Are the courageous writers [*452] who have risen against oppression and tyranny not worthy of gratitude because they could not themselves free mankind from fetters and captivity? And shall we fail to honor Lomonosov because he did not understand the rules of dramatic poetry and wore himself out in writing epics, because in his poems he was wanting in sentiment, because he was not always penetrating in his judgments, and because even in his odes he sometimes employed more words than ideas? But listen! Before the beginning of time, when existence had no firm support and everything was lost in eternity and infinity, everything was possible for the Source of power: all the beauty of the universe existed in His thought, but there was no action, no beginning. And behold, an Almighty Hand thrust matter into space and gave it motion. The sun began to shine, the moon received its light, and the revolving bodies on high were formed. The first impulse in creation was all-powerful; all the wonders, all the beauties of the world [*453] are only its consequences. Thus do I understand the influence of a great soul upon the souls of its contemporaries or descendants; thus do I understand the influence of mind upon mind. Lomonosov is the first upon the path of Russian literature. Away with you, envious crowd! Posterity will judge him, and it knows no hypocrisy.

But, dear reader, I have talked too much —. Here we are already at Vsesvyatskoe —. If I have not wearied you, wait for me at the crossroads; we shall meet again on our return journey. Now good-bye! Drive on, coachman!

MOSCOW! MOSCOW!!!

With the permission of the Department of Public Morals

THE EMPRESS CATHERINE II'S NOTES ON THE *JOURNEY*

[These notes were first published by Osip Maksimovich Bodyansky in *Chteniya*, LIV (1865), book III, sect. V, pp. 67–77, and were reprinted in Radishchev's *Complete Works*, ed. Borozdin, Lapshin, and Shchegolev, II, 300–308. The starred pages here refer, of course, to the pages of Radishchev's original edition of the *Journey*.]

NO. 1

This book was printed in 1790 without mention of the printing press and without any visible permission at the beginning, although at the end it says: "With the permission of the Department of Public Morals." This is probably a lie, or else carelessness. The purpose of this book is clear on every page: its author, infected and full of the French madness, is trying in every possible way to break down respect for authority and for the authorities, to stir up in the people indignation against their superiors and against the government.

He is probably a Martinist or something similar. He has learning enough, and has read many books. He has a melancholy temperament and sees everything in a very somber light; consequently he takes a bilious black and yellow view of things.

He has imagination enough, and he is audacious in his writing.

The citation on page *36 shows the malicious bent of the author's mind, *il cite un fait atroce*, which does not belong here at all. The English suffocated from the oppressive heat of Calcutta, but you can hire a fishing boat without asking any commander quicker than you can get one by his command, and you can't accuse a man who was sleeping because they didn't wake him up.

The author is maliciously inclined on page *60. This is particularly evident from the following pages. Pages *72, *73. They show clearly enough the purpose for which this whole book was written. It is a safe bet that the author's motive in writing it was this, that *he does not have entrée to the palace.* Maybe he had it once and lost it, but since he does not have it now but does have an evil and consequently ungrateful heart, he is struggling for it now with his pen. On page *75. Our babbler is timid. If he stood closer to the sovereign, he would pipe a different tune. We have seen a lot of such humbugs, especially among the Raskol'niki. The firmer their hearts, the more they change when the time comes.

I do not know how great the lust for power is in other rulers; in me it is not great.

Page *76. The fledglings teach the mother bird. *Malice* is in the malicious; I have none of it.

"The murder called war": What do they want, to be left defenseless to fall captive to the Turks and Tatars, or to be conquered by the Swedes?

In criticizing the poor execution of our commands, they are accusing themselves.

Pages *77, *78 are written with a seditious purpose, and the care taken in rooting out an evil is criticized adversely.

Page *79, at least he does not mention Chichagov. Page *80, they have eaten up all the wisdom, and only the Sovereign is left without a grain of sense. On this same page the granting of amnesty is censured.

Page *81 is full of abuse, invective, and an evil-minded interpretation of things. This villainy continues through the following pages: *82, *83, *84, and *85. But withal they were unable to censure the intentions, and so were obliged to turn to their fulfillment; hence they are criticizing society, and not the Sovereign's good heart or intentions.

*86. He himself says that he had a *delirious dream*.
Page *88. He refers to "information: what I have had the good luck to learn." I think that information was picked up in Leipzig; hence the suspicion falls on Messrs. Radishchev and Chelishchev, the more so since they are said to have established a printing press in their house.
Pages *92, *93, *94, *95, *96, *97 preach the doctrines of the Martinists and other theosophists.
Page *98 is so indecent that it cannot even be mentioned.
*99, *100, *101. Speaking of Novgorod, of its free government, and of Tsar Ioann Vasil'evich's cruelty to it, he does not say anything about the cause of this punishment, which was that, having accepted the union, Novgorod had surrendered to the Polish Republic; consequently the Tsar punished the apostates and traitors, in which, to tell the truth, he did not keep within bounds.
*102. The author cries: "But what right did he have to rage against them? What right did he have to take Novgorod for himself?" Answer: the old right of sovereignty and the law of Novgorod and of all Russia and of the whole world, which punishes rebels, and apostates from the Church. But the question is raised here only to deny monarchical rights, and should therefore be left without an answer.
On *103. The questions brought up here are the ones over which France is now being ruined.

NO. 2

Everything which is established and ordered in the world today is established and ordered by experience, which demands that everything be based on precedent, and not on arbitrary will. If it were otherwise, it would be worse, for the better is an enemy of what is good today, and it is better to hold fast to what is known than to lay out a path to what is unknown.
Page *108. He is well acquainted with the details of mer-

cantile deception, such as one may observe at the custom house.

*109. *110. *111. About the same. On the last page there is a sortie against the commercial law, and the author himself does not know what he wants, with which he ends page *112. Pages *113, *114, *115, *116 show that the author is a complete deist and does not conform to the doctrine of the Eastern Orthodox Church. These reflections end on page *118.

Page *119 and the following serve to demonstrate the author's purpose, which is to point out the defects of the present form of government and its vices. Here he discusses the criminal law, with which he fills up pages *120, *121, *122, *123.

Page *124 is given over to the proof of the unworthiness of advancements in the service. At the end of this page the author contradicts himself, for he points out the evil inclinations of a man of low estate, whereas, according to his system (the present French system), all estates are established equal in the name of man and his so-called rights.

On page *125 there is another reference to "lowly origin," from which we may conclude that the author is not well grounded in his principles. But he tries to shower his malice on the court and courtiers. These slanders he got partly from books to which the courtiers have never made any reply, and yet it is possible to make a defense against such accusations.

Pages *126, *127, *128, *129, *130, *131, *132, *133 are an oratorical invention for the tale of the beastly behavior of the landed proprietor with his peasants and the murder of the master and his three sons.

Pages *134, *135 serve as a justification for that murder. On p. *136 there begins an illegal discussion.

On *137 the French venom is poured out, and this continues on *138 and *139. But this whole argument can easily be overthrown by one simple question: if someone does evil, does that give someone else the right to do even greater evil? Answer: of course not. The law permits one to strike in self-defense, but it demands proof that death could not have been averted otherwise. Hence the whole of the author's discussion is irrelevant, illegal, vain philosophizing.

Page *140. The governor is accused of bribery, and yet only his legitimate interpretation of things is adduced as proof. At the end of page *141 the custom of visiting the governor is criticized. But it is necessary if he is to know those whom he has to work with and if they are to know him. Or does the general welfare demand that people should not know one another and not visit one another, but should live far apart like wolves in the forest?

On *142 there is a sally against the governor's conceit. Of course he is a person of distinction, and it is improper to have any dispute with him on legal matters, for even a wise man may turn out to be a fool here.

Pages *143, *144, *145, *146 advocate principles which are completely destructive of the laws and which have turned France upside down. It would not have been surprising if the governor had arrested the loose talker.

On page *147 he continues to bewail the sad fate of the peasants, although it cannot be denied that our peasants who have good masters are better off than any in the world.

Pages *154, *155, *156 describe the nobleman's entrance into service in the same malicious colors as the rest.

*156, *157, *158. In these pages may be seen the author's *haughtiness of soul* and his *dissatisfaction with the magnates*, which he is trying to disseminate in his book, like the calumnies on everything else that is established and accepted. On page *159 this becomes even clearer.

NO. 3

*160, *161, *162, *163, *164, *165, *166, *167 serve to break the bonds between parents and children and are in direct opposition to the law of God, the Ten Commandments, Holy Scripture, Orthodoxy, and the civil law. And it is evident throughout this whole book that the author has little respect for the Christian teaching and that he has adopted, instead, certain ideas which are not in conformity with the Christian and civil law.

At the end of page *167 and on *168, *169, *170 are the rules of education; these are continued on *171, *172, *173; at the end we are told why the children were taught English and Latin.

Pages *174, *175 are very well thought out; *176 and *177 continue with the education of the children; so do *178, *179, and *180. After that the pages become unbridled, like the whole book, and the author's mentality is just like it. He seems to have been born with unbounded ambition, to have prepared himself for the highest offices, but since he has not yet attained them, the gall of his impatience has poured out over everything established, and has produced this philosophizing. But it is drawn from sundry semi-sophists of the present time, such as Rousseau, the Abbé Raynal, and similar hypochondriacs; but in metaphysics he is a Martinist.

Page *181 speaks of marriage in the same way.

*182. The rules of social life begin here. The author says: Ask your heart; it is good; do whatever it tells you. He does not command us to follow our reason. This proposition cannot be correct.

On *183 he speaks of the contradictions of customs, habits, laws, and virtue.

On *184 he cites the example of Socrates and gives the rule that one should prefer virtue to everything, but it remains unknown wherein virtue consists.

On *185 this is confirmed and virtue is discussed. It is either individual or social.

On page *186 is the example of Curtius, and some rules for the conduct of life are given. These prove that the author is a true egotist and more concerned about himself than about anything else.

On *187 the author has come back again to his favorite subject: the attendance upon prominent persons. He says that this custom is abominable, meaningless, and subservient, while in the person called upon it is evidence of conceit and a weak intellect.

*188. This is confirmed, but with the exception of calling in matters of duty.

*189. On this page the author speaks of dandyism and proves that he is not mercenary.

Pages *190, *191, *192, *193, *194 prove that the author has imagination enough and loves to disseminate hypochondriac and gloomy thoughts, and here we are once again reminded of the insignificance of the power of parents over their children, a notion contrary to both the Christian and the civil law.

Page *195. He continues to expatiate on this illegal and truly vicious proposition, with which he finishes on page *196. No respect for the divine and civil laws is to be seen here, but rather a preference for arbitrary, quasi-philosophical raving.

Pages *197, *198, *199, *200, *201 describe the consequences of the shameful disease which the author had. On page *202 the blame for it is cast upon the government, and on *203 those who preach peace and quiet are abused and defamed.

Pages *204, *205, *206, *207, *208, *209 contain the story of Valdai and the monk who swam the lake, and are of no consequence.

Pages *210, *211, *212, *213, *214, *215, *216 contain the story of the maid of Edrovo, with frequent attacks on the gentry, their lawlessness and their bad treatment of the peasants.

The strongest passages occur on *217.

Page *218. This might almost be the story of Aleksandr Vasil'evich Saltykov. Here is an attack on justice; at the end of this page are the words: "No, no, he lives, he will live, if he wishes to!" These are noteworthy and truly seditious remarks.

Pages *219, *220, *221, *222 are a continuation of the story of Anyutina.

Page *223 attacks the morals of the capital, the gentry, etc.

Page *224 is a continuation of the story; also *225.

*226 compares the village mothers with the urban; this comparison is continued on page *227.

*228, *229. The author's reflections on Anyuta of Edrovo.

*230. He describes the pernicious custom, in the country, of marrying ten-year-old boys to grown-up girls. The author does not know that such marriages are forbidden, or he does not wish to know it, for he says: The law *should* forbid it. His discussion of matrimony runs counter to Orthodoxy, for matrimony is a sacrament. At the end of page *231 there is another attack on the gentry: Why should a man of fifty marry a girl of fifteen? We have a proverb: One swallow does not make a summer.

Pages *232, *233, *234, and *235 are the conclusion of this story.

NO. 4

Pages *236, *237, *238 speak sarcastically about happiness, and we are made to feel that there is no such thing. This serves as an introduction to what the author has to say about the peasants and their enslavement, and about the army, which is likewise enslaved through military organization. All this is on pages *239, *240, *241, *242, *243, *244, *245, *246, *247, *248, *249, *250, *251, *252, and the tendency is to stir up the peasants against their proprietors and the army against its commanders. The author does not love the words "peace" and "quiet."

From page *253 there begins an attack on conquests.

*254 and *255 are filled with abuse of victory, conquest,

and settlements. At the end of the latter page he returns to the agriculturists.

*256 and *257 describe the condition of peasants who have no fields of their own.

*258, how men are worn out by work.

*259 says that slaves love their fetters. N. B. All this is taken for the most part from the Abbé Raynal's book.

*260. Once again words that incite to rebellion escape him.

*261 is also worth noting.

*262. He tries to persuade the landed proprietors to free the peasants, but no one will listen to him.

*263. Continuation of this.

*264. Here it says that everything written above was found on a piece of paper which he picked up from the road.

On page *265 there is a project for the emancipation of the agriculturists in Russia; this project takes up *266 and *267.

*268, *269, *270, *271, *272, *273, *274, *275, *276, *277 are written to bring into contempt those landed proprietors who take the fields away from their peasants. The author lashes out at them, and the government catches it, too.

Pages *278, *279, *280, *281, *282, *283, *284, *285, *286, *287, *288 are on the abolition of court ranks. Here monarchs catch it badly, and it ends with the words: "how power can be joined with liberty for mutual advantage." One must assume that he is thinking of the vicious example of France today. This is the more likely because the author seeks occasion everywhere to attack the sovereign and the government He is doing this now.

Pages *289, *290, *291, *292, *293, *294, *295, *296, *297, *298, *299, *300, *301, *302, *303, *304, *305 contain abuse of the censorship of books, and here he speaks quite boldly and insultingly about authority and government, which, it is evident, are despised by the author.

*306, *307, *308, *309, *310, *311, *312, *313, *314, *315, *316, *317, *318, *319, *320, *321, *322, *323, *324, *325,

*326, *327, *328, *329, *330, *331, *332, *333, *334, *335, *336, *337, *338, *339, *340 are also on the censorship. The strongest passages are marked in pencil. On the last page are these words: "he was an emperor. Tell me, in whose head can there be more inconsistencies than in an emperor's?" The author does not love monarchs, and wherever he can vilify love and respect for monarchs, he does so with rare audacity and greedy relish.

On page *341 begins the pitiful story of a family sold at auction for their master's debts, and this continues on *342, *343, *344, *345, *346, *347, *348.

On *349 it ends with these words: "freedom is not to be expected from their counsels (the landed proprietors), but from the heavy burden of slavery itself." That is, he puts his hopes in a peasant rebellion.

Pages *350 to *369 contain, in the guise of a discussion of prosody, an ode most clearly, manifestly revolutionary, in which tsars are threatened with the block. Cromwell's example is cited and praised. These pages are of criminal intent, completely revolutionary. Ask the author what is the meaning of this ode and by whom it was composed.

Page *370 and the following, to *394, the story of the levying of recruits, of oppressed peasants, and the like, which serves for the propagation of liberty and the eradication of the landed proprietors.

*395 through *400. Another attack on the wealthy magnates and courtiers.

From *401 through *409 is the story about the blind man.

From *410 through *416 is again about the peasants' miserable existence.

NO. 5

Tell the author that I have read his book from cover to cover, and that in the course of reading it I have come to wonder whether I may in some way have offended him. For I do not want to judge him without hearing him, although he judges sovereigns without hearing their justification.

From *401 through *409 is the story about the blind man to whom he gave the scarf.

*410, *411, *412, *413, *414, *415, *416 continue to describe the miserable condition of the peasants.

On *418 begins the eulogy on Lomonosov, which continues to the end of the book. This contains praise of Mirabeau, who deserves not once but many times over to be hanged. Here the Empress Elizabeth Petrovna is treated with disrespect. Here it is evident that the author is not a true Christian. And it seems probable that he has appointed himself the leader, whether by this book or by other means, in snatching the scepters from the hands of monarchs; but, since one man alone could not do this, and since there are indications that he has a few accomplices, he should be questioned on this matter, as well as on his real intentions. And, since he himself writes that he loves the truth, he should be asked to say how the matter stood. If, however, he does not write the truth, I shall be compelled to seek evidence, and things will be worse for him than before.

On *453 the author promises a continuation of this book "on our return journey." Where is this work? Was it begun, and where is it?

Of the line "With the permission of the Department of Public Morals" I will say that it is a deceitful and contemptible act to add anything to a book after the permission has been signed. It must be determined how many copies were published and where they are.

BIBLIOGRAPHY

NOTES

INDEX

BIBLIOGRAPHY

I. EDITIONS OF THE *Journey*

Radishchev's own edition, *Puteshestvie iz Peterburga v Moskvu*, St. Petersburg, 1790. All copies that could be found were burned. Eighteen copies are extant in Russia, including the one which belonged to Pushkin. There is also a copy in the Library of Congress in Washington, D.C., and another in the Houghton Library of Harvard University. A photolithographic reprint of this edition was published by "Academia" (Moscow and Leningrad, 1935), together with a companion volume: see below, Section II, Barskov.

Herzen's edition, London, 1858. Herzen published Radishchev's *Journey* and Prince Mikhail Shcherbatov's work *On the Corruption of Morals in Russia* in a single volume, with two prefaces.

P. A. Efremov's edition, St. Petersburg, 1872. This was confiscated.

Edition at Leipzig, 1876, in volume XVIII of E. L. Kasprowicz's "International Library." This was a stereotyped copy of Herzen's edition.

A. S. Suvorin's edition, St. Petersburg, 1888. This was a limited edition of one hundred copies, printed on very expensive paper.

P. A. Kartavov's edition, St. Petersburg, 1903. This was forbidden at the last moment by the censorship.

P. E. Shchegolev and N. P. Pavlov-Sil'vansky's edition, St. Petersburg, November 1905. This was a complete scholarly edition, distributed without hindrance. Since the Revolution of 1905, the *Journey* has appeared in a great many editions. Only a few of the most noteworthy will be mentioned.

A. K. Borozdin, I. I. Lapshin, and P. E. Shchegolev's edition, in volume I of *Polnoe sobranie sochineniy A. N. Radishcheva* (Complete Works of A. N. Radishchev), 2 vols., St. Petersburg, 1907. This edition of Radishchev's complete works has been used here for works other than the *Journey* and is cited hereafter as Borozdin, *Complete Works of Radishchev*.

I. K. Luppol, G. A. Gukovsky, and V. A. Desnitsky's edition, in volume I of their Complete Works of Radishchev, Moscow and Leningrad, 1938.

D. D. Blagoy and L. B. Svetlov's edition, Moscow and Leningrad, 1950. This is a beautifully illustrated edition, in honor of Radishchev's bicentennial in 1949.

German translation by Arthur Luther, *Reise von Petersburg nach Moskau*, Leipzig, 1922, vol. IV of *Quellen und Aufsätze zur russischen Geschichte*, ed. Karl Stählin. This translation is readable and faithful to the original; an altogether excellent work, unfortunately out of print.

German translation by Anneliese Bauch, "unter Heranziehung der Übersetzung von Arthur Luther," Berlin, 1952. This translator uses a more colloquial language than does Luther. Two passages (*Journey*, pp. *141, *175; Bauch, pp. 121, 141) are omitted, though probably not (to judge from the context) deliberately. The translation contains a good and useful "Kleines Lexikon" of persons, heroes, and gods mentioned in the *Journey*.

II. SELECTED WORKS ON RADISHCHEV

Barskov, Yakov Lazarevich, and M. V. Zhizhka. *Materialy k izucheniyu "Puteshestviya iz Peterburga v Moskvu" A. N. Radishcheva* (Materials for the Study of A. N. Radishchev's "Journey from St. Petersburg to Moscow"). Moscow and Leningrad, 1935. This is a companion volume to a photolithographic reprint of the original edition of the *Journey*. It contains a biography of Radishchev, notes to the *Journey*, and textual apparatus, principally the work of Barskov. It is an excellent piece of work.

Bodyansky. *See* Catherine II, Empress.

Borozdin, A. K. "Aleksandr Nikolaevich Radishchev." Biographical sketch in Borozdin, *Complete Works of Radishchev*, I, vii-xxxviii.

Catherine II, Empress. "Radishchev. Zamechaniya na sochinenie ego Gosudaryni Imperatritsy Ekateriny II" (Radishchev. Notes of Her Imperial Majesty Catherine II on His Work), ed. Osip Maksimovich Bodyansky, *Chteniya v Imperatorskom Obshchestve Istorii i Drevnostey Rossiyskikh pri Moskovskom Universitete* (Publications of the Imperial Society of Russian History and Antiquities at Moscow University, hereafter cited as *Chteniya*), LIV (1865), book III, section V, pp. 67-77.

———— "Sobstvennoruchnoe chernovoe nastavlenie Ekateriny II dlya molodykh Russkikh, otpravlennykh v Leyptsig dlya izucheniya yurisprudentsii, i sovremennyya izvestiya o prebyvanii ikh tam" (Autograph Instruction of Catherine II for the Young Russians Sent to Leipzig to Study Jurisprudence, and Contemporary Accounts of Their Stay There), *Sbornik Imperatorskago Russkago Istoricheskago Obshchestva* (Publications of the Imperial Russian Historical Society), X (1872), 107-131. Cited hereafter as "Autograph Instruction of Catherine II."

Evgen'ev, Boris Sergeevich. *Alexander Radishchev: A Russian Humanist of the Eighteenth Century.* London, 1946.

Kashin, N. P. "Novy spisok biografii A. N. Radishcheva" (A New Copy of a Biography of A. N. Radishchev), *Chteniya*, CCXLI (1912), book II, section III, pp. 1-26.

Khrapovitsky, Aleksandr Vasil'evich. *Dnevnik A. V. Khrapovitskago* (Diary of A. V. Khrapovitsky), ed. Nikolay Platonovich Barsukov, Moscow, 1901. Cited hereafter as *Diary of A. V. Khrapovitsky*.
Kuz'mina, V. D., and M. I. Kostrova, eds., *Radishchev v russkoy kritike* (Radishchev in Russian Criticism). Moscow, 1952.
Lapshin, I. I. "Filosofskiya vozzreniya Radishcheva" (Philosophical Views of Radishchev) in Borozdin, *Complete Works of Radishchev*, II, vii–xxxii.
Lossky, A. "Aleksandr Nikolaevich Radishchev." *Russky biograficheskiy slovar'* (Russian Biographical Dictionary), XV (St. Petersburg, 1910), 382–388.
Orlov, Vladimir Nikolaevich. *Radishchev i russkaya literatura* (Radishchev and Russian Literature). 2nd ed. Leningrad, 1952.
"Protsess Radishcheva. Offitsial'nye materialy i svidetel'stva sovremennikov" (The Trial of Radishchev. Official Materials and the Testimony of Contemporaries) in Borozdin, *Complete Works of Radishchev*, II, 295–354.
Pushkin, Aleksandr Sergeevich. "Aleksandr Radishchev," in Pushkin's *Polnoe sobranie sochineniy* (Complete Works), ed. D. D. Blagoy, V. D. Bonch-Bruevich, S. M. Bondi, M. A. Tsyavlovsky, D. P. Yakubovich, *et al.* 16 vols., Leningrad, 1937–1949, XII, 30–40. Cited hereafter as Pushkin, *Complete Works*.
Radishchev, Nikolay Aleksandrovich. "A. N. Radishchev," a biographical sketch edited by Nikolay Platonovich Barsukov, in *Russkaya starina* (Russian Antiquity), VI (1872), 573–581.
Radishchev, Pavel Aleksandrovich. "Aleksandr Nikolaevich Radishchev," *Russky vestnik* (The Russian Messenger), XVIII (1858), 395–432.
Semennikov, Vladimir Petrovich. *Radishchev: ocherki i issledovaniya* (Radishchev: Essays and Studies). Moscow and Petrograd, 1923.
Sukhomlinov, Mikhail Ivanovich. *A. N. Radishchev, avtor "Puteshestviya iz Peterburga v Moskvu"* (A. N. Radishchev, Author of "A Journey from St. Petersburg to Moscow"). St. Petersburg, 1883. Cited hereafter as *A. N. Radishchev*.
Vorontsov, Prince Semyon Mikhaylovich. *Arkhiv knyazya Vorontsova* (Archive of Prince Vorontsov), 40 books in 32 vols., Moscow, 1870–1895, particularly vol. V (1872) and vol. IX (1876). Cited hereafter as *Archive of Prince Vorontsov*.
Zavadovsky, Count Pyotr Vasil'evich. "Otvet Gosudaryu ot pervago chlena Kommissii o Sostavlenii Zakonov, Grafa Zavadovskago, na zapros o medlennosti Kommissii" (Answer of the Chairman of the Commission on Revision of the Laws, Count Zavadovsky, to the Sovereign's Question about the Dilatoriness of the Commission), *Chteniya*, XXXII (1860), book I, section V, 61–64. Cited hereafter as "Answer of the Chairman."

Since this book first appeared, in 1958, there have been a great many studies of Radishchev and the *Journey*. I can mention here only a few of these. There are now two full-length lives of Radishchev in English: David Marshall Lang, *The First Russian Radical: Alexander Radishchev, 1749–1802* (London: George Allen & Unwin, Ltd., 1959), and Allen McConnell, *A Russian Philosophe: Alexander Radishchev, 1749–1802* (The Hague: Martinus Nijhoff, 1964). Each of these works includes a bibliography. In addition, there is a very useful German translation by Erich Salewski of Radishchev's *Ausgewählte Schriften* (Berlin, 1959). This is translated from I. Ya. Shchipanov's edition (Leningrad, 1949) of Radishchev's selected philosophical works.

R. P. T.
July 1966

NOTES

See Bibliography for full titles of works here cited in abbreviated form. R. signifies Radishchev. In the Notes to the *Journey*, the starred number in parentheses following the note number indicates the page of the original edition to which the note refers.

EPIGRAPH

Vasily Kirillovich Tred'yakovsky (1703–1769), *Telemakhida* (St. Petersburg, 1766), a translation of Fénelon, *Les aventures de Télémaque* (Paris, 1699). Fénelon's and Tred'yakovsky's monster is Cerberus, R.'s is serfdom. R. has changed Tred'yakovsky's line from "with three mouths" to "hundred-mouthed." R. uses essentially the same figure of speech on pp. *239, *259, and *359.

NOTES TO INTRODUCTION

1. Benedict Humphrey Sumner, *Peter the Great and the Emergence of Russia* (London, 1950), p. 158.
2. Law of January 24, 1722, *Polnoe sobranie zakonov Rossiyskoy Imperii, s 1649 goda* (Complete Collection of the Laws of the Russian Empire, from the Year 1649), (St. Petersburg, 1830), VI, 486–493, No. 3890 (hereafter cited as *P. S. Z.*). In the Table of Ranks, there was no office of the first grade listed for the Court Service. In the second grade, the court office was "Ober-Marshal." No court office was listed for the thirteenth grade. Choristers and barbers were among those in the fourteenth court grade.
3. Laws of April 6, 1722, *P. S. Z.*, VI, 638–641, No. 3939; June 26, 1724, *P. S. Z.*, VII, 310–318, No. 4533; November 26, 1718, *P. S. Z.*, V, 597, No. 3245.
4. Laws of December 31, 1736, *P. S. Z.*, IX, 1022, No. 7142; May 6, 1736, *P. S. Z.*, IX, 809–810, No. 6951; February 18/March 1, 1762, *P. S. Z.*, XV, 912–915, No. 11444; January 17/28, 1765, *P. S. Z.*, XVII, 10, No. 12311.
5. *Journey*, p. *261.
6. April 21/May 2, 1785, *P. S. Z.*, XXII, 344–358, No. 16187.
7. "Autograph Instruction of Catherine II," p. 107.
8. Gabriel Bonnot de Mably, *Observations sur l'histoire de la Grèce ou des causes de la prospérité et des malheurs des Grecs* (Geneva, 1766), pp. 170–171. Radishchev's translation, *Razmyshleniya o grecheskoy istorii ili o prichinakh blagodenstviya i neschastiya Grekov*

(St. Petersburg, 1773), pp. 126–127. The two passages are printed side by side in Mikhail Ivanovich Sukhomlinov, *A. N. Radishchev*, pp. 26–27. For an excellent account of Mably, see Ernest A. Whitfield, *Gabriel Bonnot de Mably* (London, 1930).

9. Catherine II's Notes on the *Journey*, *Chteniya*, LIV (1865), book III, section V, p. 76. A complete translation of Catherine's notes is included in this volume.

10. The full text of the Ode was published in Borozdin, *Complete Works of Radishchev*, I, 318–330. Stanzas 12–22, 23, 48–49, 34, 45, 46, 47 are referred to above. Stanza 46 is a close paraphrase of part of the eighth section of Raynal's work; see Guillaume Thomas François Raynal, *Révolution de l'Amérique* (London, 1781), p. 92.

11. Catherine's Notes, pp. 67, 76.

12. *Ibid.*, p. 67.

13. *Diary of A. V. Khrapovitsky*, p. 199. Entry for July 7/18, 1790.

14. *Archive of Prince Vorontsov*, IX, 181.

15. Ivan Ivanovich Lapshin in Borozdin, *Complete Works of Radishchev*, II, vii. Radishchev's "O cheloveke, o ego smertnosti i bezsmertii," *ibid.*, pp. 1–141.

16. Letter of May 2/13, 1791, *Archive of Prince Vorontsov*, V, 308.

17. "Pis'mo o kitayskom torge" (1792), in Borozdin, *Complete Works of Radishchev*, II, 201–242.

18. Only the proem and the first canto are extant. The editors of the 1807 edition of Radishchev's works said that eleven cantos had been written, but that the other ten had been lost. But they had seen all that had been written and gave a prose summary of the entire work. This appears with "Bova" in Borozdin, *Complete Works of Radishchev*, I, 235–263. See also *The Romance of Sir Beues of Hamtoun*, ed. Eugen Kölbing, 3 vols. (London, 1885–1894, Early English Text Society); Aleksandr Nikolaevich Wesselofsky (Veselovsky), "Zum russischen Bovo d'Antona," *Archiv für slavische Philologie*, VIII (1885), 330; IX (1886), 310.

19. Pushkin, "Aleksandr Radishchev," Pushkin's *Complete Works*, XII, 35.

20. *Ibid*. Radishchev, "Os'mnadtsatoe stoletie," in Borozdin, *Complete Works of Radishchev*, I, 334–335.

21. Radishchev's two opinions are printed in Sukhomlinov, *A. N. Radishchev*, pp. 96–102.

22. Count Zavadovsky, "Answer of the Chairman," p. 61. Pavel Aleksandrovich Radishchev, "Aleksandr Nikolaevich Radishchev," pp. 424–425. N. P. Kashin, "A New Copy of a Biography of Radishchev," p. 22.

23. Pavel Aleksandrovich Radishchev, p. 422.

24. Aleksandr Kornil'evich Borozdin, "Aleksandr Nikolaevich Ra-

dishchev," in Borozdin, *Complete Works of Radishchev*, I, xxxvii. Pushkin, *Complete Works*, XII, 34. *Journey*, p. *191. Marcus Porcius Cato Uticensis (Cato the Younger) in Plutarch's *Life of Cato*, LXX, 1.

25. For Beckmann, see "Torzhok," n. 11. *Journey*, pp. *173, *352, *353. Pavel Aleksandrovich Radishchev, pp. 399, 402.

26. Raynal, *Histoire philosophique et politique des établissemens* [sic] *et du commerce des Européens dans les deux Indes*, 6 vols. (Amsterdam, 1770). For a careful, scholarly account of Raynal, see Anatole Feugère, *Un précurseur de la Révolution: l'abbé Raynal (1713-1796)*, (Angoulême, 1922). *The Letters of Horace Walpole, fourth Earl of Orford*, ed. Mrs. Paget Toynbee, 16 vols. (Oxford, 1903-1905), VIII, 222, letter to the Countess of Ailesbury, December 29, 1772. Edmond Scherer, *Etudes sur la littérature au XVIIIᵉ siècle* (Paris, 1891), pp. 277-278. *Journey*, p. *449.

27. John Bennett Black, *The Art of History: A Study of Four Great Historians of the Eighteenth Century* (London, 1926), pp. 117-141. William Robertson, *The History of America*, 2 vols. (London, 1777), II, 306 (Book VII). *Journey*, p. *285.

28. Mably, "De la législation, ou principes des loix" (1776), book I, ch. III, *Collection complète des oeuvres de l'abbé de Mably*, 15 vols. (Paris, the Year III of the French Republic [1794-1795]), IX, 79. *Journey*, p. *256.

29. *Journey*, p. *98. Pierre Bayle, *Dictionnaire historique et critique*, 2 vols. (Rotterdam, 1697, and many later editions). *Journey*, pp. *104-*105, *366, *440, *337, *301, *451, *450, *449, *419-*453, *125, *23, *107. Catherine's Notes, p. 67.

30. Laurence Sterne, *A Sentimental Journey through France and Italy*, 2 vols. (London, 1768), I, 56-61.

31. Pyotr Ivanovich Chelishchev (1745-1811), *Puteshestvie po severu Rossii v 1791 godu* (A Journey through the North of Russia in the Year 1791), ed. Leonid Nikolaevich Maykov (St. Petersburg, 1886). Nikolay Mikhaylovich Karamzin (1766-1826), *Pis'ma russkago puteshestvennika* (Letters of a Russian Traveler). Karamzin traveled during the years 1789-1790 and published the Letters serially after his return to Russia. An abridged English translation of Karamzin's *Letters* has just appeared, translated and abridged by Florence Jonas, with an introduction by Leon Stilman, New York, 1957.

32. Peter Yershov, *Science Fiction and Utopian Fantasy in Soviet Literature* (New York: Research Program on the U.S.S.R., 1954), p. 6. Cesare Bonesana, Marchese di Beccaria, *Dei delitti e delle pene* (Milan, 1764). A French translation appeared in 1766. As noted, the Empress Catherine II made use of Beccaria in her *Nakaz*.

33. *Journey*, pp. *353, *442-*443, *440, *308, *395, *251, *285, *449, *353, *397, *352, *90, *352, *353, *118, *90, *93-*94, *90, *290-*292, *402-*403.

260   NOTES: INTRODUCTION

34. Pushkin, *Complete Works*, XII, 35–36.
35. On Radishchev's language, see Viktor Vladimirovich Vinogradov, *Ocherki po istorii russkogo literaturnogo yazyka XVII–XIX vv.* (Outlines of the History of the Russian Literary Language, XVIIth–XIXth Centuries), (Leyden, 1949), pp. 144ff.
36. *Journey*, pp. *72, *185, *193, *381; *242, *249, *379–*380, *402, *403; *14, *35, *150, *154–*155; *30–*31, *64–*65, *253, *426.
37. *Journey*, pp. *281–*282, *399. For Mark Twain, see *A Connecticut Yankee in King Arthur's Court* (1889), ch. XXII, "The Holy Fountain." For William Faulkner, see especially *A Fable* (New York, 1954), pp. 50–52.
38. "— ibo i krest'yanki lyubit' umeyut! — " Karamzin, "Bednaya Liza" (Poor Liza), 1792, in *Sochineniya* (Works), ed. Aleksandr Smirdin, 3 vols. (St. Petersburg, 1848), III, 4.
39. "Liberty: An Ode," stanza 47, in Borozdin, *Complete Works of Radishchev*, I, 329. Ivan Petrovich Pnin, *Sochineniya* (Works), ed. Ivan Kapitonovich Luppol and Vladimir Nikolaevich Orlov (Moscow, 1934), p. 62.
40. Pushkin, *Complete Works:* "Bova," I, 64. "Vol'nost': Oda," II, 45–48. "Derevnya," II, 89–91. *Journey*, pp. *269–*270, *341.
41. Pushkin, Letter to Sergey Aleksandrovich Sobolevsky, November 9/21, 1826, *Complete Works*, XIII, 302–303. Roderick Page Thaler, "The French Tutor in Radishchev and Pushkin," *The Russian Review*, XIII (1954), 210ff. Pushkin, *Complete Works*: "Kapitanskaya dochka" (1836), vol. VIII, ch. I, pp. 279–280; "Puteshestvie iz Moskvy v Peterburg," XI, 223–267, 249. *Journey*, pp. *389–*394.
42. Pushkin, "Ya pamyatnik sebe vozdvig nerukotvorny," *Complete Works*, III, 424, 1034. Horace, "Exegi monumentum," *Odes*, III, 30; "Odi profanum vulgus," *Odes*, III, 1. *Journey*, p. *453.
43. Preface dated "Putney, 25th May 1858." Aleksandr Ivanovich Gertsen, *Polnoe sobranie sochineniy i pisem* (Complete Works and Letters), ed. Mikhail Konstantinovich Lemke, 22 vols. (Petrograd, 1919–1925), IX, 271, 277.
44. The Review appeared in *Sovremennik* (The Contemporary), January 3/15, 1858. Nikolay Aleksandrovich Dobrolyubov, *Pervoe polnoe sobranie sochineniy N. A. Dobrolyubova* (The First Complete Collection of the Works of N. A. Dobrolyubov), ed. M. K. Lemke, 4 vols. (St. Petersburg, 1911), I, 571–577. Pushkin, Letter to Aleksandr Aleksandrovich Bestuzhev, June 13/25, 1823, *Complete Works*, XIII, 64.

NOTES TO THE JOURNEY

Dedication — Aleksey Mikhaylovich Kutuzov, R.'s fellow student at Leipzig and lifelong friend. He translated Gottlieb Friedrich Klopstock's *Der Messias* (an epic poem in hexameters, on the redemption of the world by Christ) into Russian. He was in Berlin when the *Journey* appeared.

Tosna — 1. (*10) Razryadny Archive, the office which kept records of the names of men who had served in the army and the ranks they had achieved. Some of the new gentry, when they had acquired rank and wealth, also began to acquire noble ancestors. Although after the abolition of mestnichestvo (see n. 4), one's ancestry was no longer to determine one's place in the service, some people still liked to have their "ancestry" recorded.

2. (*10) Vladimir Monomakh, Vladimir II, 1053–1125; Grand Prince of Kiev, 1113–1125. One of the best and most beloved of the early Russian rulers. Rurik, traditional founder of the Russian state, supposed to have come from Scandinavia to Novgorod ca. A.D. 862.

3. (*11) Fyodor Alekseevich, Fyodor III, 1661–1682; Tsar of Russia, 1676–1682.

4. (*11) *Mestnichestvo*, a system whereby members of noble families were appointed to offices in the state service in accordance with their hereditary precedence. For example, members of the Odoevsky family had the hereditary right to be appointed to higher offices than members of the Buturlin family. See Vasily Osipovich Klyuchevsky, *A History of Russia*, tr. C. J. Hogarth, 5 vols. (London, 1911–1931), II, 45–57. Mestnichestvo was abolished by a law of January 12, 1682, P. S. Z., II, 368–379, No. 905. Under the Table of Ranks, introduced forty years after mestnichestvo was abolished, ancestry was to count for nothing in the service. A man of the humblest origin could become a field marshal, as Menshikov did under Peter the Great.

5. (*11) Novgorod nobility. After Ivan III's conquest of Novgorod, the Novgorod nobility were transported wholesale to the region of Moscow, ca. 1488. Many of them eventually entered the Muscovite state service, but all other noble families which had entered it earlier had precedence over them. The Novgorod nobility were traditionally poor and underprivileged.

6. (*11) Table of Ranks. See Introduction, n. 2.

7. (*11) Charter to the Gentry. See Introduction, n. 6.

Lyubani — 1. (*15) Commutation tax (*obrok*), money or produce which a serf gave to his master instead of working on the master's land. Although the master could demand obrok in whatever amount he pleased, the amount tended to remain relatively constant. Paying obrok was considered less burdensome than working on the master's land.

2. (*15) Dissenter (*Raskol'nik*), one who refused to accept the decisions made at the Church council held in Moscow in 1654. The council had decided, among other things, that Christ's name should be spelled "Iisus," not "Isus," and that the sign of the cross should

be made with three fingers, not with two. Those who refused to accept these decisions included many of the most devout members of the Church. The loss of these people greatly weakened the Church. Many of the Raskol'niki were the most oppressed and discontented of the peasants, and in peasant uprisings against the government and landlords, Raskol'niki often took the lead.

3. (*15) Three fingers indicate that he is Orthodox.

4. (*15) Work on the master's fields (*barshchina*), compulsory, unpaid labor of serfs on the manorial fields, that is, on the master's own demesne lands. Barshchina was generally considered the worst and most burdensome form of serfdom, and people generally thought of barshchina when they thought of serfdom.

5. (*18) Crown and manorial peasants, those on lands belonging respectively to the crown and to individual landed proprietors.

Chudovo — 1. (*21) My friend Ch———, probably Pyotr Ivanovich Chelishchev (1745–1811), Radishchev's fellow student at Leipzig.

2. (*23) A verst is .6629 mile or 1.067 kilometers.

3. (*23) Paphos and Amathus, centers of the worship of Aphrodite on the southwestern coast of Cyprus.

4. (*23) Claude Joseph Vernet, 1714–1789, French marine painter, whose best-known painting is "The Storm." By tradition, during a storm at sea he had himself tied to the ship's mast so that he could have a better view of the storm.

5. (*27) Turkish War in the Archipelago, the Russo-Turkish War of 1768–1774; specifically two Russian naval victories, one in the Chios Strait on June 24/July 5, 1770; and one in Chesme Bay on June 26/July 7, 1770.

6. (*37) Guillaume Raynal, *Histoire philosophique . . . dans les deux Indes*, 10 vols. (Geneva, 1781, hereafter cited as Raynal), II, 196–198, Book III, ch. xxxv. We have followed the translation of John Obadiah Justamond, 8 vols. (London, 1783), II, 168–169.

Spasskaya Polest' — 1. (*43) The giant Polkan was the villain, Bevis (Bova) the hero of the tale of "Bova Korolevich." See Introduction, p. 14. Nightingale the Robber (Solovey Razboynik) was a wicked monster who overpowered people by his whistling. He was finally captured by the hero Ilya Muromets.

2. (*43) The Viceroy was probably Prince Grigory Aleksandrovich Potemkin.

3. (*45) Troika, a carriage drawn by three horses abreast.

4. (*47) A rhymed proverb, "No Tsar' zhaluet a psar' nezhaluet." The unmerciful "dogkeeper" ("psar' ") is the Tsar's official.

5. (*52) That is, a wealthy man and private citizen, not a poor government official who might have had to take bribes to keep his head above water.

6. (*53) Anyone who reached the eighth rank or higher in the Table of Ranks automatically became one of the gentry.

7. (*54) That is, that the attachment did not apply to property acquired after the decree had been issued.

8. (*54) The host had been telling the story himself, although he had started by making his guest tell it. Now he suddenly returns to the guest as narrator.

9. (*58) "... edu ... kuda glaza gledyat." It makes no difference to him where he goes; he goes wherever chance leads him.

10. (*72–73) Radishchev seems to say that faithful subjects are ready to see the government lose a war, because its defeat might lead to liberation — an attitude curiously foreshadowing the attitude of some Russian revolutionaries at the time of the Russo-Japanese War of 1904–1905.

11. (*73) See Catherine II's note on this sentence.

12. (*75) See Catherine's note.

13. (*75–76) The story of the fairy Truth, who gives the king a ring that pricks his finger whenever he does wrong, is in the French *Cabinet des Fées*, and is delightfully told in English by Andrew Lang as the tale of "Prince Darling," in *The Blue Fairy Book* (Philadelphia, 1930), pp. 325–339.

14. (*76) See Catherine's note.

15. (*78) See Catherine's note.

16. (*80) Captain James Cook (1728–1779) was killed while exploring the Hawaiian Islands.

17. (*82) Castalia, a fountain on Mt. Parnassus; Hippocrene, a fountain on Mt. Helicon, both sacred to the Muses and hence, sources of inspiration.

18. (*84) That is, the pilgrim who would dare to tell the truth, to whom Truth herself had already referred.

19. (*85) See above, n. 13.

Podberez'e — 1. (*86) "Na vsyakago mudretsa dovol'no prostoty"; Ostrovsky wrote a play with this title in 1868.

2. (*86–87) Praskov'ya, a variant form of Paraskeva. St. Paraskeva, usually called "Paraskeva Pyatnitsa," was a martyr at the time of Diocletian's persecution of the Christians. Her day is October 28 in the Orthodox calendar of saints.

3. (*87) Kvas, a kind of beer made from rye or barley. Countess Alexandra Tolstoy (*Tolstoy: A Life of My Father*, trans. Elizabeth Hapgood, New York, 1953, p. 111) says that kvas was still used as hair tonic in 1859.

4. (*89) Kuteykin (Radishchev, by a typographical error, spells it "Kuteynik"), a teacher in Denis Ivanovich Fonvizin's comedy, The Minor (*Nedorosl'*). The speech referred to is in Act II, Sc. 5. The play was presented in 1782 and published in 1783. It is

available in English as "The Young Hopeful," trans. George Z. Patrick and George Rapall Noyes, in *Masterpieces of the Russian Drama*, ed. George Rapall Noyes (New York and London, 1933); see p. 44.

5. (*90) Sir William Blackstone's *Commentaries on the Laws of England*, 4 vols. (Oxford, 1765-1769), was translated into Russian by S. E. Desnitsky in three parts, which appeared respectively in 1780, 1781, and 1782. This conversation may therefore have taken place in 1781.

6. (*91) In 1782 a commission was appointed, with Count Zavadovsky as chairman, to study the question of founding new schools and universities. In 1787 it recommended establishment of universities at Pskov, Chernigov, and Penza, but nothing was actually done, probably because of the war with Turkey, which began in 1787. No new universities were actually started until the reign of Alexander I.

7. (*93) Martinist, an adherent of the doctrines of Louis Claude de Saint-Martin, 1743-1803, French philosopher and mystic, whose teachings were very popular with the Russian Masons, including Radishchev's friends Novikov, Kutuzov, and Count Aleksandr Vorontsov. Emanuel Swedenborg, 1688-1772, Swedish scientist, philosopher, and mystic, founder of the Church of the New Jerusalem.

8. (*94) Frederick the Great provided for religious toleration in his code and welcomed Voltaire to his court.

9. (*95) This may be a reference to Luther's battering down of what he described as "the three walls of the Romanists." See Martin Luther, "An den christlichen Adel deutscher Nation von des christlichen Standes Besserung" (1520), in *Werke. Kritische Gesammtausgabe*, ed. J. K. F. Knaake (Weimar, 1888), VI, 406-415.

10. (*98) Pierre Bayle, *Dictionaire [sic] Historique et Critique*, 2 vols. in 4 (Rotterdam, 1697), I, 156-157. We have followed the translation of Pierre Des Maizeaux *et al.*, 2nd English ed., 5 vols. (London, 1734-1738), I, 173-174.

Novgorod — 1. (*100) *Posadnik*, an elected official in charge of the civilian government in Novgorod, comparable to a mayor. *Tysyatsky*, an elected official who commanded the troops and had control of the police of Novgorod.

2. (*101) Novgorod was not actually a member of the Hanseatic League, but maintained close commercial relations with it. The League had a permanent trading station in Novgorod.

3. (*101-102) Ivan III (reigned 1462-1505) "took Novgorod for himself" in 1471. The sort of punishment described by R. was meted out in the course of a later rebellion of the Novgorodians.

4. (*103) See Catherine's note.

5. (*103) Cf. Rousseau, *Contrat social*, Book I, ch. III.

6. (*105) Not actual excerpts from the Chronicle of Novgorod,

but written after the style of the Chronicle, and factually correct according to it.

7. (*105) Merchants of the third guild were those having a capital of from five hundred to one thousand rubles. The class of "honorable citizens," established by the Charter to the Towns, was exempt from corporal punishment and had various other privileges. Law of April 21/May 2, 1785, *P. S. Z.*, XXII, 358–384, No. 16188.

8. (*107) The Aleutian Islands at this time belonged to the Russian Empire.

9. (*107) Johann Kaspar Lavater (1741–1801), Swiss poet and physiognomist, author of *Physiognomische Fragmente zur Beförderung der Menschenkenntnis und Menschenliebe*, 4 vols. (Leipzig, 1775–1778).

10. (*108) White powder: "3 puda belil." A pood is 36.113 pounds or 16.38 kilograms. Rzhev, a town roughly one hundred miles west of Moscow, two hundred miles southeast of Novgorod.

11. (*110) One hundred kopeks make a ruble.

12. (*111) Here Borozdin, Lapshin, and Shchegolev supply a line not in Radishchev's own edition: "Nevestka vstan' da podnesi gostyam." "Daughter-in-law, get up and pour for the guests." See *Complete Works of Radishchev*, I, 93.

Bronnitsy — 1. (*113) "This city [Kolmogard] was where the village of Bronnitsy now is, and its hill [kholm] was renowned for its great holiness . . . . In pagan times, Kolmogard was renowned for its holiness throughout the North. . . Many, not only simple folk but northern kings, came there to pray." Vasily Nikitich Tatishchev, *Istoriya rossiyskaya s samykh drevneyshikh vremen* (Russian History from the Most Ancient Times), ed. Gerhard Friedrich Müller, 5 vols. (Moscow, 1768–1848), I, 45, 46, 271.

2. (*115) Perun, the old Slavonic god of thunder.

3. (*116) See Catherine's note.

4. (*118) Joseph Addison, *Cato* (1713), V.i.27–31.

Zaytsovo — 1. (*124) Under the Table of Ranks, ranks in the Court Service had been made to correspond with ranks in the Military and Civil Services.

2. (*124) A man who reached the rank of Collegiate Assessor became one of the gentry.

3. (*125) See Catherine's note.

4. (*125) As one of the gentry, he could buy a village of serfs.

5. (*125) William Hogarth, 1697–1764.

6. (*125) See "Novgorod," n. 9.

7. (*127) The fortification or fastness of the Zaporozhian ("beyond the rapids") Cossacks on islands among the rapids of the Dnieper River. All ate the same sort of food, at the general expense. There

were very strict rules, and very severe punishments for anyone who broke them. The fastness was destroyed in 1775.
 8. (*136) See Catherine's note.
 9. (*142) See Catherine's note.
 10. (*146) See Catherine's note.
 11. (*147) See Catherine's note.
 12. (*147) Baba, the country estate of A. A. Naryshkin, about three miles from St. Petersburg. It had its own canals with gondolas, ponds with swans and pelicans, and even an English park, and was a favorite outing place for the gentry.
 13. (*148) Duryndin, a name formed from "durynda," an augmentative form of "durak," means "a particularly big fool."

Kresttsy — 1. (*156) Literally, "on her chicken legs," a favorite Russian folklore expression.
 2. (*160) See Catherine's note.
 3. (*168) See Catherine's note.
 4. (*171) "... netverdya, kak to govoryat po poslovitse, kak soroka yakova." The proverb goes, "Zatverdila soroka Yakova, odno pro vsyakago." Vladimir Ivanovich Dal', *Poslovitsy russkago naroda* (Proverbs of the Russian People), (Moscow, 1862), p. 437.
 5. (*173) R. himself learned English well enough to read Shakespeare and Milton in the original. See Pavel Aleksandrovich Radishchev, "Aleksandr Nikolaevich Radishchev," pp. 399, 402.
 6. (*173) R. was strongly opposed to dueling. Dueling was actually condemned in an Imperial manifesto, April 21/May 2, 1787, P. S. Z., XXII, 839–846, No. 16535.
 7. (*175) Aegis, the shield with which Zeus and Pallas Athene protected themselves and, occasionally, mortals who were dear to them.
 8. (*179–180) Cf. Horace, *Odes*, II, x, 5.
 9. (*184) See Catherine's note.
 10. (*185) Cf. Milton, "All wickedness is weakness." *Samson Agonistes*, 834.
 11. (*186) By tradition, in 362 B.C. Marcus Curtius jumped, fully armed, on horseback, into a tremendous chasm caused by an earthquake. As he jumped, he said that no blessings were more truly Roman than arms and valor. The chasm closed around his body, and the rest of the people were saved. Livy, VII, vi, 1–6.
 12. (*186) See Catherine's note.
 13. (*191) See Introduction, p. 19 and n. 24.
 14. (*193) Cf. Psalm 51:17.

Yazhelbitsy — 1. (*199) As noted in the Introduction (pp. 28–29), this episode should not be taken at face value as applying to Radishchev and his sons. With this scene, compare the gravediggers' scene in *Hamlet*, V.i, especially ll. 268ff.

    2. (*200) One of his sons was cut off before his time at the tender age of eighty-six.

    3. (*203) See Catherine's note.

Valdai — 1. (*204) Aleksey Mikhaylovich, 1629–1676, Tsar of Russia, 1645–1676. Russia was at war with Poland, 1654–1667. Valdai was "raised to the dignity of a city" in 1772.

    2. (*205) Lada, in Old Slavonic, the personification of love.

    3. (*206) Nikon, ca. 1610–1681; Patriarch of Moscow, 1652–1666; founded the Iberian Monastery in 1653. Its name was derived from Iveria, an old name for Russian Georgia.

    4. (*209) The most famous poem on this theme, Christopher Marlowe's *Hero and Leander*, is quoted and alluded to by Shakespeare in *As You Like It*, III.v.81–82; IV.i.94–108. It looks almost as though R. might have borrowed the words of the fourth-act passage. "Gero i Leandr. Pontiyskaya povest'" ("Hero and Leander. A Pontic Tale") appeared in Novikov's *Moskovskoe ezhemesyachnoe izdanie* (The Moscow Monthly), 1781, part II, pp. 102–121.

Edrovo — 1. (*210) Cf. Pushkin's story "Mistress into Maid" in the *Tales of Belkin* for a similar comparison of city and country girls.

    2. (*210–211) R. seems not to have had a very high regard for dentists, but to have thought better of oculists and urologists. Cf. pp. *70, *201.

    3. (*213) A span is nine inches.

    4. (*218) Emel'yan Pugachev, pretending to be Emperor Peter III.

    5. (*218) Catherine noted: "This might almost be the story of Aleksandr Vasil'evich Saltykov."

    6. (*219) Lomonosov wrote an article, "O sokhranenii i razmnozhenii rossiyskogo naroda" ("On the Preservation and Increase of the Russian People"), in 1761, attacking forced marriages of peasants, especially those in which the wife was decidedly older than the husband.

    7. (*228) Cf. Gogol' 's epigraph to *The Inspector General*: "Na zerkalo necha penyat', koli rozha kriva." "Don't blame the mirror if your face is ugly."

    8. (*230) There were laws against marriages of persons of such unequal age, but they were not enforced. Laws of August 5/16, 1775, P. S. Z., No. 14356; December 10/21, 1781, P. S. Z., No. 15295. Cf. Catherine's note.

    9. (*234) In Russian, "cousin" is literally "brother in the second degree."

Khotilov — 1. (*239) Literally, "glorified" (slovuty).

    2. (*246) Cf. p. *238, where he says one third. Actually, according

to the census of 1783, about 94.5 per cent of the Russian people were peasants. Of these, about 55 per cent were manorial serfs, 39 per cent crown serfs, and 6 per cent free peasants.

3. (*247) Cf. Adam Ferguson, *An Essay on the History of Civil Society* (Edinburgh, 1767), pp. 401–418. See Catherine's note.

4. (*251) "premeni imya, povest' o tebe veshchaet." This is clearly Horace's "Mutato nomine, de te fabula narratur." Horace, *Satires*, I, i, 69–70.

5. (*253) Probably a reference to the Montgolfier brothers, whose linen balloon, inflated with hot air, went up on June 5, 1783, at Annonay, France.

6. (*255) "Muchitel' ": literally, "torturer," tormentor. Catherine, also called the Great, had also conquered both desert and settled areas.

7. (*257) See Catherine's note.

8. (*258) Cf. Thomas Jefferson, "The whole commerce between master and slave is a perpetual exercise of the most boisterous passions, the most unremitting despotism on the one part, and degrading submissions on the other. Our children see this and learn to imitate it. . . ." *Notes on the State of Virginia*, Query XVIII. This was published in Paris, in English in 1784, in French in 1786.

9. (*259) See Catherine's note.

10. (*260) See Catherine's note.

11. (*261) Pugachev.

12. (*262) See Catherine's note.

13. (*267) Cf. pp. *104, *340, and *369. Gogol', in *Dead Souls*, often does the same sort of thing, ending a chapter or breaking off a train of thought by going back to the horses.

Vyshny Volochok — 1. (*271) Genesis 3:17.

Vydropusk — 1. (*285) Numa Pompilius, traditional second King of Rome, reigning from 715 to 672 B.C. Livy, I, xix, 4–5.

2. (*285) Manco Capac, traditionally the first of the Incas, supposed to have lived in the eleventh century. This thought is borrowed from William Robertson. See Introduction, pp. 25–26.

3. (*288) See Catherine's note.

Torzhok — 1. (*289) By a law of January 15/26, 1783, P. S. Z., XXI, 792, No. 15634.

2. (*290) Mitrofanushka, the pampered, spoiled, and stupid "minor" in Fonvizin's comedy of that name. Cf. "Podberez'e," n. 4.

3. (*290) Johann Gottfried von Herder, "Vom Einfluss der Regierung auf die Wissenschaften und der Wissenschaften auf die Regierung" (1780), *Sämmtliche Werke*, ed. Bernhard Suphan, 33 vols. (Berlin, 1877–1913), IX (1893), 357–358, 361.

4. (*290) R. says only "permission" ("dozvolenie"), omitting Her-

der's "eine gute Sache zu treiben" without indicating the omission (as he does elsewhere) by dots.

5. (*291) R. says "much less its censor, whether in a hood or with a sword-knot," referring to the ceremonial sword worn by government functionaries. Herder says simply "geschweiger ihr bekutteter Zensor."

6. (*292) R. omits Herder's parenthetical "mit einiger Einschränkung nach seiner Situation und Lage."

7. (*294) The Empress Catherine II's *Nakaz*, 1767, ch. XX, especially articles 480–484.

8. (*297) Instead of the Orthodox three. Cf. "Lyubani," n. 2.

9. (*297) Such as the example of martyrs.

10. (*301) See Charles J. Stillé, *The Life and Times of John Dickinson, 1732–1808* (Philadelphia, 1891), pp. 223–242, on Dickinson's election as President of the Supreme Executive Council of Pennsylvania (he served from 1782 to 1785) and the anonymous attacks on him by "Valerius." "Valerius" is conjecturally identified as General John Armstrong (later Secretary of War under Madison), pp. 421–423. Dickinson's "Vindication" is printed, pp. 364–414.

11. (*306) Radishchev's principal source for the greater part of this discussion, through the end of p. *331, is Johann Beckmann, *Beiträge zur Geschichte der Erfindungen*, 5 vols. (Leipzig, 1786–1805), I, 95–108; II, 246–253. The whole of volume I appeared in 1786, the whole of volume II in 1788, but each volume appeared gradually, in several separate parts. The parts containing the material R. used, part I of volume I and part II of volume II, appeared in 1783 and 1785 respectively.

12. (*307) Protagoras, ca. 480–411 B.C., Greek Sophist who said "Man is the measure of all things." In 411 he was accused of impiety by Pythodorus, one of the Four Hundred, and his book *On the Gods* was condemned to be burned. Diogenes Laertius, *Lives of Eminent Philosophers*, IX, viii, 50–56. Cicero, *De natura deorum*, I, 23.

13. (*307) 181 B.C. Livy, XL, xxix, 3–14.

14. (*307) 13 B.C. Suetonius, *Lives of the Caesars*, II ("The Deified Augustus"), xxxi, 1.

15. (*307) Cf. Catherine's note on p. *80.

16. (*308) Lucius Annaeus Seneca Rhetor, "the Elder Seneca," ca. 54 B.C.–A.D. 39, father of Seneca the philosopher and playwright. The passages quoted are from his *Controversiae*, book X, preface 5–8. Titus Labienus, not Caesar's general, but perhaps the general's grandson. An orator and historian, he committed suicide ca. A.D. 12.

17. (*309) Benito Arias Montano, 1527–1598, Spanish theologian, was the chairman of a committee of theologians who, at the request of the Duke of Alba, published an *Index expurgatorius librorum* at Antwerp in 1571, a kind of supplement to the Index published by the

Council of Trent in 1564. Arias Montano is better known as the editor of the famous Antwerp polyglot Bible, *Biblia sacra hebraice, chaldaice, graece et latine Phillipi II Regis catholici pietate et studio ad Sacrosanctae Ecclesiae usum, cura et studio B. A. M.*, 8 vols. (Antwerp, 1569–1573). León de Castro, Professor of Oriental Languages at Salamanca, attacked the earlier volumes and charged Arias Montano with heresy in 1571, but Pope Gregory XIII gave both the polyglot Bible and Arias Montano himself his blessing on August 23, 1572. See A. Lambert, "Arias Montano," *Dictionnaire d'histoire et de géographie ecclésiastiques*, IV (Paris, 1930), 129–145.

18. (*309) Cf. Blackstone, *Commentaries on the Laws of England*, IV (1769), 151 (book IV, ch. 11, sect. 13): "By the law of the twelve tables at Rome, libels, which affected the reputation of another, were made a capital offence: but, before the reign of Augustus, the punishment became corporal only. Under the emperor Valentinian it was again made capital, not only to write, but to publish, or even to omit destroying them. Our law, in this and many other respects, corresponds rather with the middle age of Roman jurisprudence, when liberty, learning, and humanity, were in their full vigour, than with the cruel edicts that were established in the dark and tyrannical ages of the antient *decemviri*, or the later emperors."

19. (*310) A.D. 25. Tacitus, *Annals*, IV, 34–35. Aulus Cremutius Cordus, Roman historian in the time of Augustus and Tiberius. It was not Cassius Severus whom Cremutius called the last Roman, but Caius Cassius Longinus, Brutus' fellow conspirator against Caesar. Cremutius, condemned by the Senate, committed suicide, A.D. 25. Cassius Severus (ca. 50 B.C.–A.D. 33), Roman orator and satirist, was banished by Augustus ca. A.D. 9, and again by Tiberius ca. A.D. 24.

20. (*310) Antiochus IV Epiphanes, ca. 200–164 B.C.; Seleucid King of Syria, 175–164 B.C.; burned the Sacred Books of the Jews ca. 168 B.C. See (in The Apocrypha to the Old Testament) The First Book of the Maccabees, 1:10–6:16.

21. (*311) Diocletian, A.D. 245–313; Roman Emperor, 284–305; on February 23, 303 issued his edict commanding that the Christian Scriptures be burned. See Eusebius of Caesarea, *Historia ecclesiastica*, VIII, 2; and Lactantius, *De mortibus persecutorum*, ch. 12.

22. (*311) Arnobius Afer, *Adversus Gentes* (ca. A.D. 297–303), III, 7.

23. (*313) The Council of Nicaea anathematized Arius, and the Emperor Constantine I ordered his books burned, A.D. 325: Sozomen, *Historia ecclesiastica*, I, 21; Socrates Scholasticus, *Historia ecclesiastica*, I, 9, letter of Constantine to the bishops and people. Nestorius was condemned by the Council of Ephesus, A.D. 431: Mansi, ed., *Sacrorum Conciliorum Nova et Amplissima Collectio*, IV (Florence, 1760), 1211. The Emperor Theodosius II in 435 ordered Nestorius' writings burned:

Sacrorum Conciliorum, V (Florence, 1761), 413. The *Codex Iustinianus*, book I, title 5, section 6, sub-section 1, contains an order for the burning of Nestorius' books. Eutyches was excommunicated by the Council of Chalcedon, A.D. 451: *Sacrorum Conciliorum*, VI (Florence, 1761), 745ff. In 452 the Emperor Marcian ordered that the writings of Eutyches be burned: *Sacrorum Conciliorum*, VII (Florence, 1762), 501ff. In Justinian's *Pandects* (*Digests*), book X, title 2, Section 4, sub-section 1, it is ordered that books of magic and other objectionable books be destroyed.

24. (*314) Ambrosius Autpertus, born in Gaul, wrote ten books of commentaries on the Apocalypse, became abbot of the monastery of St. Vincent on the Volturno in Italy, died in 778. See *Maxima Bibliotheca Veterum Patrum, et Antiquorum Scriptorum Ecclesiasticorum*, ed. Marguerin de La Bigne *et al.*, 27 vols. (Lyons, 1677), XIII, 403-404, for his letter to the Pope; and XIII, 404-657, for his commentaries on the Apocalypse.

25. (*314) *Sacrorum Conciliorum*, XXI (Venice, 1776), 559-570.

26. (*315) Illuminati, a benevolent society founded in 1776 by Adam Weishaupt, a professor at the University of Ingolstadt, Bavaria. Closely associated with the Masons, they had three classes of membership — novices, freemasons, and priests. The lower classes were pledged to obey their superiors. In the late eighteenth century, the Illuminati had the reputation of being politically subversive. Thomas Mann includes an interesting discussion of the Illuminati in *The Magic Mountain*, trans. H. T. Lowe-Porter (New York, 1953), pp. 509ff. The fullest account is Leopold Engel, *Geschichte des Illuminaten-Ordens* (Berlin, 1906).

27. (*316) Beckmann, I, 98, speaks of "the Heidelberg edition of the book *Nosce te ipsum* of the year 1480." I have not seen this book. Maffeo Gerardo was Patriarch of Venice from 1466 until his death in 1492.

28. (*317) *Codex diplomaticus anecdotorum, res Moguntinas, Francicas, Trevirenses, Hassiacas, finitimarumque regionum nec non ius Germanicum et S. R. I. historiam vel maxime illustrantium*, ed Valentin Ferdinand, Freiherr von Gudenus, *et al.*, 5 vols. (Göttingen, Frankfurt, and Leipzig, 1743-1768), IV (1758), 469-471, 473-474. Hereafter cited as *Codex*.

29. (*317) *Codex*, p. 469, says "of the Holy Roman Empire in Germany."

30. (*319) *Codex*, p. 470, says literally: "which, because of the magnitude of the danger, we fear even more in the case of the sacred writings."

31. (*320) R. inserts the word "Apostle," not in *Codex*.

32. (*320) *Codex*, p. 470, says literally "in this our golden Mainz."

33. (*321) *Codex*, p. 471, says "within."

34. (*321) *Codex*, p. 471, says "of whatsoever rank, order, profession, dignity, or condition they may be."

35. (*322) R. begins a new sentence with "But." *Codex* continues with the old sentence.

36. (*323) *Codex*, p. 471, says "and let no one dare, without special authorization from us, to absolve anyone from the punishment for having violated this decree."

37. (*324) R. inserts "presume to," not in *Codex*.

38. (*328) R., by a typographical error, says "1507." Rodrigo Lenzuoli Borgia, 1431–1503, was Pope Alexander VI, 1492–1503. His bull, *Inter multiplices*, of June 1, 1501, is published in Peter de Roo, *Material for a History of Pope Alexander VI, His Relatives, and His Time*, 5 vols. (New York, 1924), III, 467–470. The bull as found in de Roo is hereafter cited as *Inter multiplices*.

39. (*329) R. omits the Pope's words "as We are obliged by Our pastoral office to do": *Inter multiplices*, p. 468.

40. (*329) *Inter multiplices*, p. 469, says "or their vicars general in spiritual matters or their officials." R. says "ili ikh namestnikami."

41. (*330) *Inter multiplices*, p. 469, says "catholic."

42. (*330) *Sacrorum Conciliorum*, XXXII (Paris, 1902), 912–913.

43. (*331) The partial text of the edict of September 7, 1650, establishing the civil censorship, is printed in Edmond Werdet, *Histoire du livre en France* (Paris, 1861), II, 196–201.

44. (*332) The legal basis for the Court of Star Chamber was the Act of 3 Hen. VII, c. 1 (1487), *Statutes of the Realm*, II, 509ff. The full text of a Star Chamber decree of June 23, 1585, regulating printing in the ways described by R., is printed in John Strype, *The Life and Acts of John Whitgift, D.D.*, 3 vols. (Oxford, 1822), III, 160–165. Blackstone, *Commentaries*, IV (1769), 152, note a, gives all the information (except on Caxton and Strafford) that R. does on censorship and freedom of the press in England, much of it in language very similar to R.'s.

45. (*332) William Blades, *The Biography and Typography of William Caxton, England's First Printer*, 2nd ed. (New York, 1882), pp. 169–171, says that probably the first book printed in the English language was *The Recuyell of the Historyes of Troye*, printed at Bruges (Flanders), probably in 1474. Blades, pp. 173–178, says that *The Game and Playe of Chesse*, translated by Caxton from *Le Jeu d'Echecs* of Jean de Vignay and printed at Bruges ca. 1475–1476, was probably the second work printed in English. *The Dictes or Sayengis of the Philosophres*, translated by Anthony Woodville, second Earl Rivers, is actually dated Westminster, 1477 (cf. Blades, pp. 188–191).

46. (*332) Secret Chancellery, a government department which arose out of Peter the Great's attempts to root out corruption. Formally established in 1718, it was most active during the reign of Em-

press Anna, 1730–1740. It made extensive use of informers, more than one of whom later admitted that he had falsely accused innocent people in hopes of being rewarded. It was abolished by Emperor Peter III in 1762.

47. (*333) Thomas Wentworth, Earl of Strafford, was executed after the passage of an Act of Attainder against him, 16 Car. I, c. 38 (1641), *Statutes of the Realm*, V, 177ff. The Court of Star Chamber was abolished by the Act of 16 Car. I, c. 10 (1641), *ibid.*, p. 110. The King was executed on January 30, 1649.

48. (*333) The Long Parliament's Order of June 14, 1643 (the immediate occasion for Milton's *Areopagitica*) is printed in *A Collection of All the Publicke Orders Ordinances and Declarations of Both Houses of Parliament, from the Ninth of March 1642 untill December 1646* (London, 1646), p. 214.

49. (*333) R., by a typographical error, says "James I." The two Acts are 14 Car. II, c. 33 (1662), *Statutes of the Realm*, V, 428; and 1 Jac. II, c. 17 (1685), *ibid.*, VI, 19–20.

50. (*333) 4 Gul. & Mar., c. 24 (1692), *ibid.*, p. 418.

51. (*333) Press censorship was abolished in Denmark under King Christian VII in 1770. Voltaire's poem to Christian was written in 1771: "Au Roi de Danemark, Christian VII, sur la liberté de la presse accordée dans tous ses états," *Oeuvres complètes*, ed. Louis Moland, 52 vols. (Paris, 1877–1885), X (1877), 421–427. In 1772 the Danish government again began to restrict the press.

52. (*334) R.'s source on freedom of the press in America is almost certainly *Recueil des lois constitutives des colonies angloises* [sic], *confédérées sous la dénomination d'États-Unis de l'Amérique-Septentrionale*, comp. and trans. Regnier (Philadelphia and Paris, 1778). Hereafter cited as *Recueil*. Here, following *Recueil*, p. 69, Radishchev says "An expositive declaration. . ." Except where otherwise noted, I have followed the standard English text of *The Federal and State Constitutions . . . of . . . the United States of America*, comp. and ed. Francis Newton Thorpe, 7 vols. (Washington, 1909). Hereafter cited as Thorpe. The reference here is to V, 3083.

53. (*334) *Recueil*, pp. 115–116. Thorpe, V, 3090.

54. (*334) This "Project" is printed in small type at the bottom of each page, section by section accompanying the "Plan or Frame of Government" in *Recueil*. Section 35 appears on pp. 115–116. It does not appear in any other collection, French or English, that I have seen. A careful search of the Library of the Pennsylvania Historical Society, with the generous help of the archivist, failed to turn up any trace of the English original.

55. (*335) *Recueil*, p. 159. This is not in Thorpe. I have followed the text of *The Constitutions of the Several Independent States of America*, ed. William Jackson (London, 1783), p. 216.

56. (*335) *Recueil*, p. 206. Thorpe, III, 1690.
57. (*335) Radishchev, following *Recueil*, pp. 270–271, makes it section 14. It is actually section 12 of the Virginia declaration.
58. (*335) This actually is R.'s effective condensation of the original: "That the freedom of the press is one of the great bulwarks of liberty, and can never be restrained but by despotic governments." Thorpe, VII, 3814. *Recueil*, pp. 270–271.
59. (*336) Argus, in Greek mythology, was sent by Hera to watch Io, whom Zeus loved. But Zeus sent Hermes, who played so sweetly on his flute that he put Argus to sleep. Briareus was the gods' name for him whom men called Aegaeon. Aegaeon, who had a hundred arms and fifty heads, with his brothers fought and defeated the Titans, thereby helping Zeus to become king of the gods.
60. (*337) Jean Paul Marat (1743–1793) edited a paper, *L'Ami du Peuple*, in which he frequently criticized the National Assembly. This paper was paged continuously from number to number, and appeared in book form. Marat was arrested in December 1789, and tried in a court known as the Comité des Recherches. The Marquis de Lafayette, as commander of the National Guard, took part in his cross-examination. See Louis R. Gottschalk, *Jean Paul Marat* (New York, 1927), p. 60.
61. (*338) Wilhelm Ludwig Wekhrlin (1739–1792) was editor of a magazine, *Das graue Ungeheuer*. In 1787 he was arrested by the government of Oettingen-Wallerstein for publishing a satire which was considered lese majesty against the Holy Roman Emperor Joseph II.
62. (*338) See Thomas Carlyle, *History of Freidrich II. of Prussia, called Frederick the Great*, 8 vols. (New York, 1895), III, 291ff. (book XI, ch. I).
63. (*339) See Ignaz Beidtel, *Geschichte der österreichischen Staatsverwaltung 1740–1848*, 2 vols. (Innsbruck, 1896–1898), I, 206ff., for a full discussion of Joseph II's law of June 11, 1781; and see I, 443ff., on the law of his successor, Leopold II, September 1, 1790. Hermann Gnau, *Die Zensur unter Joseph II* (Strassburg and Leipzig, 1911), pp. 255–267, gives the partial text of Joseph II's law.

Mednoe — 1. (*341) My friend: Kutuzov.
2. (*343) Field Marshal Count Burkhard Christoph Münnich (1683–1767), commander of the Russian forces in the Russo-Turkish War of 1735–1739, led an invasion of the Crimea in 1736 and defeated the Crimean Tatars, allies of the Turks.
3. (*343) In the Battle of Kunersdorf, near Frankfurt on the Oder, on August 12, 1759, the Russians under Count Pyotr Semyonovich Saltykov and the Austrians under Baron Ernst Gideon von Loudon defeated the Prussians under Frederick the Great. This, the worst defeat suffered by Frederick, made possible the Russian capture of Berlin in 1760.

NOTES: TVER'

4. (*347) In the excitement, R.'s "six" of p. *342 have shrunk to "four."

5. (*347) Radishchev's favorite philosopher Raynal was the most enthusiastic of a number of eighteenth-century French philosophers who warmly admired and praised the Quakers. See Raynal, IX, 6–24 (book XVIII, chs. 3–5), and Edith Philips, *The Good Quaker in French Legend* (Philadelphia, 1932).

6. (*347–348) Laws of April 15, 1721, *P. S. Z.*, VI, 377, No. 3770; and August 5/16, 1771, *P. S. Z.*, XIX, 293, No. 13634.

7. (*349) See Catherine's note.

Tver' — 1. (*350) See "Eulogy on Lomonosov," n. 3. Russian prosody as late as that of Prince Antiokh Dmitr'evich Kantemir (1708–1744) had followed the Polish model of syllabic verse (introduced by way of the Ukraine and Belorussia). In every Polish word, the accent falls on the penult, but in Russian the accent may fall on any syllable. Lomonosov began the use of accentual feet.

2. (*350) Aleksandr Petrovich Sumarokov (1718–1777), chiefly famous as a dramatist, also wrote songs, fables, and satirical works. In 1759 he founded a literary magazine, *Trudolyubivaya pchela* (The Industrious Bee).

3. (*351) *Semira* and *Dimitry Samozvanets* (the latter about the Pretender Dimitry who reigned briefly as Tsar, 1605–1606, during the Time of Troubles), tragedies by Sumarokov, published in 1768.

4. (*351) Mikhail Matveevich Kheraskov (1733–1807) worked on the *Rossiada* (an epic poem on the conquest of Kazan' by Tsar Ivan IV in 1552) from 1771 to 1779.

5. (*351) Vasily Petrovich Petrov (1736–1799) translated the *Aeneid* in alexandrines, 1781–1786.

6. (*352) Ermil Ivanovich Kostrov (ca. 1750–1796) translated the *Iliad* in alexandrines, 1787.

7. (*352) See note on the EPIGRAPH.

8. (*354) Voltaire's epic poem on Henry of Navarre, *La Henriade* (1726), was translated in blank verse in 1777 by Yakov Borisovich Knyazhnin (1742–1791).

9. (*355) See Catherine's note.

10. (*356) Catherine's *Nakaz*, 1767, ch. V, articles 34, 38.

11. (*356) The ode is here translated in prose. R. has his "poet" read parts of it in verse and summarize parts of it in prose. Indentions designate the parts he reads in verse. There are fifty-four stanzas in the complete ode. In the *Journey*, R.'s "poet" reads in full or in part, or summarizes, or alludes to, fifty stanzas. Stanzas 9 and 24 of the complete ode are entirely omitted from the *Journey*. Under the heading of stanza 24 in the *Journey* (26 in the complete ode), R.'s "poet" summarizes what he calls the next eleven stanzas. But they are actually the next twelve stanzas, 26–37, inclusive, of the complete ode, and

should have been numbered 24-35, inclusive, in the *Journey*. But R.'s "poet" resumes with what he calls stanza 34, instead of resuming with stanza 36, as he should have. In short, two stanzas are omitted, and there are two mistakes in counting, which reduce the total number by two more.

    12. (*356) "Sedyay vo vlasti," literally "Sitting in power." Tell: Wilhelm Tell, Swiss patriot.

    13. (*356) "Vo svet, rabstva t'mu, pretvori."

    14. (*360) cf. Romans 13: 12.

    15. (*366) Possibly a reference to the Russo-Turkish War of 1768-1774. Catherine sent a fleet which, in 1770, landed a few men and arms in Greece and tried to rouse the Greeks against the Turks. The Greeks rose, but were soon put down again by the Turks. The Russians won two naval victories in Greek waters (cf. "Chudovo," n. 5), but were unable to do anything effective on land in Greece.

    Gorodnya — 1. (*372) Economic village: A village of serfs, formerly belonging to a monastery, but since the secularization of monastic lands by the Emperor Peter III in 1762, belonging to the government and administered by the Economic College.

    2. (*374) As a peasant would be dressed and shaven, but as an educated gentleman would ordinarily not be.

    3. (*375) "Dyad'ka" is both valet and tutor, servant and mentor, like Savelyich in Pushkin's *The Captain's Daughter*.

    4. (*375) "Van'ka" is a pejorative diminutive of "Ivan."

    5. (*376) "Vanyusha" is an affectionate diminutive of "Ivan."

    6. (*389) Laws of September 29/October 10, 1766, *P. S. Z.*, XVII, 997-1015, No. 12748; January 13/24, 1769, *P. S. Z.*, XVIII, 800-801, No. 13229; July 20/31, 1770, *P. S. Z.*, XIX, 87-90, No. 13483; October 22/November 2, 1789, *P. S. Z.*, XXIII, 95-96, No. 16818.

    7. (*393) The Russian "funt," here translated as "pound," is .903 pound or .41 kilogram.

    8. (*394) On Pushkin's use of R.'s Frenchman, see Introduction, p. 35 and n. 41.

    Zavidovo — 1. (*395-396) Virgil, *Aeneid*, I, 135 *et passim*. It was Neptune, not Aeolus, who threatened the winds. Neptune even told the winds to tell Aeolus himself to behave.

    2. (*396) Cf. "Spasskaya Polest'," n. 1.

    3. (*399) Denis Ivanovich Fonvizin (1745-1792), *Vseobshchaya pridvornaya grammatika*, ch. II. Fonvizin wrote this for a journal he planned to start in 1788 — *Drug chestnykh lyudey ili Starodum* (The Friend of Honest Men or Starodum) — Starodum being the name of one of the few decent characters in The Minor. But he was refused permission to publish the journal. See *Sochineniya D. I. Fonvizina* (The Works of D. I. Fonvizin), ed. Arseny Ivanovich Vvedensky

(St. Petersburg, 1893), pp. 196–197. Available in English as "Universal Courtiers' Grammar," in *The Portable Russian Reader*, comp. and tr. Bernard Guilbert Guerney (New York, 1947), ch. II, pp. 25–27.

Klin — 1. (*401) "Aleksey chelovek Bozhy," a folk song derived from the life of St. Alexis (fl. A.D. 400. His saint's day is March 17 according to the Eastern Orthodox, July 17 according to the Roman Catholic, calendar of saints). The story came to Russia from two principal sources: "The Life of S. Alexis" in Jacobus de Voragine's *Legenda Aurea* (written ca. 1275. In English as *The Golden Legend or Lives of the Saints*, tr. William Caxton (1483), ed. F. S. Ellis, 7 vols. (London, 1900), VI, 205–212. It went east via Bohemia and the Ukraine); and the Byzantine *Anthologion*, translated by Arseny the Greek, Moscow, 1660. For a full account of the story, see Varvara Pavlovna Adrianova-Peretts, *Zhitie Alekseya cheloveka Bozhiya v drevney russkoy literature i narodnoy slovesnosti* (The Life of Aleksey the Man of God in Old Russian Literature and Folk Literature), Petrograd, 1917).

2. (*401) Catterina Gabrielli, 1730–1796, Italian operatic singer, in Russia ca. 1768–1775. Luigi Marchesi, 1755–1829, Italian singer, in Russia ca. 1785. Mrs. Francesco Saverio Todi (born Luiza Rosa de Aguiar), 1753–1833, Portuguese singer, in Russia ca. 1783–1786.

3. (*402) Goethe's *Die Leiden des jungen Werthers* appeared in 1774.

4. (*402–403) Kutuzov.

5. (*409) Cf. Laurence Sterne, *A Sentimental Journey*, "The Snuff-Box. Calais."

Peshki — 1. (*410) "golod ne svoy brat," literally, "hunger is not your brother." That is, hunger is not someone with whom you can have a friendly argument or reasonable discussion. Hunger is an imperious master who can only be obeyed. Cf. Shakespeare's proverb in *Coriolanus*, I.i.210.

Eulogy on Lomonosov — 1. (*419) See Catherine's note.

2. (*421) Kutuzov.

3. (*421) Kholmogory is near Archangel, near where the Northern Dvina River flows into the White Sea. Lomonosov lived from 1711 to 1765. There is a biography of him in English, by Boris Nikolaevich Menshutkin, *Russia's Lomonosov: Chemist, Courtier, Physicist, Poet*, tr. Jeannette Eyre Thal and Edward J. Webster (Princeton, 1952; Russian Translation Project of the American Council of Learned Societies).

4. (*427) Lomonosov's article "O pol'ze knig tserkovnykh v Rossiyskom yazyke" (On the Use of Church Books in the Russian Language), 1757.

5. (*428) Lomonosov studied philosophy and physics under Pro-

fessor Christian Wolff (1679–1754) at the University of Marburg, 1736–1739.

6. (*434) Simeon Emel'yanovich Petrovsky-Sitnianovich (1629–1680), known in Moscow as Simeon Polotsky, came from Polotsk in Belorussia. His translation of the Psalter was published in 1680. Tsar Aleksey Mikhaylovich made him tutor to his daughters by his first marriage, Sophia (later Regent), Martha, Maria, and his son, later Tsar Fyodor Alekseevich.

7. (*435) The Russians under Münnich defeated the Turks and Tatars in the Battle of Stavuchany on August 18, 1739 and captured the fortress of Khotin on August 19. Lomonosov sent from Freiberg to the Imperial Academy of Sciences in St. Petersburg his "Oda Gosudaryne Imperatritse Anne Ioannovne na pobedu nad turkami i tatarami i na vzyatie Khotina 1739 goda" (Ode to the Sovereign Empress Anna Ioannovna on the Victory over the Turks and Tatars and on the Capture of Khotin in the Year 1739).

8. (*436) Lomonosov's *Rossiyskaya grammatika* (Russian Grammar), 1755, was the first Russian (as distinct from Church Slavonic) grammar.

9. (*439) Lomonosov's *Kratkoe rukovodstvo k krasnorechiyu, kniga pervaya, v kotoroy soderzhitsya ritorika, pokazuyushchaya obshchie pravila oboego krasnorechiya, to est' oratorii i poezii, sochinennaya v pol'zu lyubyashchikh slovesnye nauki* (A Short Guide to Eloquence, Book I, Containing Rhetoric, Setting Forth the General Rules of Both Kinds of Eloquence, That Is, Oratory and Poesy, Prepared for the Use of Lovers of Literature), 1748.

10. (*440) See Catherine's notes on pp. *418ff.

11. (*443) The date of the Empress Elizabeth's accession to the throne was November 25, 1741, and the date of her coronation, April 25, 1742. Lomonosov wrote many odes in praise of the Empress on the anniversaries of these occasions. See Catherine's notes.

12. (*445) Sumarokov: see "Tver'," n. 2.

13. (*448) The "you" in this paragraph is Platon (1737–1812), son of Georgy Levshin, and Metropolitan of Moscow, 1787–1812. On August 29/September 9, 1772 he gave a solemn oration at the tomb of Peter the Great, calling him, as father of the Russian Navy, to come and see the fruit of his planting, the Russian naval victories of 1770 (cf. "Chudovo," n. 5). Catherine II sent a French translation of the speech to Voltaire.

14. (*449) William Robertson (1721–1793), historiographer to George III for Scotland, wrote histories of Scotland, the Emperor Charles V, and America. See "Vydropusk," n. 2.

15. (*449) Andreas Sigismund Marggraf (1709–1782), German chemist, chiefly famous as one of the discoverers of beetroot sugar, ca. 1747. Johann Andreas Rüdiger (1673–1731), German physician and

chemist, wrote on the pituitary gland, on the circulation of blood, on the use and abuse of technical terms in philosophy, etc.

16. (*450) Turgot's famous epigram (1778) on Franklin: "Eripuit caelo fulmen sceptrumque tyrannis." See Carl Van Doren, *Benjamin Franklin* (New York, 1945), p. 606.

17. (*450) Lomonosov's friend and fellow member of the Academy of Sciences, Professor Georg Wilhelm Richmann, was killed on July 26/August 6, 1753, while experimenting with lightning.

18. (*451) Sir Francis Bacon (1561-1626), Baron Verulam, Viscount St. Albans, Lord High Chancellor of England, published *The Advancement of Learning* in 1605. A Latin translation, *De Augmentis Scientiarum*, appeared in 1623.

INDEX

R. signifies Aleksandr Nikolaevich Radishchev. Pages are those of the present edition, not of the Russian original.

Abolition. *See* Emancipation; Serfdom
Academy of Sciences, Imperial, St. Petersburg, 229-230, 278, 279
Addison, Joseph, 30, 91, 265
Aleksey Mikhaylovich, Tsar of Russia, 128, 267, 278
Aleutian Islands, 86
Alexander I, Emperor of Russia, 15-19, 264
Alexander VI, Pope, 182-183, 272
America, United States of: Negro slavery in, 23, 148-149, 157, 191; freedom of the press in, 184-185, 273; mentioned, vii, 9, 176
Anna, Empress of Russia, 2, 272-273, 278
Annenkov, Pavel Vasil'evich, 36
Anticlericalism, 23-24, 57, 174-175, 189, 191, 196, 222, 235
Autocracy, 6, 21-22, 65, 66-76, 120, 214

Bacon, Sir Francis, 27, 237, 279
Barskov, Yakov Lazarevich, 253, 254
Barsukov, Nikolay Platonovich, 255
Bauch, Anneliese, 254
Bayle, Pierre, 6, 26, 82, 259, 264
Beccaria, Cesare Bonesana, Marchese di, 3, 30, 259
Beckmann, Johann, 24, 269
Belorussia, 15, 278
Bevis of Hampton, 14-15, 34, 58, 212, 213, 258
Black, John Bennett, 25, 259
Blackstone, Sir William, 8, 30, 79
Bodyansky, Osip Maksimovich, 239, 254

Borozdin, Aleksandr Kornil'evich, 18, 239, 253, 254
Bova Korolevich. *See* *Bevis of Hampton*
Burke, Edmund, 10, 26, 231

Calcutta, Black Hole of, 55, 56, 239-240
Catherine II the Great, Empress of Russia: *Nakaz* (*1767*), 3, 167, 194; *Charter to the Gentry* (*1785*), 4, 17-18, 45; on R.'s ode *Liberty*, 8, 248; on the *Journey*, 10-12, 27, 239-249; death of, 14; Coleridge on, 16; R. on, 16, 17-18, 21-22; mentioned, 2, 13, 55, 65
Cato the Younger, 19, 91, 123, 259
Censorship: of the *Journey*, 10; R. on, 24, 164-187; Pushkin on, 35; Herder on, 165-166; Catherine II on, 247-248, 249

R. on reasons for: to prevent blasphemy, 167-168; to prevent criticism of government, 167-170; to prevent pornography, 170-171; public opinion as the best censor, 171

R. on history of: in Greece, 172; in Rome, 172-174; the Christian Church, 174-175; by popes and other prelates, 175-183; in France, 183, 185-186; in England, 183-184; in United States, 184-185; in Prussia, 186; in Austria, 187
Cervantes-Saavedra, Miguel de, 30, 213
Charles I, King of England and Scotland, 8, 184, 200

Charter to the Gentry. See Catherine II
Chatham, William Pitt, first Earl of, 10, 26, 231
Chelishchev, Pyotr Ivanovich, 5, 28, 49–57, 241, 259
Chinese trade with Russia: R.'s letter on, 14, 258
Church Slavonic: R.'s use of, 31, 32, 235, 260
Cicero, 10, 30, 173, 231, 232, 234
Civil Code. See *Project*
Civil Service, 1, 6, 7, 45, 92, 93, 162
Commerce Collegium: R. an official in the, 7, 19, 157, 241–242; Count A. R. Vorontsov president of the, 12, 14
Commercial law, 62–63, 88–89
Condorcet, Marquis de, 14
Constitution: R.'s desire for Russian, 17–18
Cook, Captain James, 74
Corporal punishment, 17, 24, 166
Court Service, 1, 5, 21, 30, 94, 160–164, 214
Cromwell, Oliver, 8, 26, 199–200, 248
Custom House: R. Chief of the St. Petersburg, 7, 11, 157, 241–242

Defoe, Daniel, 28
Demosthenes, 10, 30, 231, 232, 234
Derzhavin, Gavriil Romanovich, 32
Dickinson, John, 23, 27, 170, 269
Dissenters. See Raskol'niki
Dobrolyubov, Nikolay Aleksandrovich, 36–37, 260
Drayton, Michael, 28
Dueling, 114, 115, 266

Education: R.'s views on, 8, 24, 29, 30, 78–79, 110–123, 166, 211–212, 225–227
Emancipation of serfs, vii, 7, 17, 25, 34–35, 154, 155–156, 247
England: R.'s admiration of its freedom of person and of press, 8, 15; "the citadel of liberty," 8, 199; its language above all, 115; censorship and freedom of the press, 183–184; mentioned, 12, 14, 18, 31, 173

Fénelon, 6, 257
Folk songs, Russian, 43, 187, 215–216, 277
Fonvizin, Denis Ivanovich, 31, 78, 165, 214, 263–264, 276–277
Fox, Charles James, 10, 26, 231
Franklin, Benjamin, 5, 23, 27, 236, 279
Frederick II the Great, King of Prussia, 9, 80, 186
French Revolution of *1789*, 9, 10, 25, 185–186, 231–232; Catherine II on, as inspiration of R., 239, 241, 242, 243, 247, 249
Fyodor III Alekseevich, Tsar of Russia, 45, 261

Gellert, Christian Fürchtegott, 6
Gentry. See Catherine II; Serfdom
Gertsen. See Herzen
Gibbon, Edward, 25
Goethe, Johann Wolfgang von, 5, 28–29, 30, 215–216
Government, Russian. See Autocracy; Sovereign
Grotius, Hugo, 8, 30, 79

Herder, Johann Gottfried von, 30, 165–166, 268
Herzen, Aleksandr Ivanovich, 36, 253
History, Russian: R.'s knowledge and use of, 8, 19–20; R.'s views on, 43, 82–85, 153, 209, 223, 235
Hogarth, William, 27, 94
Homer, 30, 193
Horace, 30, 36, 78, 229, 260, 268

Imperialism: R.'s opposition to, 8–9, 201, 246–247
Inland waterways, 19, 20, 156–157
Instruction *(Nakaz)*. See Catherine II

Jefferson, Thomas, 5, 268
Joseph II, Holy Roman Emperor, 9, 187, 274

INDEX

Journey from St. Petersburg to Moscow. See Radishchev, A. N.

Karamzin, Nikolay Mikhaylovich, 28, 31, 32, 34, 259
Karpovich, Michael, viii et passim
Kashin, N. P., 17, 254, 258
Kheraskov, Mikhail Matveevich, 192, 275
Khrapovitsky, Aleksandr Vasil'evich, 11, 255
Kostrov, Ermil Ivanovich, 192, 275
Kutuzov, Aleksey Mikhaylovich, 5, 8, 10, 29, 40, 187, 216, 223–224, 260–261

Lafayette, Marquis de, 26, 186
Languages, foreign: R. on, 115, 225–226
Lapshin, Ivan Ivanovich, 13, 239, 253, 255
Lavater, Johann Kaspar, 27, 86, 94, 265
Law: R.'s plans to reform the, 3, 8, 15–19, 154–156
Leipzig, University of, 5, 11, 18–19, 241
Levées: R.'s opinion of, 101, 121, 243, 245
Livy, 30, 78, 172, 269
Lomonosov, Mikhaylo Vasil'evich, 5, 10, 24, 27, 32, 35, 191, 192; R.'s "Eulogy on Lomonosov," his life and works, 222–237
Luther, Arthur, 253–254
Luther, Martin, 81, 175, 183, 264

Mably, Gabriel Bonnot de, 6, 26, 257–258
Manco Capac, 26, 163, 268
Marggraf, Andreas Sigismund, 27, 236, 278
Mestnichestvo, 45, 261
Military Service, 1, 6, 45, 92, 93, 162
Milton, John, 24, 30, 192, 193, 266, 273
Mirabeau, Honoré Gabriel Riqueti, Comte de, 10, 26–27, 231, 249
Mohammed, 82, 163
Montesquieu, 3, 6, 8, 28, 30, 79

More, Sir Thomas, 29, 30

Nakaz (Instruction). See Catherine II
Nationalism, R.'s Russian, 8, 9, 12, 142–143, 149, 161–162, 194, 201, 223, 235
Negroes, 23, 149, 157, 191
Nikon, Patriarch of Moscow, 129, 267
Novgorod: government of, 82–84; *Chronicle* of, 85; Catherine II on, 241; mentioned, 19, 26, 45, 78, 261
Novikov, Nikolay Ivanovich, 264, 267

Ostrovsky, Aleksandr Nikolaevich, 32, 263

Paul I, Emperor of Russia, 14, 15
Pavlov-Sil'vansky, Nikolay Pavlovich, 253
Peasants. See Serfdom
Peter I the Great, Emperor of Russia, 1, 2, 32, 45, 235, 257, 278
Peter III, Emperor of Russia, 2, 4, 272, 276
Pindar, 30, 233
Pitt, William, the Elder. See Chatham
Pitt, William, the Younger, 5
Platner, Ernst, 6
Platon, Metropolitan of Moscow, 23–24, 235, 278
Pnin, Ivan Petrovich, 34, 260
Potemkin, Grigory Aleksandrovich, Prince, 32, 58–61, 262
Press, freedom of. See Censorship
Project of a Civil Code, R.'s, 17–18
Proverbs, 58, 60, 65, 77, 85, 104, 114, 142, 187, 210, 219, 246
Pugachev Rebellion, 4, 5, 6, 7, 11, 134–135, 153
Pushkin, Aleksandr Sergeevich: on R., vii, 15, 16, 18–19, 30, 32, 35, 36, 37; works of, influenced by R., *Bova,* 34, *Liberty: An Ode,* 34, *The Village,* 34–35, Letter to S. A. Sobolevsky, 35, *The Captain's Daughter,* 35, *Journey from Mos-*

INDEX

cow to St. Petersburg, 35, Aleksandr Radishchev, 35–36, *Exegi Monumentum*, 36

Quakers, 23, 190, 275

Racine, Jean Baptiste, 30, 193
Radishchev, Aleksandr Nikolaevich: *Journey:* historical background, 1–4; R.'s motives for writing, 7, 8, 34, 40, 239, 240; composition of, 9, 10; censorship of, 10; Catherine II's criticism of, 10–12, 239–249; descriptive, 19–20; on serfdom, 20–21, 23; the sovereign, 21–22; officials, 22; gentry, 22; peasants, 22–23; the United States, 23; the clergy, 23–24; education, 24; censorship, 24; historical source material and points of departure, 24–27; literary analogues or sources, 27–30; language, style, literary technique, 30–34; influence and aftermath, 34–37

Life: birth, family, schooling, 4–5; at Leipzig, 5–6; Military and Civil Services, 6–7; marriage, 6; knighthood, 7; patriotism, desire for reforms, 7–8; suspected by Catherine II as author of *Journey*, 241, 242; imprisoned for writing *Journey*, sentenced to death, 11; commuted to Siberian exile, 11–12; second marriage, 13; friendship of Count A. R. Vorontsov, 13–14; released from exile by Paul I, 14; fully rehabilitated by Alexander I, 15; member of Commission on Revision of the Laws, 15–19; ardent Anglophile, 18; hopes for reform in Russia, 18; threatened with exile again, 18–19; suicide, 19

Works: Translation of Mably's *Observations sur l'histoire de la Grèce*, 6; *Liberty: An Ode*, 8–9, 34; *Conversation about Who Is a True Son of the Fatherland*, 12; *On Man, on his Mortality and Immortality*, 13; Letters to Count A. R. Vorontsov, 13–14; *Letter on Chinese Trade*, 14; *Bova Korolevich*, 14–15, 34, 58, 212, 213, 258; *The Eighteenth Century*, 15–16; *Project of a Civil Code*, 17–18; on censorship, see Censorship; on serfdom, see Serfdom
Radishchev, Moisey Nikolaevich (R.'s brother), 12
Radishchev, Nikolay Afanas'evich (R.'s father), 5, 7, 14, 21
Radishchev, Nikolay Aleksandrovich (R.'s son), 12, 255
Radishchev, Pavel Aleksandrovich (R.'s son), 13, 17, 24, 36, 255
Radishcheva, Anna Vasil'evna (R.'s first wife), 6, 12
Radishcheva, Elizaveta Vasil'evna (R.'s second wife), 12–13, 14
Radishcheva, Fekla Stepanovna (R.'s mother), 5, 7, 14
Raskol'niki, 10, 23, 46–47, 168, 240, 261–262
Raynal, Guillaume Thomas François, 6, 8, 24–25, 55–56, 235–236, 244, 247, 259, 262
Reform: R. for, not revolution, vii, 7–8, 10, 18, 21, 153–154, 185–186; Pushkin likewise, 34–35; unless instituted, revolution to be expected, 190–191, 209
Regicide, 8, 34, 184, 199–200
Religious beliefs, R.'s, 16, 17, 24, 53, 55, 66, 80, 89–91, 124, 167–168, 189, 222, 237; Catherine II on, 240, 241, 243–244, 245, 246, 249
Religious toleration, 17, 23, 90–91, 142–143, 167–168, 174–175
Revolution. See Reform
Revolution, French. See French Revolution
Richmann, Georg Wilhelm, 27, 236, 279
Robertson, William, 25–26, 236, 259, 278
Rousseau, Jean Jacques, 6, 23, 25, 29, 244, 264
Rüdiger, Johann Andreas, 27, 236, 278–279
Rurik, 45, 261

Seneca the Elder, 173, 269
Serfdom: Peter the Great and, 1; reasons for, 2; effects of, 2–4; powers of serf-owners, 2–3; Pugachev Rebellion, 4, 134, 153; R.'s father on serfdom, 5; R. for emancipation, 7, 17, 30, 34–35, 154, 155–156; R. on evils of, 7–8, 10, 12, 20–21, 22–23, individual and social, 143–147, economic, 151–152, 157–160; Paul I's limitation of, 15; R.'s hopes for further reforms, 15–16, 17–18; equated with Negro slavery, 23, 148–149, 157, 191; as punishment for criminals and enemies, 30; in Russian literature, 33–34; *obrok* and *barshchina* illustrated, 46–49; crown and manorial peasants contrasted, 48, 157–160; landlords' abuse of peasants, exploitation of men, violation of women, 94–104, 134–135, 189; forced marriages of peasants, 135, 140–141, 189–190, 207–208, 221–222; as slavery of both master and serf, 152; dangers of, to life and property, 153; auction sale of serfs, 187–191; levying of serfs as recruits, 202–212; serf sent to army as punishment, 203–208; poverty of peasants, 219–221; mentioned, 194, 197–199
  Catherine II on, 242, 243, 245, 246, 248, 249; Herzen on, 36; Mably on, 26; Pushkin on, 34–35, "following R." for emancipation, 36; Raynal on, 25, 55–56
Shakespeare, William, 24, 30, 192, 193, 267
Shchegolev, Pavel Eliseevich, 239, 253
Slavery. *See* Serfdom
Slavonic language. *See* Church Slavonic
Smith, Adam, *The Wealth of Nations*, 14
Sobolevsky, Sergey Aleksandrovich, 35, 260
Sorcerers, 70, 214–215

Sovereign, the Russian, 2, 3, 4, 6, 8, 18, 21–22, 65; R.'s dream of himself as, 66–76; as source of Russian laws, 120
Stählin, Karl, 253
Sterne, Laurence, *Sentimental Journey*, 27–28, 259
Stowe, Harriet Beecher, *Uncle Tom's Cabin*, vii, 21
Suicide: R. on, 18–19, 29, 44, 123, 148, 189–190, 206, 215–216
Sukhomlinov, Mikhail Ivanovich, 255, 258
Sumarokov, Aleksandr Petrovich, 191, 192, 234, 275
Sweden: Swedish-Russian War (*1788–1790*), 9, 11, 73, 240
Swedenborg, Emanuel, 80, 264
Swift, Jonathan, 28, 29–30

Table of Ranks, 1, 17, 30, 45, 59, 156
Tacitus, 25, 30, 78, 174, 235–236
Tasso, Torquato, 30, 193
Telemakhida. *See* Tred'yakovsky
Thaler, Alwin, viii *et passim*
Tred'yakovsky, Vasily Kirillovich, *Telemakhida*, 192, 257
Trial by jury, 17, 18, 30, 155
Turkey: Russo-Turkish War of *1735–1739*, 10, 188, 229; War of *1768–1774*, 3, 6, 52, 199, 235, 262, 276; War of *1787–1791*, 9, 72–73, 240

United States. *See* America
Ushakov, Fyodor Vasil'evich, 5, 10, 18–19

Vernet, Claude Joseph, 27, 50, 262
Virgil, 30, 31, 78, 192, 193, 212, 229, 276
Vladimir II Monomakh, Grand Prince of Kiev, 45, 261
Voltaire, François Marie Arouet de, 6, 24, 25, 30, 80, 184, 192, 193
Vorontsov, Aleksandr Romanovich, Count, 12, 13, 14, 15, 18
Vorontsov, Semyon Mikhaylovich, Prince, 13

Vorontsov, Semyon Romanovich, Count, 12

Walpole, Horace, fourth Earl of Orford, 25
Washington, George, 9
Wasson, R. Gordon, viii

Wiener, Leo, vii, viii
Wolff, Robert Lee, viii

Yershov, Peter, 30

Zavadovsky, Pyotr Vasil'evich, Count, 17, 18, 19